REINVENTING LOVE

ALSO BY MONA CHOLLET

In Defense of Witches

REINVENTING LOVE

How the Patriarchy Sabotages
Heterosexual Relations

MONA CHOLLET

Translated by SUSAN EMANUEL

ST. MARTIN'S PRESS
NEW YORK

CONTENTS

INTRODUCTION: Illusion of an Oasis   1

PROLOGUE: Between Conformism and Nihilism   25

1. MAKING YOURSELF LESS NOTICEABLE TO BE LOVED? The Inferiority of Women in Our Romantic Ideal   57

2. REAL MEN: Learning Domestic Violence   99

3. GUARDIANS OF THE TEMPLE: Is Love Women's Business?   153

4. THE GREAT DISPOSSESSION: Becoming Erotic Subjects   220

NOTES   263

INDEX   285

REINVENTING LOVE

INTRODUCTION

Illusion of an Oasis

As soon as I got my first smartphone, I chose to upload a certain image as my home screen, and I have never changed it. It is an Indian miniature from 1830 called *A Lady Comes to Her Lover's House in a Rainstorm*.[1] The colors are splendid: the orange-red of her sari, which she holds in two hands over her head as she runs across the garden, drenched by the storm; the rosy white of his outfit signaling to her from a covered balcony on a house's upper floor; the pale green of the grass, of a tree bent by the wind, of the hills undulating in the background; the black of an angry cloud striated by lightning that roils the skies over them. The lover is captured at this delicious moment when she is still being mangled by the elements, but when she is already about to reach her goal. Soon she will be under shelter. She will be able to not only take off her soaked sari, dry herself, get warm, and smell the perfumes of a bedroom, but also join the man she desires, hold him in her arms, roll with him on a bed. I imagine her running, the freshness of the raindrops on her face, the acceleration of her heartbeat along with the rhythm of the rain. Having this scene in front of my eyes every day, I no longer think much about its meaning, but it accompanies me, like a screen saver is supposed to. It reminds me of the existence of love, or at least of its possibility. Love gives me the feeling of igniting a great flame under the cauldron of life, to the point of dilating it, making it denser, a little like writing does. Like writing, it helps me to become one with the world. "Happiness in love," writes Alain Badiou, "is the proof that time can accommodate eternity."[2] And Annie Ernaux at the end of *Passion simple* sums up her liaison with the one she calls "A" in these terms: "Thanks to him, I was able to approach the frontier separating me from others, to the extent of actually believing that I could sometimes cross over it. I measured time otherwise, with all my body."[3]

Every day, apart from the moments spent with those close to us, we have to deal in our social and professional lives with people who might inspire in us sympathy as much as indifference, boredom, irritation, or even detestation. We resign ourselves to these constraints and to superficiality, to the solitude that this implies. But from time to time, a stupefying phenomenon occurs: suddenly, usually at a time when we are least expecting it, when we let down our guard, thanks to fate's gratuitous generosity, when faced with someone we have known a few seconds or a few days (or even sometimes a few years), a veil falls with a discreet hiss, announcing the impending and hence ineluctable fall of clothing to the ground. The scales fall from our eyes. We understand who this person is, just as this person understands who we are—and find it marvelous. This seems too beautiful to be true. A gift falls into our hands, an intoxicating bond, an immediate and crazily benevolent intimacy with someone who could have been totally unknown to us.

This big bang engenders an energy that could take us around the Earth three times. Here is something like the dice throw in the game of Chutes and Ladders of my childhood that permits a spectacular shortcut to the summit while other players continue to progress laboriously from square to square.

By making two existences mingle, love places the couple's lives into commonality: combined wisdom, life stories, financial resources, heritages, and ways of benefiting from life, their friends, and their countries. It multiplies connections and possibilities. Inside our identity, it opens doors we didn't know were there. It lays at our feet the possibility of a new life. I am thinking of a springtime day in Cannes, more than thirty years ago, when my friend K invited a young man with brown hair who for days had been throwing her languorous looks to join her at the terrace of a café. They were both accredited film critics at the Cannes Film Festival (yes, hard to find a classier venue for a meeting!). They started to converse in English, and I don't know whether she was aware of the world that was opening before her at the moment she asked him where he came from and he replied, "Greece." A country where she had never set foot, in which she was never particularly interested, but that she was about to discover and adore; a country where she would live for seven years, whose language she'd learn; a country to which, even after their divorce, she would continue to return each year, before buying a house there. A country to which she would offer a new citizen, in the person of their daughter, whose spirit on that day in the café must have trembled because her future parents were sharing a café table for the first time.

I cannot imagine a better representation of the imprint left by love in our lives than an event that occurred in 2010 at the opening performance of Marina Abramović's *The Artist Is Present* at the Museum of Modern Art in New York. The setup was as follows: Abramović, dressed in a long red gown, was seated on a chair in front of a table and another empty chair, in a large cleared area. Visitors walked by, sat for a few moments in the other chair, and bore her gaze in silence, then made way for the next person. Without her being forewarned, her former lover and creative partner, the artist Ulay (gray beard, trainers, and a black suit), suddenly sat down opposite her. When she raised her head and saw him, her eyes filled with tears that flowed down her cheeks. They had not seen each other since 1988, when they each had walked half of the Great Wall of China to find each other in the middle and say farewell. (In the beginning of their relationship, they had thought of getting married there, but didn't, given the time to obtain authorizations, etc.). That evening in New York, everything in their silent exchange, in the way they looked at each other, the nods of their heads, the flickering of their eyelids, and their timid smiles, conveyed nostalgia, tenderness, regrets. Breaking the protocol of her own performance, Marina Abramović launched herself forward and offered him her hands, which he took on the table that separated them, while around them the audience burst into applause and cheers. A few years later, Ulay sued his former companion, a lawsuit that he would win, over the rights to one of the works they created together. Yet they had time to reconcile before his death, on March 2, 2020.

MAKING THE GREAT LEAP

I would adore being able to speak of love only in this way, going on about the most beautiful stories I've heard. There is a close kinship between the amorous impulse and the narrative impulse, and I have never been able to resist a good story. Falling in love is to have the sensation of crossing the page or the screen and seeing one's own life generating all these highly enjoyable moments that, usually, come out of the genius brain of a good writer or a good screenwriter. When I close a novel that has held me breathless for days or weeks or reach the end of a TV series that I have particularly savored (wavering between the temptation to devour pages or binge-watch episodes, as opposed to economizing to prolong the pleasure), I feel a sentiment similar to a breakup: nostalgia, the impression of leaving an enchanted world, of depriving myself of a form of privilege and being returned to a daily life that is dreary and uninteresting. I have the sense that a state of grace is ending—which, as long as it lasted, had introduced a protective layer between me and everything that is harsh and wounding in the world and in life.

I would love to be able to speak of love as an oasis, a sanctuary. But I increasingly stumble upon obstacles. I've observed in society at large, among my circle of friends, and in my own life a spectrum of situations, ranging from revolting oppression to misunderstandings (which are certainly less tragic but terribly frustrating). These observations increased my desire to come to grips with the subject of heterosexual love. During my adolescence, nothing challenged the idyllic vision of love and romance I derived from films and novels; I must have long

nourished the illusion that inequality, domination, and violence were absent from emotional lives. There was something
very stressful and destabilizing about eventually comprehend-
ing that people suffer from these things, particularly in places
where some of their deepest aspirations are concentrated, where
they are most vulnerable. At the very least, it is disturbing to
think that among the ninety-eight women killed by a partner
or ex-partner in France in 2020,[*4] probably some were at first
intensely happy upon meeting the person who would later become their persecutor and murderer.

I have often heard women compare their discovery of feminism to the moment in the film *The Matrix* when Neo (played
by Keanu Reeves) chooses the red pill—that of lucidity—which
enables him to enter the Matrix, rather than the blue pill, which
would guarantee him blissful ignorance. When it comes to love,
I would have willingly continued to swallow the blue pill like
candy. I panic at the prospect of damaging the core beliefs driv-
ing one of my most essential and vital impulses. But it has become difficult to ignore the attacks upon those beliefs, and I
realized just how difficult when I plunged into *A Vindication of
Love* by the American journalist Cristina Nehring. I found her
flamboyant style magnetic from the first lines, but I quickly understood that I could not subscribe to her views without reservations. She confirmed my feeling of finding myself up against
a wall, of being obliged to give up my unconditional "love of
love," since she holds out a mirror offering me the spectacle of

---

[*] In 2018 there were 1,014 intimate acquaintance killings in the United States, compared to 120 in France. Rose Hackman, "Femicides in the US," *Guardian,* September
26, 2021, theguardian.com/us-news/2021/sep/26/femicide-us-silent-epidemic.

her own obstinacy in wanting to preserve that "love of love." She encourages her readers to love with courage, with audacity, with combativeness, to take on the risk of failure—there can be more nobility in a failure than in many successes, she correctly states. "At its strongest and wildest and most authentic, love is a demon," she writes. "It is a religion, a high-risk adventure, an act of heroism. Love is ecstasy and injury, transcendence and danger, altruism and excess. In many ways, it is a divine madness—and was recognized exactly as that as early as the time of Plato."[5]

When she recounts celebrated love stories, Nehring is luminous in her sense of the tales and in the lessons she draws from them, whether they are about characters we French know only slightly (the feminist journalist Margaret Fuller, the poet Edna St. Vincent Millay) or those we thought we knew by heart (Héloïse and Abélard, George Sand and Alfred de Musset, Frida Kahlo and Diego Rivera). I even forgave Nehring for her digs at certain feminist figures. However, my doubts did not take long to resurface.

First, I was seduced: she defends love as a sort of supreme lucidity, a rare state that enables us to see clearly inside somebody—not a state of blindness or being caught in an illusion, as the cliché would have it. But then she tells the story of a woman named Mary Bain Pikul, whom we will meet again in chapter 2 of this book. We are in 1987: this New Yorker fell in love with the father of her school friend—he was a man accused of murdering his wife. She's left everything for him and now, in the middle of the night, he is chasing her in the forest surrounding the house where they live. She'd thought he was innocent but is coming to understand that he truly did kill his wife. So, can love give access to supreme lucidity? Shouldn't we examine more closely the mechanisms that sometimes make us fall in love? "We may be seduced by the plea that love itself cannot be wrong, because the language of the heart is surely the language of freedom itself. Such romanticism, however, may be precisely what conceals power the most, in theory as in experience," observed the scholar Wendy Langford.[6]

Finally, I braked sharply when Cristina Nehring praised the disequilibrium in power between partners. She asserts in her book that this disequilibrium is much more propitious for erotic tension than equality would be. She speaks of the "aphrodisiac effects of inequality," without ever envisaging that they might be explained by the fact that we have learned to eroticize masculine domination. She gives examples drawn from literature where the cards are indeed constantly reshuffled, where it is sometimes the woman rather than the man who has the upper hand in the relationship, where love confers power sometimes to one, sometimes to the other. Then hierarchy within the couple, she says, becomes an occasion "to tease and provoke, bait and flirt." On paper this is beautiful, but I know of innumerable examples in which the concept of hierarchy has served only to crush women who'd thought they were free and consenting.

Nehring rejects the idea that most men do not want companions who are more successful than they are, though this has been shown in many studies: "[Men] do not want partners who are exactly *as* successful as they are," she claims. "They prefer—as women do—dating *either* down or up. Sideways is dull." She is also blind when it comes to the attraction of certain women to "difficult" men, explaining that "girls *like the challenge*." She believes that "the choice of a challenging love object signals strength and resourcefulness rather than insecurity and psychological damage."[7] Unfortunately, this hypothesis does not resist even a cursory analysis.

Denial will not save us. It is better to make the great leap, to confront the questions that arise and dismantle the edifice of love, in the hope of reconstructing another, one more beautiful and more solid. My initial readings as background for this book produced a violent sobering up that left me both relieved—to the extent that it blocked certain harmful patterns—and sad, because it made me miss the intensity. If I had set a goal for writing this book, it would have been that it might enable me to rediscover the momentum of desire, but with other dynamics. My goal would not have been to avoid suffering at all costs—love is always risky, heaven and hell are conjoined there—but to believe that when one is a woman, there is suffering and then there is *suffering*.

As I started this book at the beginning of 2020, I had the impression of seeing this questioning pursued inside the heads of other women and inside my own. Gathering force in the autumn of 2017, by revealing the scale and breadth of sexual violence, the #MeToo movement produced a domino effect that, in a fascinating manifestation of collective intelligence, gradually came to challenge all aspects of the relations between women and men. We started to talk about consent, the burden of domestic duties (family logistics usually rest on the shoulders of wives, female companions, and mothers), and even about the orgasm gap (the fact that women reach orgasm less often than their male partner during sexual relations). And, little by little, we approached the heart of gender relations.[8]

The subject is in no way easy. Many people remain persuaded that our feelings and our attitudes in this domain are products of individual choices that are entirely free and escape social conditioning. It seems to them as if culture did not shape us from the start, fashioning even what we believe to be most intimate and personal about ourselves, but is rather just a little coat of varnish applied after the fact to a human nature that would have existed independently of it. We are all fabricated, writes Amandine Dhée: "It is only when you recognize this that you can invent yourself a little."[9]

Trying to describe the way in which we are "fabricated" might trigger fear of falling into caricature, into exorbitant generalizations. The comic book author Liv Strömquist helped me overcome these inhibitions by attacking the subject fearlessly, with a mixture of ferocity and humor.[10] She persuaded me that it was worth facing the risk of hawking clichés; by keeping in mind their limits and their exceptions, we may attempt to discern and analyze the major laws of heterosexual love. She showed me how good it might be for women to see laid out on the page some situations they previously experienced in solitude and confusion. The closed romantic environment is intoxicating when everything is going well, but it can also weaken us terribly. We need public discussion to break this isolation.

It is a perversity of our societies to bombard us with injunctions to be heterosexual, while methodically educating and socializing men and women so that they are incapable of understanding each other! Ingenious, right? In fact, partners who conform exactly to their respective gender scripts have every chance of making themselves very unhappy. These scripts produce, on the one hand, a woman who is sentimental and dependent, subject to tyrannical demands, and overinvested in the affective and romantic world and, on the other hand, a mute and rough-hewn man barricaded in by the illusion of his own fierce autonomy who seems always to be wondering by what dramatic lack of vigilance he could have fallen into this domestic trap. Even when we are not completely incarnating these roles, we might rediscover elements of this dualism inside ourselves. At least we can be conscious of the existence of these roles, that they create problematic interferences—in particular the former, with the female role functioning as a deterrent.

Of course, from conjugal violence to the tense misunder-standings that arise between persons who respect each other, the situations I will discuss are not of the same gravity. Conjugal vio-lence threatens the physical and psychological health of women, even their lives; it voids them of their life energy and their self-esteem, it cuts these women's wings. Meanwhile, tensions in a relationship prevent mutual understanding and trust; they de-prive individuals of the pleasures of a true complicity and they compromise the relationship in the shorter or longer term. This book is born of my own sense of the wastefulness of these roles, of my desire to dissolve these obstacles and to supply all women and men with ways of developing more fulfilling relationships.

LOVE AND ANGER

I must be specific about my own past because this necessarily influences how I deal with this subject: I am lucky enough to have reached the end of my forties while maintaining rather serene relations with men. I had a father who was gentle and benevolent. I have a marvelous brother. I have never experienced a toxic relationship. Never having wanted a child, I have never known the abrupt disequilibrium in the sharing of domestic tasks that a birth often provokes. Nor have I gone through one of those destructive divorces that I see around me. I remain (or rather, I have become again) very close to the man with whom I lived for eighteen years, and I still love him deeply. I once had a troublesome employer, who would interrupt me to praise my beauty and then natter about my companion, whom he had once met; but I did not see much of this employer and was able to quit the job before the situation became unbearable. Finally, I was able to escape the two assaults that I can remember. One night as an adolescent, coming home through the deserted streets of Geneva, I thought I heard footsteps behind me and I closed the bolt when I had just gotten into the building. I saw the face of the man who was following me through the upper half of the door that had a window pane; meanwhile he was trying to push that door open with all his weight. Around the same period, in the Swiss mountains three guys wearing gorilla masks (Carnival had just begun), reeking alcohol through all their pores, burst into the chalet where I was staying with my brother and a female friend of the same age. When one of them bent over me and demanded a kiss, I managed to push him off and rushed along a corridor, with him on my heels, and then locked myself in the bathroom. He spent some time (which seemed very long to me) shaking the door and shouting, while I was crouched on a toilet seat; his two acolytes emptied the bottles in the chalet. They eventually made a quick getaway because our friend (we were at her place) had recognized one of them from his voice, thereby ending his anonymity. Thirty years later, I still have trouble sleeping in a house where the door is not locked, and as a woman I detest having to pay constant attention to my security, but I have escaped any trauma. I have never felt that deep rage—oh, how justified—that inhabits many rape victims, although I feel solidarity with them.

I am surprised by the ease with which lucidity and idealism, fury and exaltation, can coexist within me. Basically, I know that the same aspiration is being expressed in every case, but in different modes. As the novelist Joumana Haddad says, "I have two sources of energy: anger and love. One might believe they are contradictory, but they are complementary: I draw from one what I do not find in the other."[11] However, that does not usually stop me from expressing only the angry side in my books. No doubt this is because when I write to be published, I instinctively go for the most gratifying posture, the most self-assured. For example, I savor the feminist wisecracks by which I can exorcise my conditioning to wait for a Prince Charming, a savior. I adore Ellie Black's cartoon in the *New Yorker* in which the knight arrives to save the princess from the dragon and she welcomes him with folded arms and a defiant look on her face, alongside the animal, who tells him: "She does not want to see

you, man." But I also sense that a wisecrack is not enough, or
no longer enough.

But speaking about love requires accepting one's vulnerability, one's desires, one's weaknesses and doubts—one's sentimentality, too, this distressingly feminine trait that we learn
to despise and censor. "Our sustained longing for love has not
been fully addressed, for fear that to name it would somehow
undermine an image of powerful, self-actualized feminist
womanhood," proclaimed the writer bell hooks in 2002.[12] She
noticed that we may speak of our desire for power, but "Our
longing for love must be kept secret. To give voice to such
longing is to be counted among the weak, the soft."[13] Recently,
as I told my friend that I was increasingly being recognized in
the street, she commented: "You mean that you are no longer
sure of remaining anonymous when hanging on the neck of a
man in public?" Then she added, maliciously: "Or when you
cling to his leg and beg him not to leave?" I snorted at imagining the effect that such a scene would produce after my bold
harangues on feminine independence in the *Witches* book.[14]
Shortly after I discovered, thanks to Cristina Nehring, that the
tumultuous emotional life of the English philosopher Mary
Wollstonecraft caused her to be disowned, even by some of her
sisters, who were embarrassed that the author of *A Vindication
of the Rights of Woman* (1792) had twice tried to kill herself
because of a man (the same man both times: this woman was
single-minded). For her part, Nehring sees no contradiction
in this, quite the contrary, and I more or less agree with her:
the strength of ideas and the strength of feelings both testify to
the same passionate temperament and the same fearlessness.[15]

Reading *All About Love* by bell hooks, I perceived that unwittingly I had begun my book in the same way she did hers: with the description of a piece of daily life that is equivalent to a proclamation of faith. Bell hooks evokes not an Indian miniature but four photographs on the wall of her kitchen, graffiti from a construction site that she passed every day when she was teaching at Yale University: "The search for love continues even in the face of great odds." When the graffiti was whitewashed over, she located the artist and he gave her the photos of it. "From the time we met, everywhere I have lived I have placed these snapshots above my kitchen sink," she writes. "Every day, when I drink water or take a dish from the cupboard, I stand before this reminder that we yearn for love—that we seek it—even when we lack hope that it really can be found."[16] Among hooks's circle, her interest in love arouses perplexity and embarrassment. Her friends don't see this as a legitimate intellectual quest, but instead as a rather embarrassing weakness. They cut short discussions by suggesting that she go in for therapy. The subject, she remarks, is considered serious and legitimate only when it is theorized by men, although "women are more often love's practitioners."[17] This produces the same phenomenon as cooking, a domain in which great male chefs are celebrated, while women are denied their own expertise, although they are the vast majority of those preparing meals every day.

In choosing this subject, I know that I am dooming myself to roll lamentably at the foot of the podium of radical feminism. Some militant lesbian feminists, in particular, bring out the popcorn when one of their heterosexual sisters unwittingly tries to justify her problematic habit of forming loving and sexual relations with men. And, in truth, these women should not deprive themselves of that choice. Considered quite coldly, heterosexuality is an aberration. After all, as Patricia Mercader, Annik Houel, and Helga Sobota have remarked: "Amorous relations between men and women have this particularity: they are the only relations of social domination where the dominant and the dominated are supposed to love each other"[18] (maybe alongside relations between parents and children). The lesbian journalist and activist Alice Coffin writes in *Le génie lesbian*: "Women's heterosexuality remains for me a painful problem," alluding to a famous radio program from 1971.[19] She adds: "For them, too, judging from many conversations."[20]

This perplexing issue has long been a subject of controversy. In 1972, in New York, women of the Gay Liberation Front published a declaration in which they argued that straight women seem to "believe that through their attempts to create 'new men' they will liberate themselves. Enormous amounts of female energy are expended in this process, with little effect."[21] In France, Emmanuèle de Lesseps* wrote an article in 1980 for the journal *Questions féministes*: "A few days ago, I was talking with a feminist and asked her if she defined herself as heterosexual. 'Yes, alas!' she replied. She told me she would 'prefer to be homosexual' because we both agreed that 'relations with men are shitty.'"[22] That same year, the American feminist poet and essayist Adrienne Rich published the landmark essay "Compulsory Heterosexuality and Lesbian Existence,"[23] in which she argues that "the bias of compulsory heterosexuality" has meant

---

* One of the nine demonstrators who on August 26, 1970, at the Arc de Triomphe in Paris laid a wreath to the wife of the unknown soldier, giving birth to the Women's Liberation Movement (MLF).

that "lesbian experience is perceived on a scale ranging from deviant to abhorrent, or simply rendered invisible." Recent books have questioned this bias: heterosexuality might have nothing to do with a "preference" but rather something that must have been imposed, directed, organized, spread by propaganda, and maintained by force. Rich cites twelve aspects of male power that contribute to heterosexual pressure; a year earlier the French feminist theorist Monique Wittig had given a lecture that theorized heterosexuality as a political regime.

In 2017, this statement by the French feminist Virginie Despentes, who had become a lesbian at age thirty-five, caused a sensation:

> To get out of heterosexuality was an enormous relief. From the start I was probably not a very talented hetero. There is something within me that does not suit this kind of femininity. Plus, I do not know many people for whom it has been a success over the course of a lifetime. So the impression of going to a different planet was dazzling. As if your head were put on backward as you were gently turned around. Wow! That was a terrific sensation. As if I had suddenly lost forty kilos. Before, I could be seen as a woman who was not enough like this or who was too much like that. In a flash, the weight of that was lifted. This no longer involved me! Liberated from heterosexual seduction and its dictates! Now I cannot even read a woman's magazine. Nothing concerns me anymore! Not blow-jobs, not fashion.[24]

Like Despentes, in her book *The Tragedy of Heterosexuality* the American essayist Jane Ward reveals her relief at escaping straight culture, its conformity, its boredom, its oppressions, its disappointments, and its frustrations—a feeling that is widely shared in her circle, she says. Of course, writes Ward, the dominant heterosexual norm causes suffering for lesbians and gays: "This story about queer suffering under the force of heteronormativity is true; but it is also only a sliver of the story about queerness, and it is one that masks not only queer joy and pleasure but also queer relief not to be straight."[25] And she wonders if homophobia could be motivated by an obscure jealousy: "Queers are hated and envied because we are suspected of having gotten away with something." Observing that at the end of the twentieth century, majority culture often reproached gay attitudes as "too flamboyant—too spectacular, too loud, too sexual, too animated, too exposed—overall just too much," Ward concludes that if this culture is "too much" then heterosexual culture is "too little": too colorless, too uptight, too unimaginative. The refrain of straight women who lament "not being lesbians" seriously irritates many of her friends: "Why don't you be one, then? It's not *that* hard."

THE DREAM OF "PROFOUND HETEROSEXUALITY"

Despentes's statement helped to reanimate debates on political lesbianism within French feminism. However, we run the risk of idealizing homosexual relations, which are not necessarily free of relations of domination—even if this does not involve structural domination, as in masculine domination. And moreover, can one choose one's sexual orientation? I am not going to launch into this debate here, but whatever the case, it is worth excavating the construction of heterosexual relations. This is what Jane Ward herself wanted to do in her book: to actualize heterosexuality rather than deconstruct it. Some women and men insist on sticking to their mutual attraction—while seeking to overcome the structural difficulties they run up against. It seemed to Ward that her experience and her point of view as a lesbian might be useful to them.

For this purpose, she immersed herself in straight culture, going so far as to attend, as an observer, seminars designed to teach men how to pick up women. ("As I watched men take notes on this most nauseatingly heteronormative of monologues, I struggled not to roll my eyes with queer repulsion.") Ward stresses that lesbians have often provided positive examples to heterosexuals with respect to sex and love relationships. "We can thank lesbian feminists for the spate of well-lit, shame-free, and education-oriented sex shops (like Good Vibrations or Toys in Babeland) where average straight couples can now buy sex toys without feeling like deviants. We can thank lesbian feminists for the concept of ethical nonmonogamy, the existence of feminist porn, the bold notion that people can remain friends and family with ex-lovers, the emphasis on consent and care within kink practices, and the radical idea that women can strap on dildos and penetrate people, including their boyfriends and husbands."[26]

One of the major problems identified by Ward is the "misogyny paradox" (a paradox of which Donald Trump was certainly the ultimate incarnation): a paradox that allows heterosexual men to express their desire for women within a culture that encourages them to despise and even hate women. This association between heterosexuality and misogyny has become so naturalized that the absence of machismo is interpreted as a sign of homosexuality. In one of her courses (she teaches at the University of California, Riverside), Ward mentioned the experience of a writer, Jason Schultz, who organized an alternative bachelor party, in the course of which he and his straight friends, instead of hiring a female stripper, told stories about their positive experiences of desire for (and sex with) women. But Ward's students were categorically dismissive: that sounded so gay. In his supercharged yet profound show *Bonhomme*, the French stand-up comedian Laurent Sciamma offers a similar insight in his anecdote about a dinner party conversation with another guest who asked him if he was gay, because he "was speaking a lot about feminism." That kind of reasoning disconcerted him. "As if it were incompatible to be a guy, heterosexual, and a feminist. How did we get here? A world that is so misogynistic and homophobic that suddenly it's like: 'Wait, you care about women? That is so gay!' The guy who thinks of the well-being of the women around him must be gay? I don't understand!"[27]

In the delicious pages of her final chapter, Ward suggests embracing what she calls "deep heterosexuality." Rather than experiencing their sexual orientation fatalistically, she says, heterosexual men and women might actively invest in it, think about it, and reappropriate it. This would be particularly useful for men, who "have been encouraged to relate to their desire for women as so physiological as to be outside of their control and so compartmentalized as to enable the disconnect between wanting women and liking them."[28] If they actually loved women, she argues, then they would truly love them. "It is possible for straight men to like women so much, so deeply, that they actually really *like* women. Straight men could be so unstoppably heterosexual that they crave hearing women's voices, thirst for women's leadership, ache to know women's full humanity, and thrill at women's freedom. That is how lesbian feminists lust for women. I do not despair about the tragedy of heterosexuality, because another way is possible."[29]

Running counter to the many reactionary books on personal development (starting with the ultrafamous *Men Are from Mars, Women Are from Venus*, published by John Gray in 1992) that postulate that there are essential and insurmountable differences between men and women, and that advise getting used to it, Ward invites heterosexual men to understand the "human capacity to desire, to fuck, and to be feminist comrades at the same time."[30] One can "desire women humanely" by seeing them as both objects and subjects. She stresses one contradiction in particular: these men supposedly feel an instinctive and irrepressible desire for women, yet often the female body must offer precise characteristics (or undergo alterations to acquire them) in order to find favor in their eyes: the body must be young, thin, hairless, and perfumed. . . . Here again, they might take inspiration from lesbians, who are more capable of desiring a woman in her totality, with her scars, her bulges, her wrinkles, her experience, her personality. Thus, Ward concludes, a deep heterosexual can become an "authentically straight man . . . and not a psuedoheterosexual who uses women to impress men."[31] The tendency of some to lose all interest in a woman once they have slept with her could also be interpreted as a sign of this pseudo-heterosexuality, or superficial heterosexuality: such men are not interested in the person or in the relationship as such, in the ways they might enrich their lives, but instead have a simple need for "conquest," for narcissistic gratification, in order to improve their status or their image. Ward encourages her straight female readers to be "bold enough to expect this from men, to demand so much more of straight men's ostensible love of women."[32] In short, "deep heterosexuality" would be a kind of heterosexuality that breaks with patriarchy and its interests,* a heterosexuality that would betray patriarchy.

However, seeing the source of all the problems within heterosexuality itself would mean leaving aside a finer vision of everything about it that might be contested, reinvented, rearranged. In her 1980 article, Emmanuèle de Lesseps judged that the desire of heterosexual women ought to be liberated as well: "In fact we have suffered since childhood from pressure to be heterosexual rather than homosexual. But I would like to remind women that above all we have suffered from the pressure not to be 'sexual' at all." She notes the contradiction between being a radical feminist and actually loving men: "If feminist radicalism ought to consist of rejecting any contradiction, of being satisfied with pure and hard principles free from error, then it would be incapable of accounting for reality, incapable of dealing with it, of making use of this reality, incapable of representing, and hence of helping, women as a whole."[33] Like her, I admit that I love the tensions

---

* Patriarchy is a system of social organization in which men exercise the power and hold authority in all domains.

and discrepancies in heterosexuality; I find them particularly fertile and interesting. When I read Alice Coffin,[34] I realized that my own feminism would never be as free of complexes as hers. Her kind of desire leaves her elbow room, while mine induces an irreducible share of pangs of regret and conflicts of loyalty. But I am interested in working from the basis of these pangs and conflicts. And then if one condemns the violence and injustice suffered by women, or just takes the trouble to highlight the most insidious manifestations of sexism, it is because one believes in a way out of the obstinately patriarchal world in which we live; one believes this system may be subverted. And hence, one can also believe in the possibility of a change in our intimate and personal relationships.

I will start in the prologue by examining the cultural background to how love is deployed in our society; a canvas marked, it seems to me, by faintheartedness and lack of imagination, but also, at the other extreme, by a certain complacency about failure, tragedy, and death. Both these attitudes express an incapacity to embrace love, to experience its everyday reality in ways that are both inventive and confident. Next, I will examine how our romantic representations are constructed on the sublimation of women's inferiority, such that many of them take it to signify that they are "too something" to find grace in a man's eye: too tall or too strong (in the physical and literal sense of both these terms), too brilliant, too creative, etc. However, women who seem to tick off all the correct boxes and not to threaten the masculine ego are not necessarily happier in love—and for a good reason, since it is difficult to build one's fulfillment upon the negation or the limitation of oneself (chapter 1).

Then I deal with the mechanisms of conjugal violence, not as an anomaly or deviance but as the logical culmination of the behaviors prescribed for men and women by social norms (chapter 2). In chapter 3 I explain the very different value that women and men are driven to grant to love, the often much stronger investment that women make in the relationship, as well as the disequilibriums and dysfunctions that this creates, and the ways of remedying this imbalance. Finally, I will speculate on how women might get out of their normative role and offer men a mute image that corresponds to their fantasies—in order to become desiring subjects themselves. But can we avoid the problem that arises immediately: Are our fantasies truly our own? How can we reconquer an imagination of our own when we have been immersed our whole lives in the universe of masculine domination (chapter 4)?

I do not believe that heterosexual love exists simply to serve patriarchy, like a Trojan horse invading the hearts of women. "If women desire men it is because a man cannot be defined in his whole being as oppressor, any more than a woman can be defined entirely as oppressed," wrote Emmanuèle de Lesseps in 1980.[35] But their tie is well and truly poisoned by domination. And if you actually love love, you have to have the courage to study this poisonous aspect lucidly. Such is the "high-risk adventure, the heroic act" that it is up to us to take.

PROLOGUE

Between Conformism and Nihilism

L ove stories as we hear them usually stop at the moment when, after all sorts of troubles and twists and turns, the two protagonists finally confess their feelings for each other. Our fairy tales end with the ritual and remarkably evasive formula: "They lived happily ever after and had many children." We seem disconcerted when it comes to describing what happened next, the way in which this love continued to be experienced and to evolve over time. We reckon there is nothing to say about this, so we stumble, our imaginations suddenly paralyzed. I think of this lacuna as I watch *Normal People*, the TV series adapted from the novel by the young writer Sally Rooney (who coauthored the screenplay). We follow Marianne and Connell, two high schoolers living in a small Irish town. They fall in love and their story continues after their entry into university in Dublin. Rooney's view is innovative in many respects, especially for the sensitive and empathic masculinity incarnated in Connell, played on-screen by the impressive Paul Mescal. But she does not break this spell of focusing only on love's first fruits. In the story of these two adolescents, there are separations born of strong and legitimate reasons, but there is also one split—prolonged and with important consequences—

that seems truly far-fetched: they break up because of a misunderstanding that could have been cleared up in three or four
text messages, or in ten minutes around a cup of coffee. Of
course, lovers do indeed separate for stupid reasons. But this
one seems to express a sort of nervousness on the part of the
scriptwriters, as if they feared there would be nothing to tell if
Marianne and Connell did not have plenty of obstacles between
them. The writers seem hung up on this proven narrative device
because viewers' anxieties are aroused when two characters love
each other but have a hard time getting together: Are they going
to end up admitting their desire to be together, yes or no? "It is
far easier to talk about loss than it is to talk about love," writes
bell hooks. "It is easier to articulate the pain of love's absence
than to describe its presence and meaning in our lives."[1] There
is often a thin line between acceptance of adversity and complacency about it, as if adversity were paradoxically reassuring.

In some cases, this lack of interest in what happens *after* the
recognition of mutual love results from the conventional view
that there is nothing to discuss, since once they are united the
protagonists have only to follow the universal recipe: marriage
(ideally), moving in together, mutual fidelity, procreation. We
pose few questions about this sequence and assume it should be
suitable for everybody. Not only does our emotional insecurity
push us to require carefully codified proofs of love from others,
but the importance of our conjugal and familial status for our
social prestige also dissuades us from departing from well-beaten
paths and exposing ourselves to unflattering judgments. Moreover, even when lovers follow the prescribed program to the
letter, they find themselves on their own when faced with dif-

ficulties or disillusionments. The models offered by our family and friends, by popular common sense, by romantic comedies, and by social regulation all subtly and constantly influence us. A thousand and one stories reiterate and constantly reinforce the clichés of happiness, and we measure the success of our lives by the fidelity with which we reproduce them. There are more-or less veiled injunctions against those who do not conform to the script. Too bad about the suffering that ensues when reality is revealed to be less idyllic than the representations.

In other cases, the refusal to take an interest in how longer-term love is experienced seems to result from contempt for life-as-a-couple, which is usually considered prosaic, bourgeois, boring. This disdain helps explain a widespread taste for impossible love stories, those that are cut short or end badly by a murder, a suicide, or both. Not only do the tragic outcomes— Juliet dying on Romeo's corpse, young Werther putting a bullet in his head because his beloved is married to somebody else—supply the opportunity for great emotional effusions, but they also dispense with having to imagine any way of durably experiencing love.

In the twilight of his life, the ecologist and thinker André Gorz became aware of the prejudices that had long prevented him from realizing how lucky he'd been to share his life with his companion, Dorine. To repair this injustice toward her, in 2006 he published *Lettre à D.*, a book in which he finally tells her of his love and gratitude. He reproaches himself for mentioning "in this dismissive, condescending way," in a youthful work he wrote when they were already living together, that he preferred to dissect at length his breakup with another woman.

Looking back, he analyzes the reasons for this distortion of his lived experience: "Being passionately in love for the first time, being loved in return—this was apparently too banal, too private, too *common*; it wasn't the kind of material that would allow me to rise to the universal. A love affair that's hit the rocks, that can never be—now that, on the other hand, makes for high literature. I'm comfortable with the art of failure and annihilation, not with the art of success and positive affirmation."[2] Another example: in a dual journal that the journalist and writer Benoîte Groult kept with her third husband, Paul Guimard, we witness the genesis of her feminist consciousness in an entry dated October 27, 1952, "Just read Paul's diary. Every time he speaks of what should be called our happiness, he draws from it an impression of melancholy, I don't know why. As described by him, a happy conjugal life appears monotonous, drab, 'comfortable and conventional.'" And she exclaims, "'Conventional'! Convention and banality mean not being happy. Risk and adventure mean being happy."[3]

Gloomy and tortured stories permit men (especially intellectuals, novelists, filmmakers) to speak of love while remaining "serious" by offering merely an illusion of depth, without exposing themselves to ridicule or being compromised by annoyingly feminine sentimentality. Anne-Marie Dardigna noted that in *L'âge d'homme* (1939) the writer Michel Leiris accused his father of having always manifested a "sentimental sensuality" that exasperated the son, particularly when he sang the romantic arias of Massenet. "I do not conceive of love other than in torment and tears," wrote Leiris.[4] In effect, for a writer to maintain a virile dignity means sacrificing the feminine—not only what is interpreted as feminine (and hence negative) inside the self, but also occasionally sacrificing a female *character*. In the courageous stories of doomed love that take up so much space in libraries and on media outlets, the murders of women are surrounded by a romantic (even heroic) aura—which nourishes the complacency with which actual feminicides are greeted. For example, I am thinking of a French film that marked the 1980s: *37°2 le matin*, by Jean-Jacques Beineix (1986), adapted from the novel by Philippe Djian, whose hero (played by Jean-Hugues Anglade) ends up smothering his lover (Béatrice Dalle) with a pillow. Having thus conjured away the threat represented by Betty as the incarnation of bestiality and chaos, he can finally realize his vocation as a writer.

Our culture of love is thus both conformist and morbid—and misogynistic. In *Love in the Western World* (1939), Denis de Rougemont wrote that we are torn between two contradictory moralities: the bourgeois one, which valorizes marriage and stability, and the passionate or romantic one, which makes us dream of tempestuous and tormented loves that are as irresistible as they are impossible. In this captivating archeology of emotions, de Rougemont goes back to the origin of the Western taste for this particular form of passion: the medieval troubadours who sang of a lady both idealized and inaccessible. He saw this as the influence of the Cathars, those presumed heretics who wanted to be "pure" and "perfect" but who despised the flesh and earthly life. According to him, the myth of Tristan and Isolde represents the occult matrix of our aspirations and our emotions; even if we have never read or heard it, "the nostalgic dominion of such a myth . . . is manifested in the majority of novels and films, in the popularity these enjoy with the masses, the acceptance which they meet with in the hearts of middle-class people, from poets, from ill-assorted couples, and from the seamstresses who dream of having a miraculous love-affair."[5] As de Rougemont defines passion here, the Other is a simple way to supply transporting emotion. We prefer this Other at a distance rather than near; we love the state of rapture more than the person. Through their impossible love (Isolde is supposed to marry King Mark), Tristan and Isolde aspire to the absoluteness of death, which they finally attain. "To love in the sense of passion-love is the contrary of to live. It is an impoverishment of one's being, an *askesis* without sequel, an inability to enjoy the present without imagining it as absent, a never-ending flight from possession."[6] In other words, Eros leads to a longing for death. But it is hard to persuade readers to accept a critique of this predisposition, since those who give themselves over to passion take pride precisely in their persistent error: "To succumb to passion is precisely to rest content with being in the wrong according to the world—in the great, irrevocable wrong of preferring death over life."[7]

BELLE DU SEIGNEUR

Among the famous works that reflect this "choice of death" is a novel by Albert Cohen, *Belle du Seigneur*, first published in 1968.[8] Its protagonists, Ariane and Solal, embody, in the most extreme manner, the incapacity to venture beyond the state of their initial encounters. This will eventually lead them to suicide by poison in a final scene that is undeniably very moving—you close the book and brush away your tears. *Belle du Seigneur*, considered to be the greatest novel about love in twentieth-century French literature, might be read as a fictional map of all the mistakes into which the cult of passion leads us. It is worth lingering over.

Its protagonists meet each other in Geneva of the 1930s. Solal is a Mediterranean Jew who serves the League of Nations as undersecretary general; Ariane, from the Genevan aristocracy, is married to Adrien, an ineffectual man who works in Solal's department. (Denis de Rougemont signaled that the "concrete existence of a *husband* symbolizes its character, husbands being despised by courtly love," which is the most obvious of the obstacles that nourish passion. In the myth of Tristan and Isolde, Isolde's husband, King Mark, provides the archetype.)[9] To get rid of his subordinate and seduce his wife more easily, Solal sends him on a long mission abroad. When the husband comes back, the lovers flee together to the South of France, where they live in total seclusion, first at a hotel, then in a sumptuous rented villa. Their isolation is half-suffered, half-chosen. Having become pariahs in the high society they used to frequent, they find themselves banished and rejected, and yet, they feel bound to act as if they have no need of others, as if they are sufficient to each other. Even in this situation, they could have kept alive the intensity of their love face-to-face, but instead they choose to endlessly replay the beginnings of their love story—they have made a fetish of memories—in a sort of funereal pantomime. Very quickly, and without admitting it, they are bored to death with each other; the only means they find to rekindle the flame is to make each other suffer. Solal occasionally resorts to sudden and gratuitous cruelty, his only goal to frighten his mistress, to arouse in her the fear of losing him. Meanwhile, Ariane arouses his jealousy by speaking for the first time of a lover she had before he came along.

Setting up a long-lasting relationship would require each accepting the other in his or her reality as a human being, which Ariane and Solal are incapable of doing. They never appear to each other except in alluring clothes and demeanor. Ariane panics at the slightest inopportune gurgling of her digestive system, and even leaves the room when she feels she is going to sneeze. In the hotel they occupy separate rooms. When they move into the rented villa, Ariane distances herself from Solal for the time it takes for renovations, like installing toilets in each of their respective bathrooms. For even more discretion, she has the builder install a communicating door between her bedroom and her bathroom. In other words, she is ready to move heaven and earth to preserve her image as an ethereal creature, and although Solal's internal monologues are ironic on the subject, it seems to suit him that she strives to preserve that image. The paradox is obviously that their bodily functions, like anything that is repressed, come to assume an invasive place in their relationship. When the maid Mariette witnesses their prudishness, she comments, "If that's love then I want no part of it, why me and my hubby would have rather had to spend a penny together than be parted and that's what real love is say I."[10] We may figure out that it is she who lives in truth, but then Mariette is not the great lover, the heroine who is given to us to admire, with whom we are invited to identify. (The acceptance of the body of the Other remains on the side of sordid conjugality, for example, the boorish husband who details his intestinal problems to his wife.) By stopping in the middle of fording the river, Cohen's novel encloses us more firmly in the vision of love that it claims to condemn. We perceive its ambiguity: Cohen once defined *Belle du Seigneur* as a "passionate pamphlet against passion."[11] In fact, he is denouncing the clichés of passion . . . but meanwhile feeding them.

Ariane and Solal do not succeed in breaking out of the trajectory of all doomed lovers, though most couples usually manage to at least negotiate their way through domesticity: continuing to love each other after having seen the partner first thing in the morning, and accepting the fact that this light-filled being does possess a digestive system, which somehow had not been mentioned at the first rendezvous! This is a moment of particular vulnerability for women, who are strongly incited by social norms to groom themselves during the day, thus increasing the distance from their nighttime appearance. This is the moment when a woman discovers whether she is loved as a real and familiar person or as an icon, an idealized and disincarnated figure, like the lady whom the troubadour fantasizes about from afar—placing her "on a pedestal sufficiently high that there is no longer a need to touch her," in Anne-Marie Dardigna's phrase.[12]

In her study of contemporary love relationships, the sociologist Eva Illouz encountered Claudine, age forty-eight, whom she described as being "strikingly attractive." Claudine recounts that one day her lover came back from a trip unexpectedly and saw her in the morning while she was still in her nightgown. She had not brushed her teeth or done her hair and makeup. "He came in and I saw the look on his face. He said to me: 'What happened? Are you sick? Are you OK? You look so different from usual.' . . . I hugged him, I thought he would kiss me but he didn't. It made me think whether this guy would love me when I am old and wrinkled."[13]

Women are supposed to be like goddesses or fairies, guaranteed to lack innards but with a pink button between their buttocks: the fault of "patriar-caca."[14] "Girls tend to be toilet-trained earlier than boys," explains Nick Haslam in *Psychology in the Bathroom*.[15] (And, of course, having inculcated shame about their bodies, we deride girls when they demonstrate prudishness.) The most basic bodily processes are sometimes reduced to the last extremity to dissimulate the awful truth. One evening in 2017, a young British woman on a Tinder date (which had been going well up until then) realized with horror after using her date's toilet that the flush was not working. She tried to get rid of the compromising packet by throwing it outside, but unluckily it fell between the two window panels. She had to explain the situation to her host, Liam, and with his help she managed to get the fecal packet back and throw it down the toilet, but she herself remained stuck upside down inside the window. The firemen had to come to free her. The story went viral, illustrated by photos (happily for the anonymity of the young acrobat, the window glass was murky),[16] which summarizes the general fate of our efforts at discretion. Liam launched a Go-

FundMe campaign to repair his window. Having collected ten times the necessary sum thanks to a burst of worldwide solidarity, he spent the surplus on an association that builds toilets in Southern countries. The last news was that he intended to recontact his guest one evening to invite her for a coffee.[17]

In this context, the joyful scatology of Rachel Bloom, the creator of and actress in the American series *Crazy Ex-Girlfriend*, assumes an almost political dimension. Similarly, the Australian-Canadian writer Fariha Róisín, when asked about her beauty regimen by the American website *Into the Gloss* in 2019, vaunted not only the merits of her Chanel mascara or her Santa Maria Novella honey shampoo but also her Squatty Potty stool, which allows her to poop more comfortably. "Women are told not to question most things about our bodies, and you're so cloaked in shame all the time that you just accept it when things are off," she declared.[18] (Hitting all the taboos at once, she went on to mention her mental health problems and her marijuana consumption, and specified her preferred brands of lubricant and dildo.)

For Solal in *Belle du Seigneur*, not only does the physiological body pose a problem but so does the sexual body. He is annoyed with women because he is attracted to and seduced by their beauty, which he considers false and superficial. In his eyes, eroticism, which is associated with a hideous and grotesque animality, cannot be justified unless it is sanctified by the highest kind of passion. He is irritated that his mistresses want to talk after lovemaking instead of leaving him "in peace to purge [his] shame!"[19] His repugnance, as well as his possessiveness, bursts out in scenes of jealousy when he learns that Ariane had another lover before him. He proceeds to ravage their hotel room, to mutilate himself, to humiliate her. It does not matter that he had had other mistresses *during* their romance: he is horrified to imagine *his* Ariane, whom he wanted to believe so "pure," has been soiled by bestial sexuality. These are pages where Cohen's retrograde ideas appear most clearly. Interestingly, his third wife, Bella Cohen (hired first as a secretary, and who had typed from dictation the manuscript of *Belle du Seigneur* four times because he was constantly adding text to the nearly thousand-page book), told him in 1980 that she was personally opposed to these scenes and wanted him to cut them. "She was wrong," he peremptorily concluded.[20]

Passion thus allows the male protagonist to remain enclosed in his immature and defiant view of woman, which serves as a screen for an elitist posture that despises earthly and quotidian life and carnality. The misogynistic view that associates women with carnality is much more common and conventional than its supporters want to believe. There is little doubt about the misogynistic convictions of Solal, who is meant to be *the* magnificent lover in all of French literature.* For example, he does not dare admit to Ariane that he was dismissed from his post at the League of Nations after Nazism was on the rise, for ar-

---

* These views reflect those of Albert Cohen himself. In an interview on *Radioscopie* (April 4, 1980), he asserted that there should be "feudal relations" between men and women. He insisted that one say "Solal and Ariane" in that order: "Yes, the man first, of course." Of Marguerite Yourcenar, he told his scandalized host: "I haven't read anything by her, she is too ugly. Nothing great can emerge from that frightful body. . . . She is too fat. And then she loves women—all that displeases me."

guing too insistently on welcoming German Jews who were fleeing persecution, nor that he has had his French nationality revoked, making him stateless—all because he does not think that Ariane's love would survive the disappearance of his social prestige. He believes that women adore power: if they find him handsome, it is because he gives off power, a kind of force in which they recognize the faculty to kill. He is also persuaded that women are masochists. He presents himself as a good and tender man, gentle as a lamb, but who tries to appear cruel, if not violent, because that is what "they" expect. He seems to believe that if Ariane does not love her husband, it is because he is too soft, whereas the real problem with Adrien is that he is simple and desperately down-to-earth. Solal ridicules Adrien by making him unwittingly complicit in his own cuckolding, claiming this as a sad necessity for him to seduce Ariane. Deep down he actually pities his "brother," although we sense his enjoyment (and that of the author) in this ruse; and as female readers we also enjoy it, especially after the scenes of conjugal rape we witnessed at the beginning of the novel.

When I discovered *Belle du Seigneur* twenty-five years ago, I was one of those "seamstresses who dream of having a miraculous love-affair," to use Denis de Rougemont's phrase. It took me time to discover what was not right about de Rougemont's vision of love, or about Cohen's vision of women. I continue to admire Cohen's literary virtuosity, his style that is both torrential and lapidary, his lyricism, his agility, and his comic touches, but I resent him even more on account of that style. He has instilled his ideas in me all the more effectively because he did so with genius. The film adaptation made in 2012 by Glenio

Bonder (with Jonathan Rhys Meyers and Natalia Vodianova in the roles of Solal and Ariane, and Marianne Faithfull playing the maid Mariette) shows what remains when his writing is no longer there to sublimate his plot: a script full of sexism and snobbery (the class contempt—for example, when Solal observes a couple of young proletarians in a train—struck me as it did not when I first read the novel).

THE DELIGHTS OF A RELATIONSHIP OVER TIME

We need to adjust our way of conceiving of love, to breathe life back into it, by pulverizing both the bourgeois straitjacket of the obligatory trajectory of romance and the equally conventional (and limiting) view of destructive passion. We need both a little more audacity and less complacency about our neurasthenic stances. This approach can only be very personal, and the ideal of love that I am proposing now obviously cannot pretend to any universal validity. But it will at least allow my readers to know who is speaking to them, and perhaps allow them to examine the desires they nourish and clarify their own views by means of their adherence to or disagreement with mine.

After *Belle du Seigneur*, my fantasies about love were fed by very different models. I admired couples who, precisely, proved capable of establishing their story over a long time, jointly experiencing daily life with trust, happiness, and voluptuousness. For me, the ties I have woven over the years in—both love affairs and friendships—nourished by a quality specific to each person, their generosity and individual resources, the kind of relationship that deeply intermingles two existences, are what give meaning to life, the only possible victory over death. The temporal arc of a friendly or amorous relationship is a priceless gift. In my case, the fact of not squabbling with my ex-companion after our separation allows me to continue to say to him "Remember when . . . ?" to keep alive our common past, all the events only we can remind each other of. I am filled with infinite gratitude for that long liaison. Similarly, I prefer series to single films, because I love following the evolution of a character over several episodes or seasons, discovering unexpected aspects of that character, seeing displays of their richness and complexity, taking the measure of the arc covered. Some scriptwriters know how to play with this marvelously, soliciting via allusions or flashbacks the memories that the viewer has in common with the story's heroes. The writers know that this is an intensely satisfying sensation, even if with fictional beings.

Perhaps you will object that I, too, am expressing here an ideal of a conventional "forever love." This is true. This is an aspiration often considered to be romantic, naive, unrealistic, and typically feminine; moreover, my ideal is resolutely monogamous, while more and more voices are heard today claiming that it is unreasonable to expect everything from one and the same person. But for me, the attraction of love is indissociable from the act of granting a privileged place in one's life to somebody and occupying a similar place in his, to *distinguish* the Other and to be *distinguished by* that Other. Therefore "poly-love"[21] is quite simply beyond my comprehension. As for open relationships, they seem to require an immense self-confidence; I admire the people who manage it. This kind of relationship was probably raised to the rank of a masterpiece by Frida Kahlo and Diego Rivera in the course of their marriage. Both of them had intense and passionate affairs with other people, without ever putting in peril the tie that bound them. The lovers and the mistresses of the two Mexican artists, writes Cristina Nehring, "were drawn to Frida and Diego as sideshows are drawn to main shows, as candy sellers are drawn to circuses and court jesters are drawn to Shakespearean kings."[22] The queer scholar Travers Scott imagined ten types of possible arrangements that he explored with his companion, ranging from strict monogamy ("plus porn"), to monogamy plus mutually agreed upon third parties, to nonmonogamy only when out of town, to nonmonogamy only with strangers (no friends or exes), and so on.[23]

For my part, I adore the idea of an intense and captivating connection that both partners would find fulfilling. I do not believe in sacrificial fidelity: if frustration exists, it is better to separate or find an arrangement that remedies that frustration. In fact, it is not always possible to be fulfilled by a single person, but nor do I want to remove this hypothesis from the start. I believe that amorous exclusivity can bring irreplaceable pleasures, and that each man and woman is vast enough to contain the entire world and offer it to the other, and that one never finishes knowing somebody else. I rather like the spiritual definition of fidelity given by Denis de Rougemont that involves accepting the "intimate particularity" of one's lover, "in his or her own limitations and reality, choosing this being not as an excuse for excited elevation or as an 'object of contemplation,' but having a matchless and independent life which requires *active* love."[24]

In the journalist Judith Duportail's book *L'amour sous algo-rithme*, which mixes her investigation into online dating with her personal story, she recounts meeting a man on Tinder. Their beginnings are idyllic. Then one day she discovers that, like her, he had once been interviewed by a magazine for an article on dating apps, in which he stated, "When you pick a girl on Adopte un mec [Adopt a Guy], you keep your account. So even if it goes well, you are always tempted to return to the site to see if there is something better in stock." (He denied saying "in stock.") Duportail was very disturbed by these statements, but later an American anthropologist explained to her that in order to keep their users hooked, applications resort to "alea-tory and variable rewards," one of the most powerful psycho-logical mechanisms in addiction, to which slot machines—an industry with colossal profits—owe their success. Dating apps *need* their users to come back as often as possible to consult their accounts, so their economic model relies on the eternal dissatisfaction of the men and the women who use them, on their incapacity to become attached. While awaiting her Tinder match, Duportail's head was in a "whirlwind": "Will he still be tempted to go back to the app? Why does he go back all the time? What will I say? That I am hurt, at the risk of appearing tiresome? Or pretend not to care?"[25]

This logic of a regular return "to the stock" reminds me of a gardener who would neglect or trample on his plants. What could be more sinister than experiencing love as a permanent negotiation between the respective qualities of various objects? Mentioning "magazine sermons" and the happiness they dangle in front of their readers, Denis de Rougemont back in 1939 was already pointing to a fundamental contradiction: "For everything thus suggested [to be happy] introduces us to a world of comparisons in which . . . no happiness can be established."[26]

We read a lot about it being impossible to keep love alive or to maintain desire for a long duration. I wonder if this is not a hasty conclusion. It is indeed very difficult when our lifestyle reduces us to the role of harassed managers overwhelmed by family logistics. Even if one has no means of escaping the domestic role, one should be aware of the fact that disenchantment and dissatisfactions relate not to the relationship itself but to the concrete and everyday conditions into which that relationship is inserted, to everything from the outside that hinders its flourishing, which normally we do not dwell upon. A marveling young father tells me about the sweetness and ease of his whole new life; a sweetness and ease that he was not expecting, and which he attributes to the fact that both he and his female partner work from their home and are therefore the masters of organizing their time, being available both for each other and for their daughter. I remember my feeling of mourning, dispossession, and distress the day my companion since our student days became a full-time employee. (I remained an independent journalist a few years longer.) Not that I would have wanted to be stuck to him permanently—on the contrary, I need solitude—but there is something invasive about a salaried job, which sucks the blood out of you, and which, to a certain extent, captures and makes the other a stranger.[27] At first, when he came back from the office in the evening, I had the impression that he had been scooped out and they were returning to me a defrocked man who only looked like him. One gets used to and adapts to it, obviously.

I think there are many ways of existing and acting in the world, of leaving and coming back, that allow more suppleness, that do not involve this exhaustion of a particular kind, this withering of the tie to the beloved person. The pandemic confinement in the spring of 2020, although it was established for dire reasons and did harm the social fabric, nevertheless allowed some couples to find each other again in a way that would not have been possible otherwise. For example, a French teacher on extended leave, living in a small village in the Loire-Atlantique, spoke of her pleasure in having her husband at home twenty-four hours a day, when "in normal times he was absent from 8 am to 8 pm."[28] How have we been able to accept as normal this way of living in which we are profoundly deprived of the person with whom we share our home and our bed?

"IF LIFE HAS JUST BEEN A SUMMER SIESTA"*

The couple who made me dream the most—the writer, painter, and composer Serge Rezvani and his wife, Danièle, called Lula—managed to escape the fate of lovers whose relationship withers over time. They never had a child, so nothing distracted

---

* Section title from a song lyric taken from "Les grains de beauté."

them from their life as a couple. This absence of progeny arose from a deliberate and considered choice: "A child is a part of us that is hostage to the social," explained Serge Rezvani in 2003. "And we did not want to give anything of ourselves to the social."[29] After their meeting in Paris in 1950, while they were both very young (she was nineteen, he was twenty-two), they lived hand to mouth for several years, first in maids' rooms and then in an apartment on the periphery of Paris. Then one day, during a trip to the Var area of Provence, they discovered, lost at the bottom of a valley below the Maures mountains, a little cottage with walls of faded ochre, flanked by a palm tree and reached through terraced gardens. Its name was *La béate*. The owner took them in out of sympathy and agreed to a nominal rent because they had almost no money. They ended up settling in for good, hoping eventually to buy it. In this magical place (very refined, although in the first years they had neither electricity nor running water and had to fetch it from a nearby spring), they lived an enchanted life for fifty years. "Some evenings," writes Serge Rezvani in *Le roman d'une maison*, "while Danièle was reading and listening to a Beethoven quarter, stretched out on sofa cushions in the ground floor room, the cat on her knees and the dog lying at her feet, I would often go out into the night under the terraced palms and start sobbing over this excess of happiness. By the open window, I could see the love of my life in the golden light of oil lamps; I suffered, my heart painfully gripped by nostalgia for a present so delicate and perfect, whose sublime beauty could remain suspended in the eternal. No, death could never reach us here, never could it extinguish such serene perfection."[30] In "Les grains de beauté," he sings: "You laugh at the years / What do the seasons matter / If life has been just / A summer siesta?" I also love Rezvani's work because it startlingly denies the lazy prejudice that happy people have no story. "Happy families are all alike; every unhappy family is unhappy in its own way," wrote Leo Tolstoy in the opening lines of *Anna Karenina*. This sums up a widespread cliché that is flagrantly false, if you think about it for a minute. With Rezvani, happiness is a dazzling source of singularity—and of creation and reflection.

In this example, it is the love that fascinates me just as much as the home. In an earlier book on domestic living, I quoted these fine lines from Rezvani on the surprises of repetition, the marvelous interest one can find in renewing each day gestures and rituals that are laden with meaning for us, by learning to appreciate their minuscule variations, like a painting palette that one constantly enlarges and enriches. I find another paean to this idea from the writer and academic Séverine Auffret: "A continual increase in enjoyment comes to us from repeatedly hearing a piece of music. The first listen does not win our support. It is the second, the third time, and so on that affirms our pleasure, like that bodily rhythm specific to any scansion, any repetition: traveling across the same space, reiteration of the same gesture; the request that one makes during sex, like the little child you rock, throw into the air, or swing, and who cries out 'Again!'"[31] The same slightly monomaniacal trait inspires my homebody inclinations and my penchant for amorous exclusivity. It is the same taste as that for sensual intimacy, the same bet in finding hidden abundance where a superficial view sees only monotony, the same desire for an infinitely deep study, the same trust in an invisible and mysterious process that demands only that one believe in its existence, that one lets it come, that one accepts letting oneself be carried away. Writing, too, which always takes you somewhere else than you thought you were going, which makes your fingers find an unexpected thread, has taught me not to fear that the interior sources are becoming exhausted, whether in a process of solitary creation or in an amorous and sexual dialogue.

André Gorz and his wife Dorine also spent their lives together without ever tiring of each other, and they, too, ended up settling far from Paris, in a small village in the Aube. They committed suicide together on September 22, 2007, after an illness from which Dorine was suffering got worse. "Neither of us wants to outlive the other," Gorz wrote the preceding year. "We've often said to ourselves that if, by some miracle, we were to have a second life, we'd like to spend it together."[32] They, too, escaped the trap of office employment, with the constraints and separation it involves. Nor did they have a child. Moreover, in both these couples, the men were capable of sharing and appreciating daily intimacy with a real-life woman, instead of idolizing her as a distant icon. Still, I regret—a sizable regret—that only the male partner's creative activity was developed, while the women confined themselves to sustaining them. Male artistic vocations were considered to be evident, legitimate, imperious. The female companions remained silent. Both Danièle Rezvani and Dorine Gorz were fond of discretion and staying in the shadows, but women remaining silent occurs too often for that character trait to be a matter of chance. Ironically, we only know of these love stories because their male protagonists recounted them: Serge Rezvani in numerous superb books, and André Gorz in *Lettre à D*. In fact, Dorine Gorz was cultivated and charismatic, serving her husband as documentarian, adviser, conversation partner, and copy editor.[33] Danièle Rezvani (who died in 2004) was a partner and a muse. Serge Rezvani told me recently that he had kept her notebooks and was thinking of publishing them some day.

Therefore, in order to escape the usual pitfalls of love, rather than challenging the idea of an exclusive relationship, we can question the concrete conditions in which it develops. This leads me to amend the model of the two couples whom I just mentioned. The choice of an isolated retreat pleases me because it bespeaks the trust in the richness of the amorous tie, but for my part, I would need a place to live that is central enough to allow me to see my friends and to meet new ones. Above all, I do not believe that permanent cohabitation is still part of my ideal. I enjoyed it a lot; I cherish my memories of those mornings when I was in a foul mood and my companion managed to make me laugh with a well-placed joke, moments when we clasped each other in our arms while preparing coffee or tea in the kitchen before going off to work. When we separated, I dreamed of a domestic landscape where everything before my eyes belonged to me, of an apartment in which I would have chosen everything; as if I needed, after so long sharing a life in common, to gather myself, to experience who I was without him. I am very satisfied to realize this desire to be apart, even if

I sometimes feel nostalgia for the shelves where our books, our photos, and our knickknacks intermingled, the walls where our posters and respective postcards hung alongside each other, for the fusion of our two universes. I am happy that this existed. It lasted long enough to be confused with living itself, so that now when I venture into my old neighborhood, and especially into my old apartment (where he still lives), I have the impression of being a soul coming back to haunt the sites of its earthly existence.

Perhaps one day I will have a renewed desire to cohabit. But the way I see things right now, it seems preferable that each person have his or her own space, whether two separate lodgings or at least two bedrooms in the same lodging. I like the idea of having solitude as a primary state, keeping a place of retreat, being with the other for a few hours or a few days— but because I have chosen that, because both of us desire that, and not because he happens to live there, too. I like the idea of never having to endure his presence and never having mine imposed on him. "I wish you . . . riveted in my heart; but I do not desire to have you always at my elbow," wrote Mary Wollstonecraft to her husband, the political philosopher William Godwin. They each rented a flat of their own, "passing notes to each other through messengers and arranging dinner dates and amorous trysts the way courting teenagers might do," says Cristina Nehring. "Far from rendering their relationship adolescent, however, this elective distance kept it intensely engaged." Frida Kahlo and Diego Rivera did the same: "For much of their conjugal life, they maintained separate houses—Kahlo's blue, Rivera's pink—connected only whimsically by a walking bridge and divided by dozens of animal cages, fruit trees, and patches of desert."[34] The British journalist Grace Dent's perfect solution, which allows her, as she says, to have her cake and eat it, too, is to cohabit four days per week: "All human life is there: the chat, the chores, the waking ups, the teeth brushings and the joint socializing. But then for three days there is silence. And I love silence."[35]

"TWO PEOPLE WHO LOVE EACH OTHER AND ARE ONE: BUT WHICH?"

In many couples who cohabit, each enjoys the absences of the other because of the opportunity for a wave of freedom and tranquility. I find this a bit sad because it testifies to the lack of uninterrupted solitude in most people's ordinary lives. In fact, having personal space materializes one's mental space, giving what is internal its proper place. Separate living arrangements avoid the arguments that arise in shared homes, for example, about who will occupy the only office available. It may also preclude arrangements that come up from our unconscious, those spontaneous and visceral ways of interacting that solidify ways of functioning, those impulses that are impossible to root out later. Such unconscious assumptions are harmful both for the couple and for the individuals who compose it, as such friction stunts individual identity. Finally, this approach overcomes the trap that is summed up in Nancy Huston's cruel phrase: "Two people who love each other and are one:—but which?"[36] Or this remark by Rainer Maria Rilke: "When two people both give themselves up in order to come close to each other, there is no longer any ground beneath them and their being together is a continual falling."[37]

People will say separate households cost a lot, and that is true (it is also less economical). But this objection comes from people who have the means to keep separate homes, so maybe what they are expressing is conformity. People who choose to keep separate households might decide that cohabiting ultimately won't save them strife, financial or otherwise, especially if they do not have a deep desire to cohabit and suspect it might eventually damage their relationship. More generally, one solution would be to conceive of joint incomes as allowing us to live in an independent way. In *La fin de l'amour*, Eva Illouz says she sees today a multiplication of "negative relations," meaning the refusal or incapacity to form durable relationships. Among the signs of this, she cites that "single households have considerably increased in the last two decades."[38] But she implicitly assimilates cohabitation and commitment, which is a mistake. Of course, one might cherish and venerate the person with whom one lives, just as one may live alone but be a psychopath with a frigid soul. But one can also live alone and be madly and passionately committed to someone, just as one may live as a couple out of comfort, out of laziness, out of conformity, or because one has neither the means nor the courage to move out. Being captive does not mean being committed.

In 1975, the American sociologist Joseph Harris compared the lifestyles of 241 gay men in the city of Detroit (all of them in a stable relationship for at least one year) with those of heterosexual couples. While almost all the latter shared accommodation, this was the case with only three-quarters of the gay couples. The other quarter kept separate residences, which of course allowed them to avoid snoopy neighbors. The sociologist did not detect a difference in the degree of mutual commitment of these "living separately" couples in relation to those who cohabited. This arrangement, the journalist Julia Sklar concluded, "was not a barrier to the strength of these relationships, and in fact may have been the reason they were able to last in spite of social oppression and the financial strain of maintaining two households."[39] Even if many gays and lesbians would no doubt have preferred to cohabit openly, like clandestine couples of all sexual orientations they had long demonstrated that a loving relationship is not necessarily seen in the composition of a household.

Back in 1907, the American anarchist Voltairine de Cleyre argued that "the only way to preserve love in anything like the ecstatic condition which renders it worthy of a distinctive name . . . is to maintain a distance." She thought, "That life may grow, I would have men and women remain separate personalities," that each person must take care to be a "free individual."[40] I thought about de Cleyre in the spring of 2020. For my whole life (even after resuming living alone a few years ago) I had arranged to live without cooking, grazing on snacks between two meals at a restaurant or between two take-away orders. Then the first confinement of 2020 took place. Either I would condemn myself to two months of insipid food, in a context where eating well was one of the rare ties attaching me to life (other than through the screen, if I chose to turn it on), or I would get started cooking. I discovered that I was able to

get pleasure from what I cooked—a sort of gustatory autoerot-
icism! My ex-companion told me about recipe sites, he gave me
advice. As the days went by, I sent him a photo of each new
dish I had made and I complacently savored his compliments.
Had we still been living together, I would have been content
to eat the meals he prepared for me; but that would have been
a shame.

The question of children remains. What do those who have
chosen to have children together do if they do not wish to live
together? Voltairine de Cleyre was not a great fan of procreation
("We are no longer compelled to use the blind method of lim-
itless propagation to equip the race with hunters and trappers
and fishers and sheep-keepers and soil-tillers and breeders"),
and one suspects that she was irritated to have to deal with
this kind of detail. She considers that a child "may be as well
brought up in an individual home, or in a communal home,
as in a dual home." But she thinks that any alternative framework
is more beneficial and stimulating than what we would call the
nuclear family. She admits having "no satisfactory solutions to
offer to the various questions presented by the child-problem";
but she adds maliciously, "neither do the advocates of marriage."[41]

Within heterosexual couples, the principle of separate
residences is more important for women. "I believe that the
question posed by couples and cohabitation is about territory,"
wrote the journalist and feminist Évelyne Le Garrec in 1979.
"The rule for a woman, whether or not she earns her own living, studies or not for a degree, has access or not to rewarding
professions, is always having to share territory, being totally

dispossessed of the means of existing by herself in space." She saw the conjugal home as a problematic and obsolete social convention: "Institutionalized cohabitation of a couple in the same place weakens both the individual and the collective. At least the collective is meant to be a voluntary assemblage of free and autonomous individuals who construct and master that group. It seems to me that an adult would function in the dual mode of the individual and the collective, one reinforcing the other. The couple appears as a closed refuge from the fear of being confronted with one's own void and the void of a constraining collective."[42] But she knew the subject was sensitive. In February 1978, the "Common Program for Women" developed by Choisir la Cause des Femmes, the organization founded by the well-known feminist lawyer Gisèle Halimi, caused a row over a single sentence they wrote: "If the goal is the suppression of the patriarchal family, perhaps it will be necessary, in order to attain this goal, to suppress couple cohabitation for at least a generation."[43] An editorial in Le Monde (February 12, 1978) denounced "the hatred that is expressed in each page of this singular common program offered to women." (There followed the inevitable accusation about "doing disservice to your cause," familiar still today to almost all feminists: "The authors of this polemical tract discredit much more than they serve to the cause they claim to defend," etc.)[44]

Non-cohabitation solves the issue of the division of domestic tasks—by getting rid of it. "If you're not living in the same home with a guy," comments the psychologist Bella DePaulo, "then you're not going to feel obligated to do the dishes, or pick up his socks. You might not feel obligated anyway, if you lived with him, but it's a little easier to resist when they're his dishes and his sink."[45] Separate residences short-circuit the couple and the family as the means of exploiting the female workforce. Here I will return only briefly to this subject, which I have dealt with in previous books.[46] The "always on-call" duty of women to perform domestic work, which is often crushing, arises from a well-anchored social order that exceeds the individual wills of the protagonists. But what also happens is that men find the advantages procured by cohabitation quite natural, which inevitably sows doubt: Is this exploitation itself a fortuitous consequence of living together? But what is its rationale? On the Instagram account "T'as pensé à . . . ?," maintained by Coline Charpentier, a woman recounts that after "fifteen years spent running non-stop to manage everything alone," when she spoke of divorce, her husband answered, "I will have to employ a housekeeper."[47] And in the sociologist Marie-Carmen Garcia's study of extramarital couples, we stumble on this revealing fact: the married men she questioned at the start of the 2010s (not in the 1950s) thought that their single mistresses had a fine life, that they were "free" because they could dispense with the domestic service already provided by their own wives.[48]

Similarly, in a radio series titled "J'en ai marre des mecs,"[49] the host, the physician and writer Baptiste Beaulieu (himself gay and in solidarity with feminist struggles), mentioned some of the nauseating masculine behaviors observed during his patient consultations. Accused by some of having invented these anecdotes, he published on his Facebook account similar stories of bad male behavior that he received from listeners after his episode aired. A female listener remembered that when she was little, her mother had to spend three weeks in the hospital: "My brother and I ate bananas and endless spaghettis for these three weeks. Then my mother had to begin to cook again, even though she was supposed to stay in bed for a while." Christelle Da Cruz, a hospital social worker, said she could not count how many times a man told her, "My wife *has* to get out of the hospital—and quickly. I am fed up with having to cook for myself and run errands and do the housework." Coline Charpentier assembled for her Instagram account one hundred women who effectively "ran the house while they were hospitalized, receiving constant text messages along the lines of 'When are you coming home? What do we eat?' when they were undergoing operations."[50]

Popular culture takes care to not present things so crudely in the vision it presents of marriage. The popular British romantic comedy *Love Actually* (2003), for example, offers a schoolbook case of romanticizing domestic exploitation though the love story that develops between Jamie (Colin Firth), a London writer who has retired to his house in the South of France after a breakup, and Aurélia (Lúcia Moniz), his Portuguese housekeeper. When both of them return from their respective countries on impulse for Christmas Eve, Jamie finds the young woman in the café where she works as a waitress. In a highly theatrical scene, with her at the top of a staircase, he asks for her hand in marriage in front of the customers at the café and members of his family; we now discover that while they were separated, each has learned the language of the other. From now on, by the laws of plausibility, Aurélia will furnish Jamie with the same services as she had previously—she will keep house and bring him his coffee while he writes—but he no longer needs to pay her! Refusing to cohabit might enable a woman to know if one is loved for oneself or for services she renders. It would also allow certain men to acquire some useful skills and to become a "free individual," to use Voltairine de Cleyre's expression.

Perhaps you will protest that the ideal I am depicting here is not very realistic—but otherwise it would not be an ideal! In conclusion, we might usefully explore our desires, make them more precise, cultivate and refine them, follow their ramifications, independently of the possibility of realizing them, but hoping to approach them as much as possible. As we are now going to see in detail, heterosexual love is a path strewn with pitfalls. One should acquire as many strategies of survival as one can, starting with avoiding surrender to ready-made schemas about the right way to live or letting fatal conceptions sabotage our desires—noble and legitimate—for fulfillment and sharing.

MAKING YOURSELF LESS NOTICEABLE TO BE LOVED?

The Inferiority of Women in Our Romantic Ideal

In the summer of 2019, a *Paris match* cover carried a dual portrait of the former president Nicolas Sarkozy and his wife, Carla Bruni. The photo produced general laughter, because the former top model was burying her face in her husband's shoulder, making him appear to be a giant protector, while as everybody knows, she is taller than he is. Faced with jokes, the weekly magazine published a hypocritical correction: no, the photo had not been retouched; the couple had simply posed on a staircase leading to their garden, and the former president stood on a higher step than his wife.[1] Two models of desirability are telescoped here: first, the man, made irresistible by power, who can dispense with a very different criterion of conventional masculinity; and second, the trophy wife, who presents the expected characteristics of a model, starting with tall stature.

On this occasion, the journalist Pauline Thurier went back to previous *Paris match* covers featuring the couple. Each time, Carla Bruni was placed in a position of inferiority, in postures suggesting submission or fragility. We saw her perched on her husband's knees like a child, stretched out on a sofa with her head on his knees, curled up by him in a Venetian gondola, or walking alongside him on a beach, but with her head bent, as if to remain below an invisible bar set by his own stature. Charlene, the wife of Prince Albert II of Monaco, got the same treatment in family portraits after the birth of their twins, as did Diana Spencer when she was married to Prince Charles in the 1980s: in the official photos, Charles seems always to be a head taller than she, although they were of the same height.[2]

Swallowing the red pill of feminism means we should listen to the American feminist Catharine MacKinnon, who said that "male and female are created through the eroticization of dominance and submission,"[3] or as Manon Garcia summarizes this argument: "Dominance and submission are the attitudes from which gender difference is built."[4] Armed with this key to understanding, we suddenly see how our whole amorous culture tries to naturalize and even celebrate the signs of male domination and female submission, by presenting them as the secrets of a harmonious union. Moreover, the conventional idea that the growing liberation of women might ruin love relationships implies an admission: our emotional organization relies on female subordination. Is it not astonishing that this order of things is what seems so natural to us and that it is the contesting of this that offends so many people? The title of a 2010 article in the *New York Times* candidly summarized the problem of our era: "Keeping Romance Alive in the Age of Female Empowerment."[5] Female inferiority seems to be encapsulated in our amorous narrative, starting with a literal and immediately visible inferiority: in a couple, the man must be taller than the woman. "Living as a couple is less frequent among shorter men," says the sociologist Nicolas Herpin. This situation is not due to their social condition. Although working-class men are on average shorter than office workers, the effects of height on couple formation are on a par in both social milieux.[6] This gap is sought after by men, but it seems even more so by women.[7] Miriam, a young woman who is 5 foot, 11.5 inches tall, recounts how a man with whom she had a date blanched when she stood up: "He never called me back." Some of her boyfriends asked her never to wear high heels, but she refused: "Now it's a kind of protest. I do not want to make myself smaller."[8]

Does the average difference in height between men and women (which is true across the planet) arise from a biological destiny? In 2013, Véronique Kleiner's documentary *Pourquoi les femmes sont-elles plus petites que les hommes?*[9] popularized the anthropologist Priscille Touraille's hypothesis refuting this.[10] All over the world, in fact, women are less well nourished than men. According to the U.N.'s Food and Agriculture Organization (FAO), they suffer twice as much from malnutrition as men. Girls have twice the risk of dying from hunger and have a larger deficit of animal protein. Women prepare and serve the food, but they content themselves with eating the less good morsels and often go without meat. Yet during pregnancy and breastfeeding they need a diet of 30 percent animal protein and five times more iron (also necessary to prevent the risk of anemia due to menstruation) than men.

The anthropologist Françoise Héritier recounts how, during her field study in Burkina Faso, she observed that when babies demanded the breast, mothers immediately gave it to boys but they made girls wait. When she asked why, she was told that baby boys have a red body and are in danger of bursting into a fury if they are not fed right away. With respect to baby girls, the response was not physiological but sociological: they had to "learn to deal with frustration," since as women, they "will never be satisfied in their whole lives." "In this way you are creating two human varieties that are totally different in their expectations," Héritier comments. "One that will expect immediate satisfaction of all his needs and impulses, and the other who will be destined to wait upon the goodwill of someone else. This is extraordinary training by means of food."[11] The logic is the same in Europe and North America, as demonstrated in the studies of thinness by the American philosopher Susan Bordo.[12]

In the course of evolution, could this "organized food penury" have ended up making women smaller—since putting a stop to growth is the means the organism uses to resist privation? Priscille Touraille's hypothesis unleashed a barrage in the right-wing press and among anti-feminists, who turned to some scientists who disputed it. Questioned by the journalist Peggy Sastre, the biologist Michel Raymond had another explanation of the disparity: "Male gorillas fight each other and the largest have an advantage, which helps explain their larger size than their females. With men, violence is immemorial, as archeology attests, and size is not independent of social dominance. Moreover, women prefer men who are taller than they are." His colleague Robert Trivers stresses that "sexual dimorphism did not begin with our lineage in the Paleolithic era–males are taller and heavier than females among *all* our closest cousins, whether among species of chimpanzees, gorillas, or orangutans."[13] Whatever the case, though, one does not see why this superiority of the man over the woman ought to be found in *all* couples.

"A WOMAN IS BEAUTIFUL WHEN SHE IS WEAK"

While the fashion world requires models to be taller than average, many other criteria of female seduction and feminine attributes denote forms of weakness, impediments, or powerlessness. Thinness translates the obligation to take up as little space as possible. Skirts and high-heeled shoes hamper movement.[14] Youthfulness is considered more desirable, because it is associated with malleability and gullibility.[15] "A man is handsome when he is powerful. A woman is beautiful when she is weak" is how Noémie Renard summarized it in a 2016 series of articles on the subject.[16] She showed the universality of this ideal of powerlessness, though it can take many different forms. For example, the force-feeding of girls to prepare them for marriage, as practiced by the nomadic peoples of the Western Sahara, permits immobilizing women to better control them; they live cloistered and entirely dependent on men. Chinese foot-binding, used until the start of the twentieth century, had the effect of making women's walking precarious, thus suggesting delicateness and fragility; Noémie Renard cites the academic Wang Ping: "Men cannot help feeling pity for them and falling in love with them. All these are indispensable elements for Chinese eroticism and female allure."

Expression of weakness can also come through the voice. Certain women are tempted to adopt a "sexy baby" voice when they address a man: "Babies don't possess social power, economic power, or sexual power," states the sociologist Anne Karpf, who explains this temptation by a learned need to protect the masculine ego. She has noticed that many "extremely bright women" have "huge difficulty using their voice. They are terrified to use the full force of it. I've rarely encountered a man with that same problem."[17] The imperative to smile (a symbol of abnegation) and the availability and the empathy expected of women also contribute to altering their voice, since it "shortens the vocal path," explains the linguist Laélia Véron.[18] And beware of those whose timbre is considered threatening! The actress Anna Mouglalis recalls that when she left drama school, a sound expert suggested a "small modification" to make her voice less deep, which she rejected.[19]

Often the adjective "feminine" connotes constrained, reduced, limited in the expression of one's capacities. Accordingly, women are encouraged to exercise in order to have a thin and firm body, but they must be careful to develop muscles that are discreet and small, that do not suggest too much strength. "Among feminine stars, there are bombshells who are good-looking and well-built. But there are also other women who abuse exercise, especially workouts," wrote the magazine *Public* in 2013, parading the photos of some of these "monsters": Madonna, Gwen Stefani, Hilary Swank, and even the former top model Elle Macpherson, whose barely skinny arms invite us to conclude that only scrawniness finds favor in the eyes of the unforgiving female editor. "When you look at their bodies, one thing is striking: they have the arms of a Superman like Henry Cavill [the actor] or an overly muscled stomach that is frightful! So, girls, if you want to be beautiful and muscled, do glutes and abs, sprinting, cycling, swimming or else Pilates, but not excessively. You have to pace yourself. Exercise three times a week—that is the maximum."[20]

In general, the dominant taste rejects well-muscled women because they are required, above all, to offer an agreeable appearance, and these muscles are not aesthetic. But isn't this approaching the problem the wrong way, by not questioning the criteria that determine this taste preference? Is it not because we cannot bear the expression of strength in women that we do not find their bodies beautiful? The philosopher Paul B. Preciado stated in an interview: "I would prefer we begin to look at our tastes politically, learning to distrust 'the natural' in what we desire and in our tastes. Tastes are produced, they are politically fabricated. And obviously, there are tastes that are hegemonic. The more we agree with the hegemonic taste, the better we are accepted by others, and the more we are normalized and controlled, the less we are capable of constructing an aesthetic of life."[21]

Larger and sturdier than average, the writer Alice Zeniter was very annoyed to discover as a child the attributes of the ideal woman from classic literature: "delicate ankles" for Charles Baudelaire, "matchstick wrists" and calves "like elderberries" for André Breton; in Victor Hugo's *Notre-Dame de Paris*, Esmeralda is thin and fragile "as a wasp." Zeniter comments: "I was not among the beautiful women and these novels clearly told me so. A part of me was sad, awfully sad, at being excluded from the market for fine chicks even before being able to enter it, but another part of me began to roar and tell myself: 'Even better! Very well! I do not want to be one of those matchstick women, certainly not, never, because what do you do with these tiny wrists, these delicate ankles? Well, you squeeze a little and it farts, that's what is said by these guys who drool over women as fragile as porcelain dolls—and it is not me who says that but Honoré de Balzac: 'Esther was of that average size that allows a woman to be made a sort of plaything to take up, to lay down, to take once more, and to carry without fatigue'!"[22]

This censoring of women's strength on aesthetic pretexts is true even of professional women athletes, despite the evident contradiction this implies because it obliges them to remain below their potential. In 2015, while the tennis player Serena Williams was subject to a deluge of sexist and racist insults because she had a body that was considered overly powerful, the trainer of fellow player Agnieszka Radwańska explained why the young Polish athlete did not have such an athletic physique: "It's our decision to keep her as the smallest player in the top 10. Because, first of all she's a woman, and she wants to be a woman." In a less sexist world, wouldn't this male trainer have been fired for incompetence? In 2015, when she was the best paid female athlete in the world, Maria Sharapova felt obliged to declare: "I always want to be skinnier with less cellulite; I think that's every girl's wish. I can't handle lifting more than five pounds. It's just annoying, and it's just too much hard work."[23]

In the essay "The Strongest Woman in America," the writer and feminist activist Gloria Steinem recounted her surprise in 1985 when she discovered the Australian champion of bodybuilding, Bev Francis, on the occasion of a documentary about her.[24]

This "gentle, intelligent, courageous pioneer," who at the time was "pound for pound . . . stronger than Arnold Schwarzenegger," forced Steinem to confront her own prejudices. The film was shot during a female bodybuilding competition in Las Vegas, in the course of which the ultradeveloped musculature of Bev Francis very much disturbed the judges.[25] We see them in a stormy meeting to "clear up the definite meaning, the analysis, of the word 'femininity'"—no less. "What we're looking for," hammers the man who seems to be president of the jury, "is something that's right down the middle, a woman that has a certain amount of aesthetic femininity but yet has that muscle tone to show that she's an athlete." One of his young colleagues objects: "I object to being told that there's a certain point beyond which women can't go in this sport. When you say that they should look athletic but not too masculine, what does that mean exactly? It's as though the U.S. Ski Federation told women skiers that they could only ski so fast!" The president replies: "We want what's best for our sport and best for our girls. We don't want to turn people off, we want to turn them on." His young colleague rebuts, "Who are we to say what looks like a woman and what doesn't?" Eventually, the president makes his stance clear: "We're here to protect the majority and to protect our sport. If you have the majority of the girls absolutely say, 'Hey, let's go for these big, grotesque muscles and let's go to the ultimate,' so be it. Okay? But we are following what the majority wants. I just want to say that women are women and men are men, and there's a difference and thank God for that difference." Bev Francis finished eighth.

Even among Gloria Steinem's female friends, the bodybuilder aroused contradictory reactions; some were proud and enthusiastic, others hostile and disgusted—independently of their degree of feminist involvement. "In the past, the only place where women could show strength was the circus, at least we've advanced from that," Francis told Steinem. "When I was growing up, I wanted to go as far as I could. I wanted freedom. There was a TV ad in Australia that I always hated. It showed a woman dishing out food and saying, 'Feed the man meat.'[26] Why shouldn't I do more than that?" Her fiancé, Steve, was training with her. Steinem commented: "Most men might feel ambivalent about being the lover of the strongest woman in the world, but Steve, who understands her unique accomplishment in a field that is also his own, was clearly proud. Like the Olympic wrestler George Zaharias, who married and did his best to protect Babe Didrikson from the ridicule of an earlier generation, which greeted her athletic feats with charges that she was not a 'real woman,' Steve has joined Bev in creating what was clearly a mutually supportive world of their own."[27] In the "normal" world, in fact, no man is supposed to want a woman who unreservedly cultivates her physical strength.

In this respect, the treatment given to the character of Brienne of Tarth in the final season of *Game of Thrones* represents a notable step forward, especially in a production watched by millions of viewers around the world. Of an impressive height and build, covered in her armor, with a pale face and blond hair cut short, Brienne is a fearsome warrior doubled with a starry-eyed girl—at the beginning of the series we find her transfixed with love for the pretender to the throne Renly Baratheon, whom she serves and defends with passion. Her physique earns her all kinds of gibes and sneers; in her youth some boys had derisively nicknamed her "Brienne the Beauty." The day before the major battle against the Army of the Dead, she and her companions gather in front of the fireplace at Winterfell. Among them is Jaime Lannister, former commander of the royal guard and arrogantly handsome, a formerly odious and evil-doing character who has been transformed by his trials. Brienne has played a decisive role in his evolution and they have formed a strong bond with each other. That evening, flouting the tradition that a woman cannot be knighted, he invites her to kneel, takes out his sword, and dubs her, to the applause of their comrades. Once the battle has been won—thanks to a startling coup by another female warrior—and after a banquet organized to celebrate the victory, he joins her in her room and they make love, the first time for her. In this way he recognizes her as an equal while demonstrating his desire for her, whereas most of the time these two attitudes are mutually exclusive (should we be reminded that she is taller than he?).

"PLEASE DON'T SHINE TOO MUCH"

Feminine inferiority is supposed to be not only physical but also professional and economic. In a group therapy session designed for men imprisoned for domestic violence, when the female leader asked the participants if they are shocked that women might hold the same occupations as men, one of them responds: "Me, I am not shocked, as long as my wife does not have a better occupation than me. If so, that would be war—at the level of money but especially at the level of status. Imagine that I am a garbage collector and she is director of a bank. I think there would be fights; she is going to put you down. And you can only shut your mouth, because that is the reality. She's going to see you like a little pawn, and she is the boss." And if it is the inverse? "Same thing," he starts by answering. "If the man is a bank director and the wife a housekeeper, in an argument he is going to say to her: 'Remember, you are only a housekeeper.' There are always phrases that are super hurtful." The leader asks him whether the two partners should always be at the same level. "Yes," he replies without conviction, before adding with an embarrassed laugh (one senses it coming): "Or at worst, a man a little more . . . I don't know, I would not like my wife to wear the pants." He explains that when he was eighteen he became manager of a store and his companion "respected him more" than when he was a simple employee.[28] How better to say that a couple's relationship is envisaged as a hierarchical relation, as a balance of power?

This logic applies to all social classes. Magazines regularly mention women who succeed better in the social economy and earn more money than their companions, seeming in sympathy with the humiliation these men might feel—nobody imagines that a wife might exhibit the same wounded pride in the inverse situation, which is commonplace.[29] Those women who commit the capital offense of being higher up the socioeconomic ladder usually try to redeem themselves by doing more domestic tasks, and they run a high risk of divorcing.[30] Divorce also threatens actresses who win an Oscar, to the point that one speaks of a "curse of the Oscars": "The marriages of the winning actresses last on average 4.3 years, while those of the losers last 9.5 years."[31] Joan Crawford, Bette Davis, Halle Berry, Kate Winslet, Reese Witherspoon, Hilary Swank, Sandra Bullock: all of them separated from or were divorced from their husbands shortly after having won the prize. In Sweden, two researchers found that among the female candidates in municipal or legislative elections, those who won were later divorced twice as often as those who lost. As for women appointed as company directors, they divorced much more often than men who won the same kind of promotion. Whether elected officials or company directors, all these women saw their chances of finding a partner diminish, which makes improbable the hypothesis that the splits with their husbands were motivated by a flood of new candidates. An interesting detail is that the couples who broke up were often those in which the wife was much younger than the husband, or in which she was most occupied with the children. The couples who were more egalitarian from the beginning were more resilient, since when the wife was promoted, they suffered a lesser destabilization.[32] A friend told me that although she was in love with the father of her children, this was in part because he had enjoyed a startling professional success, so he did not risk taking umbrage at her own successes. Another, left by a musician with whom she had just started a relationship, told me tearfully that she thought she had committed a fatal error: she had not resisted the temptation of showing him her employment contract, with a proposed salary, that she had received from a prestigious institution and of which she was legitimately proud. It is not certain that this played a role in this man's decision to prefer another woman, but the simple fact that she might suspect this, and thus regret her impulse, is revealing. She wondered whether, in order to be loved, she should not hide her accomplishments and appear to be less brilliant than she was; whether she should, like Carla Bruni in the photos, bend her head to not exceed a certain height, but this time on the symbolic level. This is not paranoia on her part: according to an American study in 2006, men are generally reluctant to go out with women who are more intelligent or more ambitious than they are.[33]

In the case of bell hooks, she was happy to have found a man who understood and approved of her intellectual aspirations, who supported her throughout her studies. But this support was withdrawn when she obtained her doctorate and was offered a post in one of the best universities in the United States. Her friend had warned her of such a fate, saying, "My partner's willingness to affirm my intellect did not mean anything as long as my intellectual aspirations were just that, aspirations."[34] Disappointed and shocked, hooks had the impression of being caught by all the sinister prophecies—that "men really did not like smart women"—that she had heard since childhood.

Hooks remarks that those who have this kind of experience have a tendency to accuse themselves rather than the sexism of their partners. She also notes that, perniciously, the friends of women who are very invested in their work seem to presuppose that love has no or little importance in their lives: "They could not accept that a woman could be loving *and* passionately committed to work. Unable to see the way these two passions enhance and reinforce each other, they wanted to negate my right to love."[35] Often, the well-honed critical spirit of intellectual women, in particular, is interpreted "as fueled by inner ruthlessness, by a lack of empathy for others,"[36] she observes. This denial is even more unjust because they have great need of love. "Powerful women of all races and all classes are always attacked. Self-loving, high-achieving women rely on the care of our loved ones to survive brutal attacks. . . . Powerful, self-actualized women should feel no shame when we speak of our longing for a loving partner, our need to be supported by a circle of loved ones."[37]

If we borrow Eva Illouz's vocabulary, the experience of my friend with her musician can be summarized in these terms: her "social position" ruined her "sexual position." Illouz wants to identify the forces that give the advantage to men in the amorous field. The value of women, she notes, is and always has been defined as their conformity to very precise aesthetic criteria, on the one hand, and their youth on the other. Inversely, male seduction is exercised principally through their social status, independently of their age. This gives them a triple advantage: "Their sexual power is not as obsolescent as women's and even increases with time . . . They have access to larger samples of potential partners because they have access to women of their own age and much younger. Finally there is an overlap and even tight fit between men's sexual and socioeconomic goals. Men's sexual power is not distinct or opposite to their social power and each reinforces the other. Conversely, women's sexual and social positions are far more likely to conflict with each other."[38]

"EROTICIZE EQUALITY"

Yes, these laws are not absolute. In believing that they are, we risk making them self-fulfilling prophecies and rigid positions—not to mention denying the plasticity of life and of love. The American series *The Marvelous Mrs. Maisel*, which takes place at the end of the 1950s, illustrates this well. (If you are planning to watch it, skip this paragraph and the next on account of *spoilers*!) Miriam Maisel, called Midge, a Jewish mother of two young children, is married to Joel, who works in a big company but dreams of breaking into stand-up comedy. Though Midge bends over backward to be a wife, lover, and mistress of the perfect house, and supports her husband in pursuing his dreams, she is also a brilliant and witty woman, and it seems like Joel feels outshined. Soon he leaves her for his secretary, who is presented as spectacularly stupid. "I am not naive, I know that men like stupid girls," says a devastated Midge. "But I thought Joel wanted more than stupid. I thought he wanted spontaneity and wit. I thought he wanted to be challenged." Then just when she thought her life was collapsing, almost by accident, she discovers her own vocation for stand-up. She starts to appear in cabarets without her friends knowing. Soon bored with his mistress, her husband is quick to come back to her. They prepare to announce their reunion to their families when, by chance, he sees her onstage. He is devastated. Not only is she succeeding where he had failed ("She is *good*," he repeats with sobs), but he cannot bear the idea that she might make public use of her life with him: "But I just can't be a joke," he tells himself. He leaves her again, breaking her heart a second time.

Later, though, these two characters experience a passionate change. Midge flourishes as a performer and learns independence. Although she has never had a job, she gets hired as a sales clerk in a major department store while waiting for her career to take off; meanwhile Joel finally admits he has no talent for stand-up. He quits his job, and while thinking about what he really wants to do, he helps his father manage his clothing factory. After having been a real pain as a husband, he proves to be an admirable ex. Once the first shock is over, he is proud of Midge. He admires her, and this generosity makes him infinitely more appealing than the capricious, infantile, and egocentric guy he was at the end of their marriage. An incredible thing in the eyes of their friends, he looks after the children while she goes on tour. In short, he repays her a small part of the immense debt that men have accumulated with respect to women when it comes to supporting the other and helping her at self-realization. By quitting the roles into which they slipped when they married, which proved debilitating for each of them, they become much more interesting individuals than they were while spouses; and their story, in escaping social and familial control, itself also becomes more interesting. They rediscover their complicity as young lovers. While each making new acquaintances, they sleep together again regularly. One morning in Las Vegas, where Midge is performing and where Joel has joined her for a few days, they discover that the previous evening, while drunk, they got married again just after their divorce had been confirmed. . . . In this way, their relationship thwarts the rules of domination. And at the same time, as it becomes increasingly egalitarian, it becomes increasingly sexy.

While I am writing, I am looking at a button with Gloria

Steinem's famous slogan *"Eroticize equality."** It could not be better put. Most of the time, our representations remain very conventional. Even today, it is men, and not exactly the most progressive among them, who control the definition of what makes a woman seductive, as Eva Illouz reminds us: "The consumption of the image of the attractive and sexual body has considerably expanded throughout the twentieth century, increasing the revenues of a variety of visual industries exposing women but overwhelmingly owned and managed by men."[39]

The world of showbiz is conservative not only in the images and fictions it produces, but also—quite logically—in the moral behavior staged for popular consumption. Thus, when one of its members demonstrates the least bit of daring, this creates an event in the tabloids, for example the fuss created in November 2019 when the actor Keanu Reeves had his first official date with his new girlfriend, the artist Alexandra Grant. The chosen lady was the canonic age of forty-six, or "only" nine years younger than Reeves, and in addition, she did not dye her hair. The commentators in the American press were close to awarding a medal for masculine courage to the star of *The Matrix*. "An artist with white hair!" By what cosmic mystery was he able to prefer her to a twenty-five-year-old model spotted on the cover of the swimsuit issue of *Sports Illustrated*? The press reminded us of how, in 1993, Reeves had refused to comply when the director Francis Ford Coppola asked him to insult Winona Ryder to make her cry during the filming of *Bram Stoker's Dracula*, thereby sealing

---

* A souvenir of the Festival Albertine, organized in the fall of 2017 by the cultural services of the French embassy in New York, devoted that year to feminism, with Steinem as curator.

an eternal friendship between the two actors,[40] while the journalist and blogger Titiou Lecoq formulated the natural hypothesis: "Is this man perfection incarnate? Has this man descended to Earth to show men a new way in masculinity?"[41]

It is always agreeable and exciting to see a couple where one man breaks ranks. In France, this was verified when the writer Yann Moix caused a stir by calmly declaring to the magazine *Marie Claire* (February 2019) that at age fifty he was incapable of loving a woman who was age fifty. The actor Vincent Lindon refuted that: "Me, I adore women who are my age . . . There is nothing more beautiful than seeing a woman or a man who shows the marks of time. I think it is overwhelming, there is a scent, there is something sentimental, nostalgic, melancholic. Personally, I have a big appetite for nostalgia, for the acceptance of things."[42] Leaving aside the sexism here, we should welcome this kind of statement. But we have to admit that it is problematic to find ourselves praising a man simply because he deigns to love a woman for the whole of what she is—meaning that he deigns to love her—simply like women have loved men since forever. It is problematic to find myself discussing on TV whether woman age fifty are fuckable or not, when nobody imagines having this debate about men of that age. In addition, the relative rarity of these valiant knights paradoxically confers on them an even greater power and thus chains women even more to masculine goodwill. The sociologists Jean Duncombe and Dennis Marsden noticed in 1993 that if a woman stumbles on a man who is ready to live in an egalitarian relationship, she will always be structurally subordinated to him due to his status as a rare exception, both knowing that he could find better in patriarchal terms.[43] Only a change in overall mentality could really reestablish equilibrium.

Therefore, a heterosexual woman who never censors herself, who does not go for these small or large alterations of herself required by traditional femininity, risks compromising her love life, unless she meets a man who does not fear being mocked or ridiculed. According to patriarchal criteria, a man who chooses a companion who is equal gives up a part of the domination that he has the right to exercise and will be presumed to be a masochist, or else considered unconventional, or else a traitor, or all of these at the same time. He puts himself in an unusual position because it is usually reserved for women. To love a man who gives the full measure of himself is judged rewarding for a woman; whereas to love a woman who gives the full measure of herself is judged threatening for a man. Masculine attractiveness is defined by a surplus, feminine attractiveness by a deficiency.

WHAT IT MEANS TO BE A FANTASY

Do those women who correspond to the currently accepted criteria of feminine attractiveness, who do not violate the implicit laws of this tranquil and banal domination, have an easier love life? Not necessarily, one might say after reading the private diaries of the actress and singer Jane Birkin.[44] Daughter of the actress Judy Campbell, mother of the photographer Kate Barry (who died in 2013) as well as the actresses and singers Charlotte Gainsbourg and Lou Doillon, Birkin belongs to one of the great families of showbiz aristocracy. She became a myth due to her beauty, her style, and the couple she formed with the singer Serge Gainsbourg. And yet reading her notebooks we realize to what extent she has always been in a fragile position with her successive partners. The first two, John Barry and then Serge Gainsbourg, both decidedly older than she, owed their attractiveness to their talent and to their status as creators, which gave them social standing and power—power over her, and power in general. For her part, she was seductive essentially because of her beauty, indissociable from her youth. Barry married her when she was a promising eighteen-year-old actress. He was thirty-one and already a composer known throughout the world for the music of the James Bond film franchise. As for Gainsbourg, he was twenty-one years older than her when they met in 1968 and already a famous singer-songwriter.

Of course, they were very different men. As Birkin describes them, Barry was an odious character, who, before he abandoned her, would come home late and drunk, refuse to speak to her, and yell at her because her crying stopped him from sleeping. She paints a more complex portrait of Gainsbourg, with whom she would live for twelve years: that of a tyrannical and maniacal man, macho but loving, capable of tenderness and partnership. "I know now what was magical about Serge: his faults," she wrote in 1981, when she had already left him. "He is such an egoist, a small jealous thing with a dominating character, but he is funny; profoundly kind and original, even in the stupid and foolish things he does." Yet with him, she existed only as a muse and interpreter. She integrated herself into his universe and put herself at his service. "If there is one thing I would love, it is to be no longer attractive to Serge, but just be well-considered, loved as a confidante. Sexuality is not being well-considered; on the contrary, it's to be an object like all the others, not his equal. I want to be a man for him."

Her beauty was supposed to place her in a strong position with men, but she got no emotional security from this. In a world that is keen to sap their self-confidence, women rarely enjoy their beauty. Even when they are aware of it intellectually, they are rarely in contact with it. Birkin felt herself surrounded by potential rivals. Above all, she was subject to the law—omnipresent in society as a whole and even more so in her milieu—that her value is correlated with her youth. And by definition, youth passes; it is always passing away.

To summarize: a woman who exists first for her personality—her own universe, projects, opinions, successes—runs the risk of frightening away certain men. But a woman who corresponds to male fantasies, who exists amorously and socially foremost because of her beauty, runs the risk of being shunted around by male whims and desires, with the permanent and devouring insecurity that entails. She risks not finding a sufficient foundation to develop her self-esteem and the feeling of her own identity.

"A PETITE WOMAN WITH YELLOW SKIN"

Domination is reinforced another notch when a woman is not only young and beautiful but also of "exotic" origin, arousing fantasies rooted in the colonialist mentality. The

woman who succeeded Jane Birkin in the life of Serge Gainsbourg was Caroline von Paulus, a model then age twenty (he
was fifty-two), of Vietnamese and Chinese origin through her
mother. He nicknamed her Bambou (I did not know her real
name until I wrote this passage). After saddling her with this
nickname, Gainsbourg asked her to record an album titled
Made in China in 1989. The album (which was a commercial
failure) included a version of "Nuits de Chine," which the
singer Marc Lavoine covered in 2007 as a duet with Bambou. In 2016, Lavoine, age fifty-four, would fall in love with
the writer Line Papin, twenty-one and of Vietnamese origin,
whom he married in 2020. He paid her homage in a song
called "Ma Papou," in which he called her the "half Indochi-
nese doll" who "straightened the Tower of Pisa."

I know nothing of the reality of the relationship between
Line Papin and Marc Lavoine. But it is hard not to react to the
images and words inspired by their story and put into circulation in our cultural universe, since they have strong conno-
tations. Indochina was until 1954 a French colonial territory
that included Vietnam, Laos, and Cambodia. The word "doll"
has a long history of being used for Asian women. It comes up
constantly in the autobiographical novel that created Western
fantasies about them: *Madame Chrysanthème*, by writer Pierre
Loti, published in 1888, which was an enormous success and
translated throughout Europe, and which inspired Giacomo
Puccini's 1904 opera *Madama Butterfly*. In Loti's novel a French
naval officer, landing at Nagasaki for a few weeks, contracts
a temporary marriage with a young Japanese woman for the
duration of his stay, like several of his comrades. Even on the

boat, he confesses his plan to his friend Yves: "As for me, I shall at once marry. . . . I shall choose a little yellow-skinned woman with black hair and cat's eyes. She must be pretty. Not much bigger than a doll."[45]

Barely ashore, he starts the search for a fiancée. Seeing a very young dancer in the first teahouse to which he is taken, he wonders: "Supposing I marry this one, without seeking any further. I should respect her as a child committed to my care; I should take her for what she is: a fantastic and charming plaything. What an amusing little household I should set up! Really short of marrying a china ornament, I should find it difficult to choose better."[46] Finally, he finds one of them who pleases him and the ceremony is arranged. Still, this union disappoints him. Madame Chrysanthemum irritates him. He finds her too often with a mournful air: "What thoughts can be running through that little brain? My knowledge of her language is still too restricted to enable me to find out. Moreover, it is a hundred to one that she has no thoughts whatever. And even if she had, what do I care? I have chosen her to amuse me, and I would really rather she should have one of these insignificant little thoughtless faces like all the others."[47] One day on a solitary promenade, he spies a young woman who appears more seductive than his wife. But he quickly thinks twice: "It will not do to stop too long and be ensnared. . . . A doll like the rest, evidently, an ornament for a china shelf, and nothing more."

He does not experience his relationship with Madame Chrysanthemum as an encounter with a person but as an experience offered to the traveler: the temporary marriage with a Japanese woman is an "amusing" and picturesque thing one ought to do. To him, his wife does not exist as an individual but as the chance incarnation of a fantasy, as a representative of a generic model that preexisted in his head, and her role was to validate it. Madame Chrysanthemum is an element of decor that is simply a little more animated than others; she is not a protagonist in the moments they spend together. He announces this at the outset in the introduction to his novel: "Although the most important role may appear to devolve on Madame Chrysanthème, it is very certain that the three principal personages are *myself,* *Japan*, and the *effect* produced on me by that country."

The young woman is merely a foil, a support for his thoughts and reveries. In *Orientalism*, Edward Said formulated the same analysis about the meeting of the writer Gustave Flaubert with the Egyptian "courtesan" Kuchuk Hanem[48] during his "Oriental voyage" in 1850. The French novelist recounts that, after having slept with her, he watched over her until morning:

> I spent the night in infinitely intense dreams. That is why I remained. In contemplating this beautiful creature asleep, snoring with her head resting on my arm, I thought of my nights in the bordellos of Paris, of a heap of old memories . . . and of her, of her dance, of her voice singing songs without meaning or distinguishable words for me.[49]

The "Oriental" woman, comments Said, is for Flaubert "an occasion and an opportunity for Flaubert's musings[50] It is when she sleeps that he seems to have his best moments with her, as Pierre Loti did with Madame Chrysanthemum. Kuchuk Hanem is also reduced to an object, an automaton: "The Oriental woman is a machine, nothing more; she makes no difference whatsoever between one man and another man," Flaubert asserts.[51]

Women like Madame Chrysanthemum and Kuchuk Hanem are also sought after as incarnations of a worldview, as if the husband (or client) thought he could, by possessing them, also possess the country of which they are the emanation and grasp it completely.

FROM PIERRE LOTI TO MARLON BRANDO

The sexual appropriation of the female body that accompanied Western expansion forged relational models and reflexes of domination that have endured. The custom of taking a "little wife" appeared in the wake of the establishment of trading centers by Europeans in Africa and in Asia in the seventeenth century, for example by the English in India or by the French in Senegal, state Elisa Camiscioli and Christelle Taraud. These concubines were "triply subjected—as women, poor, and as 'indigenous,'" supplying a service that was domestic, sexual, and conjugal. The policy of total colonization conducted in the nineteenth century, which involved the arrival of white women in the conquered countries, never made them completely disappear. In the Belgian Congo, the institution of the "housekeeper" was justified by a "right to coïtus" for white colonists, as well as by the desire to "reestablish a 'natural' man-woman relationship that had been upset in Europe by the advance in women's rights. Throughout the colonial world, on top of this arrangement came prostitution in the strict sense, and in particular military brothels, not to mention rapes."[52]

Slavery and colonization represented the most barbaric forms of European domination, but one sees in *Madame Chrysanthème* how Pierre Loti's narrator behaves in the conquered country. (Japan had not been colonized but was forced to open up to Western commerce.) One day, because the police of Nagasaki were concerned about the validity of his marriage with his Japanese wife, he boasts about making a scandal at the station and having insulted all the men present. He delightedly describes their fright, in a country where politeness is an essential value. In addition to exercising a direct and concrete despotism, he participates with remarkable zeal in the massive production of degrading representations and fantasies of non-white people that accompanied the European occupation of the planet. This enterprise—in which images and the discourses drew their authority from each other, mutually reinforcing—lasted several centuries and had millions of contributors, famous or anonymous. Still today, victims of the stereotypes that he put into circulation, the racialized women of almost every origin, have reason—more than the men, whom he did not spare—to be angry with Pierre Loti: this great traveler skimmed over sexual fantasies at least as much as over the oceans. *Aziyadé* (1879) and then *Fantôme d'Orient* (1892) recount a love story between a naval officer and a young Turkish woman shut up in a harem; *Le mariage de Loti* (1878), a relationship with a fifteen-year-old Tahitian; and *Les trois dames de la Kasbah* (1884), the story of three Algerian prostitutes.

The case of vahine, a myth forged from a Polynesian word

for woman, shows well how a cliché of the subjugated feminine ideal can be perpetuated across the centuries, thanks to being relayed from one influential masculine figure to another. The scholar Serge Tcherkézoff recounts how the legend of an indolent, hedonistic, and slightly wild people was born. When Samuel Wallis's expedition reached Tahiti in 1767, the curious inhabitants of the island boarded the ships. The British were frightened and wanted to chase them off with saber blows and musket shot. So the islanders jumped into the water before coming back "in great number and armed. Wallis used his canons, and many Tahitians were killed." Henceforth, the inhabitants proved "pacific." They "offered" objects of value and proposed sexual encounters with their young girls. The British were thrilled by the time they left. Disembarking in 1768, Louis-Antoine de Bougainville and his crew, who knew nothing of the British cannonade the previous year, received the same welcome and marveled at the "hospitality" of this people. In his *Voyage autour du monde*, published in 1771 and quickly translated into English, Bougainville went on at length about Tahiti, this Eden "where the candor of the Golden Age still reigns," where the women were "like Eve before her sin." The book struck European imaginations. What does it matter if we know today that the young Tahitians "were placed by force in the arms of European men and could not hold back their tears"?[53] The myth of vahine was now indestructible.

The myth would be relaunched in 1878 by the publication of *Le mariage de Loti*. The fantasies aroused by reading it "largely explain Paul Gauguin's decision to go to Tahiti in 1891, in search of a paradisical environment and new sources of inspiration," writes the geographer Jean-François Staszak.[54] Even in 2017, Édouard Deluc directed *Gauguin: Voyage de Tahiti* (with Vincent Cassel in the role of the painter), which perpetuated with no hesitation the old image of Tahitians as "noble" savages with whom the great solitary artist mingled because he was misunderstood in his own country. The film skipped over the age of Gauguin's "little wife," Tehura (thirteen), having her played by the seventeen-year-old actress Tuheï Adams. The syphilis from which the painter suffered (and which spread across the island) becomes a more discreet diabetes. "The artist, presented as a loner who wanted nothing to do with the island's French colonists, in fact behaved just as they did in regard to his amorous and sexual relations," noted the journalist Léo Pajon when the film came out.[55] This fascination would endure in the twentieth century, notoriously in the form of Marlon Brando. The American actor discovered Tahiti during the filming of *Mutiny on the Bounty* in 1960. On this occasion, he met Tarita Teriipaia, a young dancer hired on the spot to play in the film. Brando made advances, but she was not interested. However, she ended up falling in love with him and became his companion. In the actor's eyes, like those of Gauguin, Tahiti was an original paradise where purity and innocence reigned, and Tarita Teriipaia incarnated all that for him. She wanted to make a career as an actress, but he forbade her. He ordered Metro-Goldwyn-Mayer to break its contract with her. He wanted her to give him children, for her to raise them and to maintain his property on the island, where he would go to visit from time to time. With Brando, too, appropriation of the feminine and appropriation of the territory go hand in hand: in 1966, he acquired the atoll of Te-tiaroa. He behaved with Tarita Teriipaia exactly like one of the oppressive American imperialists he claimed to abhor. At her birth, their daughter was also called Tarita; when he decided a while later to rename her Cheyenne (as a sign of solidarity with the Amerindian struggle), he announced this publicly without having consulted or even informed her mother. Their story, marked by eruptions of violence, ended rather quickly (Chey-enne, who was their second child, had been conceived by arti-ficial insemination), but he arranged to sabotage all Teriipaia's later amorous relationships. She had to remain his property.[56]

Relations with women born out of colonization and slavery persist today with an impressive vitality. Black women discuss their journeys and the racism from which they have suffered in Amandine Gay's documentary *Ouvrir la voix* (2014), describ-ing exactly the same old mechanisms. Sharone observes: "You are a sort of 'experience' for some whites, or even [men] of other cultures, there is a whole thing around the Black woman and sexuality that has to be tested." Zina expresses her impression of having been a "thing" for her white partners. She bitterly sums up the way in which they envisage their relationship with her: "'I have already eaten snake-meat,' 'I have already gone out with a Black woman.'" Maboula Soumahoro feels she was not seen as an individual, but as incarnating for some men a country, even an entire continent: "These guys are often 'in love with Africa.'" Marie-Julie Chalu believes the bodies of Black women are "animalized," "objectified," considered as something that one can "appropriate." "It is not 'rendered precious,'" she says:

"You are not made precious in your femininity—simply in your humanity." This casts doubt on the motivations of her partners: "When I went out with white men, I asked myself: 'Is he going out with me for that?' You cannot live your story without thinking of these things, and this damages your intimate and sexual development as a woman."

All of them have the agonizing feeling of being interchangeable, of being deprived of their personal identity. Annie sighs: "There are guys who say: 'Me, I adore Blacks,' 'Black-women guys!' Just this expression, it's not possible. And then, it is also as absurd as saying: 'Me, I adore redheads'!" Audrey says about a former boyfriend: "I realized that this person was not going out with Audrey: he was going out with a Black woman who represented a heap of fantasies." "They always project all kinds of things on you of which you are not aware," adds Sabine Pakora. "At no point are you being encountered as you are." All these women say that people project onto them an animal sexuality, reverting them to a radical otherness. "I have received comments like: 'You must really be a savage in bed,' just because I was Black, while at the time I was fifteen or sixteen and a virgin," remembers Laura. "I never heard such things said to my white girlfriends: 'Ah! You white women, you must have something. . . .' No, they are just adolescents discovering their sexuality." Some report voyeuristic questions posed about their sexual behavior or about hypothetical specificities of their anatomy, "as if we do not have the same body as white women." The journalist Rokhaya Diallo remembers having grown up with images of the Jamaican model Grace Jones, photographed in the 1980s by her partner Jean-Paul Goude, who put her onstage enclosed in a cage bearing the sign "Do not feed the animal."[57]

THE "DOUBLE FEMINIZATION" OF ASIAN WOMEN

Rokhaya Diallo and Grace Ly discuss amorous and sexual fetishization in an episode of their podcast *Kiffe ta race*, inviting the writer Faïza Guène to speak with them. There were differences among the forms of fetishization they had endured. On the one hand, Black and Arabic women aroused sexual fantasies in some white men who rarely envisaged them as life partners but rather took them as companions who could be "socially accepted." "He can boast of having 'tamed' a woman, but when it comes to starting a family, introducing her to your parents, then having Black children, suddenly it becomes more complicated," explains Diallo. "And this ambivalence places Black women in a position of being less desirable for long-term relationships." On the other hand, Asian women, because they come from a minority reputed to be "model women"—a way of insinuating there is a problem with others—are presumed to be not only sensual but also hardworking and submissive. "They are desired not only because of their 'little narrow things' [a legend maintains they have tighter vaginas], but also because they are supposed to be good mothers," as Ly analyzed it. "Hence, a matrimonial relationship with an Asian can be seriously considered. These women can be assigned to the home, to a purely maternal role."[58] In a 2021 interview, she summed it up: "Black women are supposed to be sexual beasts and we

Asians are supposed to be much more supple. It's like the Cirque du Soleil! You are a contortionist in bed, then you do a massage, and afterward you cook."[59]

Sexual submission and domestic diligence of Asian women: these prejudices and stereotypes are explained by the heritage of "little wives," but also by later historical events. The chronicler Franchesca Ramsey recalls that in the twentieth century, 85 percent of American soldiers stationed in Japan after the Second World War, or who had participated in the Korean or Vietnam wars, said they had frequented prostitutes at the time, meaning that "the first interaction that three generations of American men had with Asian women was as submissive sexual objects."[60] "Rest and Recreation Zones" had in fact been put in place for them in the Philippines, Japan, Thailand, Malaysia, and Singapore. On top of this history of prostitution came the impact of sexual tourism in the region, which of course directly derives from American military brothels.[61] Consequently throughout the whole world, many Asian women have the experience of being considered prostitutes from the start. Grace Ly remembers that one day she was in a bar with a male friend: "A guy came in and asked him, with the air of a locker-room buddy, how much he had paid to be with me."[62]

The image of the exemplary mistress of the household and educator of children was reinforced by the Philippine policy of exporting female workers in the 1970s under the presidency of Ferdinand Marcos: on average, a hundred thousand young women, trained in specialized schools, exiled themselves each year to work as domestic employees in the United States, Canada, the Near East, Hong Kong. "It is in their genes," asserted a

Belgian expatriate in Hong Kong to explain her employee's zeal. "In their culture, Philippine women are totally devoted. They adore children!"[63] The more recent stereotype of the Chinese "Tiger Mom," who is presumed to give her children a strict and ultracompetitive education, in contrast to the supposed "laxity" of Western mothers, has again reinforced this image of Asian women as ideal wives and mothers.

The philosopher Robin Zheng states that "the supposed sexual superiority of Asian women ultimately renders them inferior as whole human beings; they are more completely reduced to having value only as sexual or domestic objects." She stresses—and this applies to women of color—the enormous psychic cost of this fetishization, the considerable harm it represents in their lives. The fantasies projected onto them in effect oblige these women to be constantly on their guard, to pay attention to the motivations of those interested in them, even their lovers and partners. They are used to being hypersexualized, objectified, and blended into an indistinct mass—whereas love ought to be precisely the inverse: distinction, absolute singularization—and also harassed or assaulted because of the stereotypes associated with their appearance.[64]

Zheng observes that the stereotypes involve unconsciously attributing gender to the groups that are being singled out: "Asians [women and men] as a racialized group are stereotyped as feminine, due to their purportedly shy, soft-spoken, submissive racial 'essence,' [which] produces what might be called the 'double feminization' of the Asian woman; strikingly, the exact inverse effects are found for Blacks as a racialized group . . . due to their purportedly aggressive 'essence.'"[65] This kind of thinking harms Black women and also Asian men and, perhaps not surprisingly, these two categories are the most unpopular on dating sites. In 2014, Asian women were the most sought-after category on OkCupid,[66] and specialized sites offer to furnish men who are generally white with the Asian woman of their dreams. This superlative femininity attributed to Asian women implies that they are viewed as gathering together all the signs of inferiority that I detailed at the start of this chapter—small, thin (two traits synthesized in the word "doll"), and young—and that they hold a submissive social, professional, and economic rank. The anthropologist Marion Bottero, who interviewed Westerners living in Thailand with Thai women, remarked that the men describe their partners as "petite," "slim," "discreet," "modest," "reserved," "elegant," and "slight" (this weight consideration is often cited, she said). They appreciate the fact that their companions, who are usually much younger than they are, do not look their age. These men, economically and socially at an advantage because of their status as expatriate Westerners, enjoy an uncontested dominant position in the couple: "These girls do not come into competition with us: They remain in their place," they say.[67]

When one is in love with someone, one can of course love that person's culture or culture of origin, whether this taste preexists the encounter or flows from it. The problem arises when the fantasy obliterates the person and when it involves—consciously or not—the expectation of a certain type of behavior. Many women of color say they have learned to distrust white men who have only dated women of color, and they avoid like the plague from those who approach them while boasting about their "taste." I dug up an interview with the actor Vincent Cassel in the magazine *Closer*, in 2011, that created a stir because he mentioned his period of "jungle fever": "I was only attracted to mixed-race or Black women. Then I specialized in Asian girls, and then in little Parisian Arab chicks. I realized that when one is specific, one is not interested in people in general."[68] Despite this mea culpa, the use by Cassel—married since 2018 to the Black model Tina Kunakey—on Instagram, in February 2020, of the hashtag #negrophile4life accompanied by the middle-finger gesture, would rekindle hostilities.[69]

Raising the issue of romantic and sexual fetishization generally produces vigorous protest and accusations of wanting to "police couples." Personal inclinations, especially in this domain, are not open to debate. Therefore, it would be pure coincidence if the "personal inclinations" of millions of men led to fantasies about Asian women independent of one another. The most plausible explanation is that our tastes, here again, are dependent on the prejudices and representations circulating in our societies, by which we are necessarily influenced. The author Dalia Gebrial remarks that love, "represented as an apolitical, transcendent realm of affect into which you unwittingly fall, is actually deeply politicized, and linked to broader structural violences faced particularly by women of colour globally."[70]

Robin Zheng tries to refute what she calls the Mere Preferences Argument (MPA), the idea that preferring Asian, Arabic, or Black women is the equivalent of preferring blond- or brown-haired women. Of course, skin color and such personal traits tell us no more about a woman than the color of her hair or eyes—hence the absurdity of claiming one "adores Black women" as if you were claiming to "adore redheads." However, even without being aware of it, people project onto a person's origins some qualities not projected onto simple eye or hair color. And thereby one actualizes stereotypes, which do not emerge out of nowhere. "Blondes and brunettes as such have not suffered histories of exploitation, colonization, slavery, persecution, and exclusion on the basis of phenotype," Zheng points out. "Nor does hair or eye color track categorical differences across all social, economic, and political dimensions of life, including opportunities for health, education, jobs, relationships, legal protections, and more."[71] Grace Ly adds that "it is useless to try the usual defense that 'I prefer blondes and that is not a crime.' So if I dye myself blonde, does that change the category on porn sites where I am put?"[72]

That may be so, some say, but one cannot change one's romantic and sexual preferences. But is that so certain? Becoming aware of the fact that preferences are not as personal and intimate as generally believed also means understanding that they are changeable, and therefore this can spur us to want to make them little by little our own. Everyone experiences the fact that taste evolves, at least to a certain extent. It is worked on. It does not strictly and directly govern our intellectual trajectory or our opinions, but it still maintains some relation with them. Taste cannot be forced (there is nothing worse), but at the very least, it might be interesting to reflect on the profound reasons for our attractions, or inversely our prejudices, our rejections, and our indifferences.

"SHE DOESN'T TALK"

Also specific to the "doll" is that she does not speak, or only says what she has been programmed to say. With women of color, it seems like many white men try to realize the dream of a silent companion. They wish for a partner who fits exactly and unerringly the contours of their fantasy, and whose subjectivity never erupts into their relationship—recall Pierre Loti's contrariness when Madame Chrysanthemum's face showed a sign of sadness. They want a woman deprived of a point of view and emotions and her own desires, one whose whole being is oriented to the service of the man's well-being. They want a mixture of robot housekeeper and inflatable doll in human form. Even if they have a hard time admitting it, clinging to the idea that they are truly loved, the Westerners interviewed by the anthropologist Marion Bottero obtain what they crave thanks to their economic power. Their Thai companions take good care of them, they say. They make statements like: "She is not demanding," "As long as she has something to eat, she is happy," "She does not piss me off with metaphysical questions." Confirming that "femininity" is indeed used as a synonym for "submission," Morten (a Dane living in Bangkok) declares: "I am fed up with the masculinization of Western women. In Asia, there has not yet been women's liberation, so the relationships between men and women has not been ruined. In Thailand, there is a more sexist [*sic*] relationship between men and women, hence a more natural level."[73]

This desire involves more than Asian women. For her radio documentary *Heureuse comme une Arabe en France*, Adila

Bennedjaï-Zou went to visit the writer and collector Alexandre Dupouy, who showed her his collection of sexual photographs from the colonial period. Their discussion is fascinating. The collector finds himself confronted with a representative of the "type" from his fantasies, except that she approaches him on an equal footing, and imposes a point of view and a discourse in competition with his own. His embarrassment and his bad conscience are palpable. When she calmly asks him, "What is the particular eroticism of the Eastern woman?" he replies: "It is completely a Western fantasy. . . . She does not talk—she doesn't speak the language, or she doesn't speak *our* language, so there can be no conversation. Total submission, and then this fantasy: the sultan with his harem, all these girls, raped and hidden, taking their clothes off for him. It is magic in the head of a young Western man."[74] In the head of a "young Western man," of course—not in his own.

In his personal collection, his clichés of women from North Africa and Africa are cataloged in a file he names "Lost paradises," justifying this in a pirouette: "It's a nod and wink, because you have to classify things, and when you see these jeering young men, smiling from ear to ear, among naked women. . . . There is perhaps a sense of paradise, and then there is a sense of what has been 'lost,' because fortunately, these situations tend to exist less and less often, and the less they exist, the better human relations will go." Bennedjaï-Zou makes fun of the situation by addressing the reader as witness: "Did you hear it, the little conversation running underneath our exchanges? I ask him: 'Why am I the object of your fantasy?' and he answers: 'You are *not* the object of my fantasy.'" And she concludes: "I think what is in common between Chérifa [one of the women appearing in Dupouy's collection, photographed in front of a Moroccan brothel] and the *beurettes** is that they do not speak. Or else they just say what you want them to say."[75] Notice also that the notion of submission comes up three times in a few seconds in Dupouy's definition of the fantasy of the "Oriental woman."

Reaching the end of this chapter, I think about a conversation with a thirtysomething among my friends. She told me about her perplexity at hearing another friend assure her that in love you have to forget all the feminist principles that in any other context she would defend with conviction. This young woman did not know what to do with this advice. For my part, I am now certain (although I already doubted it) that this statement is untenable. Yes, our culture has so well normalized making women inferior that many men cannot take on a companion who does not diminish or censor herself in some way. But occasionally some men manifest enough curiosity, open-mindedness, and confidence in themselves to accept—and even seek—such a woman. Whatever the case, though, it means running a risk; more accurately, pushing a man to reveal rather quickly his true face, refusing "to make yourself small," allows a woman to protect herself. If he runs away, it is plausible he does not represent a great loss, perhaps he even represents a danger. Thus, now we can perceive the sordid and

---

* A *beurette* (the feminization of *beur*) is a French person whose family are immigrants from North Africa.

oppressive logic that underlies the fantasies around the "ideal" woman.

Among men who express these fantasies, the habit of occupying a dominant position, and the conviction that this position is natural, prevents them from seeing the personality of a woman as richness, as giving an opportunity for a real encounter with them. Instead she is an embarrassment, a nuisance. Either these men adhere to the misogynistic prejudices that circulate in society, which present women as pains in the neck, as a necessary evil who must be contained as much as possible, or else they simply adopt the habit of the dominant position, which prevents them from integrating the viewpoint of the dominated. This is Simone de Beauvoir's analysis in *Le deuxième sexe*: "Women are part of the goods men possess and a means of exchange among themselves: the mistake comes from confusing two forms of mutually exclusive alterity. Insofar as woman is considered the absolute Other, that is—whatever magic powers she has—as the inessential, it is precisely impossible to regard her as another subject."[76]

This incapacity is particularly obvious in relations with women who have been racialized, but it is not confined to them—recall that in the name of the "qualities" ascribed to them, Asian women have been raised to the rank of exemplars for *all* women. Due to their economic vulnerability, many women have no choice but to yield to the game. But for those whose survival does *not* depend on their indulgence of common masculine requirements, there is an opportunity to be seized: the chance of inventing loving relationships that are a little more egalitarian and exciting; little by little, step by step, to finally budge the monolith of a culture that places woman in front of an impossible alternative: choosing between their romantic fulfillment and their personal integrity—as if one were possible without the other, as if a truncated being could know happiness, could give and receive love.

2

REAL MEN

Learning Domestic Violence

In addition to the various forms of domination we have just examined, another factor creates a disequilibrium within heterosexual couples: what each of them has internalized about his or her role, about one's own value, and about what one should expect from the other as a man or woman. In any interaction, each brings to it what society has inculcated in them on this subject.

When the sexologist Shere Hite in the 1970s collected interviews from some 4,500 American women on their love and sex lives, many of them declared that their husband or partner had an attitude toward them that was condescending, arrogant, or clearly insulting; he would put them down or discredit them, making fun of their opinions or their interests. "He uses his tone of voice to make me feel inefficient and dumb"; "He acts arrogant, like he knows *everything*"; "What bothers me is when he gets paternalistic . . . A lot of that is stuff he picked up from his father. He recognizes it when his father does it, but he has a harder time seeing it in himself"; "His word is the law"; "There was a time when he would scold and lecture me like a child. I kept after him about it and now it has stopped."[1] At the opposite pole of this masculine assurance, women adopt a tendency not only to practice introspection and to question themselves (which is rather positive) but also to doubt themselves, to blame themselves constantly, to think that everything is their fault or their responsibility, even to excuse themselves for existing (which is clearly less good). This tendency weakens us considerably in a love relationship, especially when it turns out to be abusive.

Violence within the couple takes advantage of the fragility of the position of women in society. The American feminist Sandra Lee Bartky spoke of shame as structurally feminine, leading the philosopher Camille Froidevaux-Metterie to define shame as "a permanent feeling of inadequacy by which women think they are imperfect, inferior, or diminished, which allows the mechanisms of masculine domination to persist."[2] In this way, "shame becomes a veritable feminine mode of being-in-the-world that leads to conjugal violence and feminicide."[3] Above all, we must not claim that by their lack of confidence in themselves women give rise to the bad treatment they receive: blaming us for conditioning that serves us badly would amount to inflicting double punishment on us. The only ones responsible for violence are those who commit it and the culture that authorizes them to do so—a culture that we are going to try to study here. But just as we might remind people that the sole cause of rape is the rapist while we teach women physical self-defense,[4] women can also develop a form of psychological self-defense.

How do you acquire self-assurance and self-esteem when you have been historically deprived of them? It would take a whole book to answer this question, and such a book already exists: *Revolution from Within: A Book of Self-Esteem* by Gloria Steinem. She shows the importance of this matter as much for women as for minorities and for colonized nations—her story of the path of Gandhi, who would never have been able to become an independence leader without the personal reclamation of his pride as an Indian, is enthralling. Steinem never denies the material and concrete dimension of domination (and this would be astonishing from a woman who has spent her life as an activist for a movement that proclaims "the personal is political"). She begins to understand "that self-esteem isn't everything; it's just that there's nothing without it."[5] I refer you to this essential work, but here I will try to point out the mechanisms that spring out of the testimony about conjugal violence and analyses of it. Studying the deep roots of this violence may allow us to better understand the interactions between women and men in general, which poses the problem of the different ways they are educated. My hope is that this might allow us to prevent (or even thwart) toxic relationships. (I should point out that writing this chapter was grueling—and it might be difficult for you to read.)

I am very aware of the limits of this approach. First of all, love and coupledom are probably the area where we are most vulnerable, and even well-armed women who have a developed feminist awareness may find themselves out of their depth. The story of Marie-Alice Dibon, killed by her partner in April 2019, at the age of fifty-three, invites us to be humble. She herself shared the feminicide statistics on Facebook, and she had given a friend in a toxic relationship the book by the psychiatrist Marie-France Hirigoyen, *Le harcèlement moral,* telling her that she did not want to one day read her friend's name as a victim of crime. "She was lucid when it came to others, but not for herself," this friend stated after her death.[6] Moreover, clearheadedness is not enough. Certainly Marie-Alice Dibon and those close to her had underestimated the danger she was in by continuing to cohabitate with her partner when she had announced her intention to leave him. But even if she had left earlier, he could have easily arranged to find her again. And if she had asked for the protection she needed, nothing says she would have gotten it. In the 2017 film by Xavier Legrand *Jusqu'à la garde*, when the violent man threatens the lives of his ex-wife and their son, the response by both neighbors and the police is ideal, to the intense relief of the viewers (and especially female ones), who have shared the terror of the heroine and her little son for interminable minutes in the film. But the final scene, in which the heroine (played by Léa Drucker) can breathe at last and savor the happiness of being alive and now living in security, is precisely what in reality is denied to many women, since a lot of police officers treat the calls for help they receive in offhand ways.

NARCISSISTS OR "HEALTHY CHILDREN OF THE PATRIARCHY"?

These important reservations do not diminish our interest in better understanding how conjugal violence can prosper. In our day, the influence of feminism, writes Eva Illouz, encourages women to be "vigilant" and "scrutinize men's behavior for the signs of power and devaluation of their worth this behavior may contain." Thus, at the start of an amorous relationship, "the self develops new forms of hyper-attentiveness to signs of disinterest or emotional distance."[7] Illouz seems to attribute this attitude to a modern narcissism that inclines people to break up relationships for any little reason. It is true there is a danger of increasingly behaving like consumers in amorous relationships. On dating applications, Judith Duportail notices the increase in profiles of the "shopping list" type that describe in detail how to be (or not to be) a person who is sought after.[8] Making the same observation, Liv Strömquist shows how this attitude transforms the other into a product and prevents you from being open to the unexpected, from being overwhelmed and transformed by an encounter, from letting yourself be charmed and thrilled by a person in his or her totality.[9]

Yet with respect to women, I believe that we have to prudently apply a reading framework that is attuned to the "ravages of individualistic consumerism." A friend told me that, for ten years while he was a child and then an adolescent, his mother had an affair with a man that was complicated (not violent or abusive, but complicated). Despite everything, she made every effort for this relationship to work. She was very irritated to hear her niece declare that she had left her boyfriend because he did not believe inequalities existed between men and women. This young woman said she could not possibly pursue a relationship with someone who denied such a fundamental and decisive fact. "I deserve better," she said, and my friend's mother heard in this an echo of the famous L'Oréal cosmetic slogan "Because I deserve it"—a consumerist and capricious attitude. But isn't this an erroneous process? There is a difference between disqualifying the other person because of a small and innocent fault, like rejecting a defective product, and reacting to signs that make you fear being mistreated or lead you to foresee a profound disagreement.

Moreover, the attitude of my friend's cousin seems rather rare. I am not at all certain that women, generally speaking, are "on the lookout" for signs of mistreatment, as Eva Illouz claims. Hirigoyen expounds a very different view: "On the one hand, we educate girls to wait for Prince Charming, and on the other we warn them against all other men. So when they become women, they have not learned to trust their instincts and to filter the real dangers."[10] Above all, Illouz neglects to mention the fact that those who are really vigilant have every reason to be so. In 2000 in France, a national study of violence toward French women showed that one woman in ten has been affected, regardless of her social class. The study also revealed that it is in their life as a couple that adult women suffer the most from physical, psychological, and sexual violence. According to the study of lifestyle and safety by the National Institute of Statistics and Economic Studies (INSEE), between 2011 and 2018, 295,000 persons age eighteen to seventy-five, of whom 72 percent were women, suffered from physical and/or sexual violence on the part of a current or ex-partner. Only 14 percent of them filed a complaint.* One would like to have

---

* According to the U.S. Centers for Disease Control: "About 41 percent of women and 26 percent of men experienced contact sexual violence, physical violence, and/or stalking by an intimate partner and reported an intimate partner violence-related impact during their lifetime. . . . Over 61 million women and 53 million men have experienced psychological aggression by an intimate partner in their lifetime."

certain signs that reliably detect a potential aggressor, but this is not always possible: "There are different sorts of violent men and some of them display no outward characteristics of machismo."[11]

For Hirigoyen, psychological attacks within a couple "do as much harm as physical aggression and have more serious consequences" (since 2010, they are also punishable under French law).[12] It is impossible to separate the two: physical violence prolongs and consolidates a general enterprise of subjugation. Continual denigration, humiliation, coldness, threats, and maneuvers aiming to isolate the woman, to destabilize her, all result in a "mental wear and tear" that can lead to suicide.

"Women, too, are violent, at least psychologically." This is the argument classically used to deny the different dimensions of violence within couples. It suggests that female victims supposedly seek physical blows by emotionally mistreating their partner, aiming at what causes hurt, to the point of making him blow up. But there are other situations where men can undergo aggravation and humiliations, starting with their work. However, the blows inflicted to a hierarchical superior, a supervisor or a boss, do not amount to a social plague, and there are no statistics about the number of homicides to which they fall victim. Why is it possible to curb impulses in the professional context but not when faced with a woman? And more generally, why are men the only ones unable to control themselves when they suffer an affront or humiliation? This prejudice prevents us from seeing the many cases in which physical violence is exercised in a cold and calculating manner. Moreover, this image of women as creatures of venomous speech, capable of doing

harm in an underhanded way, like casting an evil spell, reminds me of the distrust of women's words that was manifest
in the era of witch hunts.[13] Whatever the case, alluding to
the oppression suffered in a large majority of cases by women
within a couple does not imply that they would be incapable
of the least violence, physical or psychic. However, because
they are structurally in a position of weakness and society authorizes and favors violence among men but discourages it
among women, incidents of women's aggressive words and
deeds remain ridiculously few and are essentially reactive or
defensive in character.

Violent men often act to cut their partner off from her
family and friends, whom they can alienate by their odious
behavior, or by manifesting unhealthy jealousy or possessiveness. Then the two protagonists find themselves alone in the
face of the other. But inside this tête-à-tête that can seem like a
sequestration, the outside world remains present through the
patriarchal laws the pair have both internalized, which give
the advantage to the aggressor while penalizing the victim.
"Women let themselves be trapped in an abusive relationship
because in their place in society, they are already in a position
of inferiority," writes Hirigoyen.[14] Inversely, the very few men
who suffer violence from their female companions certainly
feel a greater shame, since they find themselves in a "feminine"
position. Nevertheless, "from the outside, they continue to be
valorized as men," she remarks.[15]

Many violent men consider they have the right to behave
as they do due to their status as husband and father, as if this
confers on them a form of omnipotence. In their eyes, their wife

and children belong to them. They have not noticed the legal evolutions of recent decades to "de-patriarchalize" the family: the title "head of the family," for example, was abolished in France in 1970. A former victim of conjugal violence, Aïda, who told her story in a book that appeared in 2006 (and on which I rely in this chapter),[16] reports that her husband would say to her: "We are married. From the viewpoint of judges, I have every right over you [which is obviously not true]. If I want to sleep with you, I do." (Conjugal rape was recognized under French law in 1992.)* He even told her, when she was afraid for their child: "He is my son. If I want to kill him, I kill him." Cecile's husband, too, echoed that: "I do what I want, they are my children."[17]

Practicing a form of brainwashing, violent men play on women's inner lack of confidence—more or less aggravated by their personal history—from which they suffer due to their dominated position in society. In her book, Hirigoyen writes of a woman, Diane, who hears her husband, Stéphane, say to her: "Everybody takes you for a crazy woman."[18] She makes herself responsible for his violence: "It is because I am not sexually up to it"; "Perhaps I have not given him enough love, that I am not woman enough."[19] In getting out of a toxic relationship (without physical violence), as she relates in her podcast *Qui est Miss Paddle?*, Judith Duportail no longer "has any confidence in herself, in a literal sense": "I no longer believe in myself, I doubt all my thoughts, all my impressions. Am I really cold or am I listening to myself too much because I am a wimp? Does

---

* In America, conjugal rape was a crime in all fifty states by 1993.

that person annoy me or is it that I am incapable of appreciating people as they are?" Her mother is the first to realize that her daughter is in an abusive relationship, especially when she hears her constantly repeating: "Am I crazy? Is what I said OK? Am I not saying something stupid?"[20]

In her graphic novel *Tant pis pour l'amour*, which recounts her relationship with a manipulator and her efforts to get out of it, the thirtysomething author Sophie Lambda shows how her ex-companion persuaded her she was responsible for the harm he was causing her, for example by telling her, "I saw messages from your ex on Facebook, and it bummed me out so much I slept with my coworker," or "These hysterical fits I have started with you." She comments, "Since I am someone who has a tendency to overanalyze, the idea would end up sprouting in my head and taking root."[21] We may doubt that her lack of self-confidence is a matter of her nature: rather, it is a trait shared by a large number of women due to their education (in the widest sense, not just parental). To a lesser degree, when my friend F was with a tyrannical and manipulative man, I was desperate when she told me the incendiary comments he was making about her and the way he constantly judged her, and I heard her quickly add, "No, you know he is right, I am not perfect, I have my faults." Everybody has faults, but that in no way justifies violence, intimidation, or destabilization.

We often speak of manipulative narcissists, men who carry out this work of undermining, but we should wonder if it is not quite simply a matter of masculine domination. Rather than narcissists, the therapist Elisende Coladan prefers to speak of "the healthy children of patriarchy," an expression borrowed from

Hispanic feminist movements. She writes, "If, instead of con-centrating essentially on the psychological characteristics of these individuals, we focused on the social structures that enable them to evolve at leisure and to repeat their behavior from relationship to relationship, then the real work of education and prevention could be put in place that might bring about real change."[22]

COMPOSURE IN THE FACE OF EVERY ORDEAL

Even though she is innocent, the female victim of violence al-lows herself to be persuaded that she is guilty. And even though he is guilty, the man, used to believing that everything is owed to him, always thinks himself innocent, and may even reckon himself to be the actual victim. If they are prosecuted, some aggressors respond by countersuing their partner. The feeling of systemic illegitimacy inculcated in women is answered by the masculine sentiment of being within his rights whatever he does. Returning to Hirigoyen's example, when Stéphane is placed in custody for having locked Diane and her children in their home for twenty-four hours, and then threatening Di-ane with a knife, he tells everyone that his wife "got him sent to prison for a simple argument"; then, since the experience depressed him so much, he went out and bought a computer with money from their joint account.[23] Nathalie remembers her husband's categorical denial one morning about her black eye: "It wasn't me who did that." Then, when she insists: "Hey, you bruise easily, 'cuz I barely touched you."[24] Cécile recounts how one day her husband shot his fist toward her face. "I had the presence of mind to move my head, and so his fist collided with a wall and he completely damaged his hand, from the finger to the palm. And he lost his finger, because the tendons were broken by the violent impact. He had two operations, but his finger was twisted and he never got the full use of it back. It was me who took him to the hospital, and I am the villain."[25] In short, he blamed her for not obligingly leaving her face in the trajectory of his fist and sparing him the consequences of his own actions.

When a radio journalist joined a dozen men forced to participate in group therapy after being sentenced for conjugal violence, he recorded a chorus of protestations and denials: they all swore they had nothing to do with it. One of them, after five convictions, continued to invoke a conspiracy of his exes, who were supposedly in league against him. Another was indignant about having to spend "three days under arrest": "I thought I had committed a crime! What is this madness?" He claimed that "sometimes it's the woman who is asking for it."[26]

The idea that the victim provoked what happened to her came repeatedly from the mouth of Bertrand Cantat, the singer in the group Noir Désir, during a hearing before the judge in Vilnius in August 2003, twelve days after the murder of his lover, the actress Marie Trintignant. "Nobody is concerned about the fact that aggression can also come from someone other than me." He added, "Everything that I took, physically, nobody looked at, and from the beginning nobody paid attention to this." Then, in a repugnant scene, he pulled up his sleeves. "Here, I still have the bruises, even though it happened the Saturday before!" (According to the autopsy report, Trintignant received twenty violent blows to the head, which demonstrated relentlessness on the part of her attacker, unlike two impulsive slaps; her optic nerves were almost detached, as in cases of shaken baby syndrome, and her nose was smashed. She had a wound above her eyebrow, and also bore traces of blows to her legs and arms, on her back and stomach.)[27]

Moreover, the perpetrators' mental resistance makes any cure very difficult. Several months after his conviction, Cécile's ex-husband continued to spoil her life and those of her daughters. The problem, she said, was that he had not taken care of himself, and inevitably someone who does not do so can become a calamity for others. In *Jusqu'à la garde*, the heroine says calmly to her ex-husband, "You have to heal yourself, Antoine," a diagnosis that for the viewer seems obvious. "Who are you to tell me that?" he shouts back at her. "It is you who should heal yourself!" While group therapy is certainly very useful for those who attend sessions voluntarily (and there are some who do), its efficacy for those who are forced to participate (especially when just for a day or two) is doubtful. A journalist who witnessed one daylong workshop recounts that the only time a participant seemed ready to admit some responsibility for conjugal violence (he was shaken by seeing photos showing the injuries to his partner), another quickly dissuaded him: "Yes, but it's because she pushed you to the limit!"[28] This does not mean that a cure is impossible, but for it to have a chance, it is better not to underestimate the difficulty of success, especially if a mistaken assessment might put women and children in danger.[29]

To explain masculine composure in the face of any ordeal, the American writer, activist, and pro-feminist John Stoltenberg advances an interesting hypothesis. He observes that "the idea of one's own sexual identity must be re-created, over and over again, in action and sensation—in doing things that make one feel really male or really female and in not doing things that leave room for doubt. . . . Almost everyone thinks someone else's sexual identity is more real than one's own, and almost everyone measures themselves against other people who are perceived to be more male or more female." Therefore, "to be a man" involves interpreting a role, and interpreting it to conform to a very widespread theory of what any actor does: "To achieve recognizable naturalism, an actor must play a character as if everything that character does is completely justifiable," regardless of what the audience or other protagonists think. So even if this character commits the most abominable crimes, the actor who plays him "must have prepared for the role by adopting a belief system in which it makes moral sense to do those acts." Thus, in the value system of the violent man, "some acts are deemed 'good' and 'right' because they serve to make an individual's idea of maleness real." Of course, in the repeated cycle of conjugal violence, there is a phase of contrition in which the aggressor asks for pardon, promises to never start up again, professes his love, etc. But this does not represent any real remorse; rather, it aims to prevent the victim from leaving. "For those who strive toward male sexual identity, there is always the critical problem of how to manage one's affairs so that one always has available a supply of sustenance in the form of female deference and submission," says Stoltenberg. They need "someone female to whom to do the things that will adequately realize one's maleness," to remain male by "contrast."[30]

Alexandra Lange's story confirms the notion that violent men try to embody a virile identity such as they conceive it; without it, they would feel shaky. When she was seventeen, Lange met Marcelino Guillemin, about thirty. They had four children. After twelve years of hell, insults, and blows, one evening in June 2009 when he tried to strangle her, she killed him with a knife in the kitchen of their house in Douai, a city in northern France. In the book she published after her acquittal, she writes: "I only understood this much later, but he was living a 'false life' by marrying Sylvie (his first wife) and then me. It was a form of cover, a façade or a social alibi, call it what you will. For—now as everybody knows—he was first attracted to men. And that, he could never accept. Not him. Not a gypsy. It was inconceivable. If I had to explain his behavior—but I could never offer an excuse for it—that would be the reason. He was eaten up by the deep malaise of feeling himself to be a homosexual and never being able to admit this to anyone." Early on in their life together, he knew how to hit her without leaving any traces. But one day he shouted "Bugger yourself" and she unwisely retorted, "No, *you* get buggered." He threw himself at her. "My husband had never been so violent. That day, he was like an enraged beast. And for the first time I bore obvious signs of his blows: bruises all over my body, strangulation marks around my neck, and just above my eyebrows, a hematoma as big as a Ping-Pong ball."[31] Probably it was the reference to sodomy that made him go ballistic. Hating both women in general (he heaped sexist insults on his wife) and also what he perceived as feminine within himself, he tried to maintain his identity as a "real man" by throwing punches.

OUR REVERENCE FOR MEN'S EMOTIONS

The daughter of a violent man, Véronique remembers that her father constantly told her "shut your mouth." "He could not bear dialogue or even the smallest contradiction."[32] Not only do aggressors try to cancel the other symbolically and/ or physically, but when violent men go as far as murder, this cancellation of the woman extends into how the press treats the affair. The academics Annik Houel, Patricia Mercader, and Helga Sobota sorted through hundreds of court transcripts of cases of conjugal murders that appeared in two regional daily newspapers, *Le progrès* and *Le Dauphiné libéré*, between 1986 and 1993; they noted that the stories often made the victim disappear—for example, with headlines like "Murder in Rue Baraban: Eleven Years in Prison for René Th. . . ."[33] Much later, in 2017, when a cultural magazine published an interview with Bertrand Cantat, Houel detected the same process at work: "Marie Trintignant is reduced to the place name 'Vilnius.'"[*][34]

While the woman disappears, the man occupies all the space. The effective effacement of the victim corresponds to an inflation of the aggressor's ego, which is conveyed in self-pitying verbosity. Stoltenberg cites the testimony of a woman told repeatedly by her husband "how heavy it was for him to deal with his guilt about beating me."[35] In Alissa Wenz's novel *À trop aimer*, the narrator's partner shouts at her: "Why don't you listen to me, it's horrible what I am going through, dam-

---

* The town where Trintignant was killed.

mit!" She surprises herself by thinking: "But I do listen to you, Tristan, I listen to you, that's all I do, I never say anything anymore. For a long time my voice has been silent, it is you who interrupts yourself, I am only a listener, a gigantic and monstrous ear. It's been so long since you asked me for my news that I no longer try to give you any, I live only for you, to listen to you."[36]

Bertrand Cantat also offered every sign of this invasive egocentrism. During the night of July 26, 2003, and into the early hours of the next morning, after having given Marie Trintignant the blows that would prove fatal, he telephoned her husband, whom she had left for him, then he summoned to his hotel room her brother, Vincent, who was also in Vilnius. He vented at length to them both, describing his jealousy and torments, thus occupying the center of attention while his victim lay unconscious on the bed where he had placed her. During his hearing before the judge a few days later, he said: "I have the deep culpability of having killed the person without whom I am incapable of living." A strange sentence that invited people to be moved by *his* fate, as if he were guilty above all toward himself. And he started to sob when he described the moment when, upon their arrival at the hospital in the morning, Vincent Trintignant, understanding only that his sister's state was critical, had thrown him out. The scene is astounding: it is his "exclusion" that makes him cry, and not his guilt or the impending death of the woman he says he loves. And how could he imagine he would be allowed to remain by the side of she whom he had massacred? Whatever the case, Cantat's absorption in his own emotions was zealously echoed in certain media, particularly the magazine *Les inrockuptibles*,* which, before the feature in 2017, had already published an interview with him in 2013. The cover of the October 11, 2017, issue was spectacular: a quote nine lines long from the singer (starting with the word "Emotionally") pasted over his photo occupied the whole front page. No better way to signify the display of the masculine ego and its perceptions, their invasion of space.

After the death of Marie Trintignant, Lucile Cipriani, a Quebec professor of law and the author of a thesis on the judicialization of conjugal violence, stressed the complacency expressed by society as a whole about the discourse and effects of violent men, an indulgence that results in the effacement of victims. She explained it by the priority generally granted to the subjectivity, well-being, and emotions of men; it is incumbent on women "to bandage the psychological, affective, and psychic wounds of their partner, to protect their egos, to watch over the couple's happiness and harmony, and it is to the advantage of men that this is so. To be convinced of this, it is only necessary to notice how many books and articles aimed at women focus on conjugal success and how this subject is absent from publications aimed at men. There is no reciprocity here." It is not incumbent on men "to bandage the wounds of the souls of women. The culture ensures a space for the aggressors' discourses."[37]

In 1947, in a manual of marriage advice, an American doctor addressed wives in this way: "Don't bother your husband with petty troubles and complaints when he comes home from

---

* A French cultural magazine.

work. Be a good listener. Let him tell you his troubles; yours will seem trivial in comparison. Remember your most important job is to build up and maintain his ego (which gets bruised plenty in business)."[38] This primacy of the emotions of *all* men, not just violent men—this reflex to identify with them, with their experiences, their interests, this idea that the role of a woman is to understand everything and pardon everything—has been deeply integrated into our psyches. The philosopher Kate Manne has coined a term for this phenomenon: "himpathy" (a combination of "him" and "sympathy"). Beaten by her boyfriend, whom she left on the spot, Cécile, a thirtysomething Parisienne, decided to file a complaint, but her father dissuaded her because "everybody does something stupid."[39] Thus he spontaneously put himself in the place of the aggressor and not in the place of his own daughter, although he had seen her disfigured.

The preoccupation with men's well-being that is inculcated in women leads them systematically to put themselves in the man's place, to the point that they forget the harm men do to them, neglect their own well-being, and keep their own voice silent. Raped by a friend, Megan, an American student, reported him on the advice of the campus psychologist. After an investigation, he was suspended for a year and his credits for the current semester were nullified. "He said he was sorry I felt the way I did, but he never apologized," she said. In fact, she had to control herself from apologizing to *him*. "I hated him, but it was weird. I also wanted to give him a hug and tell him I was sorry for doing all this, for ruining his life."[40] The first time her boyfriend punched her, Véronique says he seemed shocked by what he had done and that she felt "more sorry for him than for myself."[41]

Similarly, Diane, the patient of Marie-France Hirigoyen quoted previously, invoked her husband's professional difficulties to explain his violence. She defended him so well before the judge that he was able to avoid prison with a suspended sentence.[42]

IMPOSSIBLE TO DEFEND ONE'S OWN INTERESTS

These bizarre scruples against adopting an attitude that should go without saying—i.e., resolutely taking one's own side, saving one's skin, defending one's most elementary interests and not those of the man trying to destroy us—also affected Marie-Claude, who left her husband at the end of the 1990s after thirty years of abuse. When he threatened to kill her by brandishing a pickax, she was worried that he was succumbing to depression—or that he would kill himself if she left. (In fact, he later married a woman twenty years younger than him, and had three children by her.) To prepare her escape, she went to the bank and dared to open a personal account. Between her teacher's salary and her allowance as a local official, she had money, but she did not dare withdraw all that was due her from the joint account: "I had about 90,000 francs in this savings account, and I took only 5,000 francs! I was an idiot!" After discovering her departure, her husband rushed to empty the joint account. "He told off the girl at the bank, and the director of the bank: 'By what right did you open an account for her?'"[43]

Women who finally succeeded in leaving a violent spouse say they ultimately decided to leave because they were often worried about their children—or the fact that he had started to hit them as well. They seemingly have internalized a social law that gives them the right to defend themselves only when acting as mothers. Annik Houel, Patricia Mercader, and Helga Sobota noticed this in their study of trials for conjugal murders. Liliane L., for example, tyrannized by her husband for many years, took action when their daughters reached adolescence and she could not bear the way he treated them. While he was sleeping, she killed him with the rifle with which he had threatened them earlier in the evening, which he had forgotten to put back under lock and key as usual. The jury was merciful. Simone B., after fifteen years of total submission, also killed her husband. She couldn't take it any longer when he treated her like his servant: she had already spent her life serving others, starting at age twelve as a servant to farmers, then as a chambermaid at a doctor's office and an aide at a retirement facility. Yet she did not have a right to the same indulgence in court. "Liliane L. had acted in conformity with her social role as a mother, whereas Simone B. was defending only herself and was not even a mother," commented the authors of the study. In another case, they noticed this headline: "The murder of a mother leaves four children as orphans." Thus, only maternity lends existence to this victim: "The power of the drama lies more in the fact that she left four orphans than in the fact that she was killed."[44] Similarly, in the television film *L'emprise* (2015), inspired by the story of Alexandra Lange, there is a scene during her trial when she is asked to justify the knife wound she gave her husband when he had his hands around her neck, and the accused cries: "He would have killed my children!" (The sentence does not appear in Lange's book

on which the telefilm is based.) It is as if the direct and immediate threat to her own life was not sufficient. In short, women
are expected to act in the interests of everyone in the world
before their own.

Conversely, those who suffer conjugal violence often resign
themselves for the sake of what they think is the good of their
children: they are convinced that it is always better for them
that the children's father remain in their lives, as destructive as
he might be. They privilege the pursuit of family life, even if it's
only façade. Hélène mentions her sense of guilt when she left;
she gazed at her baby and thought, "I am depriving you of your
father," even though deep down she knew that it was *he* who
was deprived of his child by brutalizing her.[45] Similarly, to
"preserve the life of [her] children," Valérie for a long time refused to envisage a separation: "Things were smooth." Smooth,
except for the fact that her husband, a senior executive in a
corporation, one day broke down the door of the toilet where
she had taken refuge so he could continue to hit her.[46] Another
example: because Krisztina Rády, the wife of Bertrand Cantat,
was trying to protect her children, she relentlessly defended
him. By swearing that he had never been violent to anyone before that night in July 2003, when he murdered his lover Marie
Trintignant, she hugely contributed to the clemency of the verdict he got—eight years in prison, although he could have been
sentenced to fifteen (in fact he was released after half that time,
in October 2007). In 2017, a former member of Cantat's band,
Noir Désir, confided to a female journalist, under cover of anonymity, that after the death of Marie Trintignant, Krisztina
Rády had asked them—his buddies and him—to keep quiet

about her husband's violent past: "She did not want her children to know that their father was a violent man."[47] Her choice to cover things up also allowed her to be instrumentalized by Cantat's defense team in media coverage of the case.

Cantat came back to live with Rády after he got out of prison; she committed suicide on January 10, 2010, in the room next to where he was sleeping. Six months earlier, she had left a message on the answering machine of her parents, who lived in Hungary, in which she said: "Bertrand is crazy. Yesterday I almost lost a tooth, my elbow is completely swollen. With a little luck, if I have the strength and if it is not too late, I will move to another country. And I will disappear, I *must* disappear." Yet she forbade her parents to alert the French consulate, as they had wanted to do.[48] After the murder of Marie Trintignant, a photo was all over the press in which, dignified and elegant, Rády had posed with a calming and protective hand on the head of her husband, hunched between two policemen, as if he were horribly tormented. That image had fed the media legend of a woman of superior wisdom, generous enough to rush to help the man who had abandoned her for another woman. Very plausibly, the truth was infinitely sadder. And all this in the name of protecting children and preserving the paternal image.

WHEN HIS FRIENDS AND FAMILY BREAK (OR REDOUBLE) THE VIOLENCE

In the context of a woman's isolation, confusion, and fragile psychological state, the response from her circle and from institutions—which depends on the background, intelligence, and reactivity of their representatives—is immensely important. "When you have lost the habit of being understood, the slightest attention can be an intense emotional shock," Alexandra Lange remembers.[49] In order to cease being a victim, a woman who has been long riddled with guilt and manipulated and made to doubt herself constantly first needs someone to tell her clearly that she *is* a victim. An outside authority must establish the wrongdoing of the violent man. Women who file a complaint and obtain a legal decision in their favor recount how important it was for them to see it recorded in black-and-white that their ex-husband was guilty. This is all the more essential because while some aggressors arouse distrust and repulsion among those close to their partner, others pull the wool over their eyes. Both the family and friends of Nathalie adored her husband so much that they repeatedly told her how "lucky" she was to have him. Then one day, after a deluge of blows that made her think that this time she would die, she fled to the house of her sister, who was "heaven-sent."[50]

Many victims mention that an outside intervention—even a discreet one—was decisive in helping them get out of their situation. A (male) emergency room nurse, without calling into question the story she was telling him (that she had cut open her chin in a fall), whispered to Cécile: "Come back when you want and you'll get a medical certificate."* Later a policeman

---

* In France, a person can receive a medical certificate from a physician testifying to their condition, which allows them to receive paid time off work. And, most importantly, it can be used as evidence in court.

told her: "What you are undergoing is no longer possible, he is going to kill you."[51] But it is hard to imagine an intervention by a greater symbolic force than the indictment delivered on March 23, 2012, by the prosecutor at the trial of Alexandra Lange for the murder of her husband. He judged that the failures of society during her twelve-year ordeal, the bottomless solitude into which she was plunged, had led to this outcome. "Alexandra was always alone. Today I do not want to leave her alone," he declared to her and the jury: "It is the public prosecutor that tells you: you do not belong in a criminal court, madame. Acquit her!"

The former partner of a violent man can also do something significant by warning the woman in his life who succeeds her. In an ideal instance, if she intervenes early enough, she can prevent the relationship from starting and thus spare another woman a destructive experience. She may be prevented from doing so by her own trauma or by the fear of reprisal, which is totally understandable. But the intervention may also come from an outside person. A woman I know transmitted a message to me from a friend we had in common: she had met a man who interested her, they had flirted, and since she knew that I knew him, she asked me what I thought of him. In fact, I knew that he had been violent in a previous relationship. My answer amounted to "Run!" She followed this advice, to my great relief. Only if the relationship is not already established can anyone from outside the couple still have a chance of being heeded. Violent men usually take care to discredit their ex to their new partner by assuring the latter that the former is "crazy."

On the other hand, an inadequate response to a violent situation can have devastating effects, since it increases the confusion with which the victim is already struggling. Like that policeman who, when Nathalie made him listen to the litany of insults and threats that she had received on her telephone, laughingly replied: "But what did you do to him to be treated like a dirty whore?"[52] Or those police who, when Alexandra Lange found the courage to call them in the first years of her marriage, did not even take the trouble to get out of their car. Observing the traces of blows on her face, they retorted, "If that is all there is, we cannot do much, madame. There is no blood," before they drove off. She remembers that "I was devastated, perhaps even more than before they came."[53] Many professionals also stress that one must never resort to mediation, since this measure presupposes that there are faults on both sides. Moreover, although some family law judges continue to be ignorant of this, mediation and reconciliation are forbidden in situations of conjugal violence by the Istanbul Convention dating from 2011 (which has the force of law in French courts, as the collective #NousToutes stresses).* Terrible mistakes are committed because those around a woman continue to treat a violent man like an ordinary husband.** Thus during one of

---

* The online activist group #NousToutes fights violence against women, www.noustoutes.org.

** In the U.S., judges still have the power to mandate mediation in family court systems. Some courts engage in a system to screen for instances of domestic violence, but the process is flawed and often inadequate in judging the nature of the threats against a woman from her male partner.

Alexandra Lange's attempts to flee, the niece of her husband, Marcelino Guillemin, revealed to him the address where she was hiding, because she saw him as "desperate" and took pity on him. And the day when Lange, thanks to enormous effort, opened up about the violence she was undergoing to a social worker, the latter, to her horror, opened the door to Guillemin, who was waiting in the corridor, to ask him for explanations; she had no choice but to retract her accusations.[54]

Perhaps the experience undergone by the thirty-something Parisienne cited previously, Cécile, best illustrates how a mistaken institutional decision can have a ravaging effect. When her boyfriend poured a torrent of insults on her, she finally gave him two slaps, which she immediately regretted. And then this man, as if he saw this as a signal, violently beat her for three quarters of an hour. In the young woman's circle, this produced an (in)famous identification with the male protagonist. Not only did her father advise her not to file a complaint, but a friend she consulted was equally hesitant: "He might get a suspended sentence, it is a risk for him, since if he does another stupid thing, he will go to prison." Supported by her mother, Cécile was not dissuaded, but she did minimize the facts in her complaint: "I did not mention the evening with my girlfriend when he charged in and smashed everything. I did not say that he dragged me along the ground by my hair. I did not say he had stepped on my face." A medical certificate established that she had a black eye and bruises; they gave her five days of leave for physical injury and ten days for psychological injury. Three months later, she learned that her ex had also filed a complaint against her . . . for the two slaps. He claimed that she had pummeled him. After a confrontation, she was found guilty on the same grounds as he and was sentenced, like him, to pursue a one-day sensitivity workshop on conjugal violence. It was as if she had received a "second black eye." She asked that at least she not be put in the same workshop as her aggressor. She was terrified of the idea of being shut up in a room "with guys who had smashed their girlfriend."

The day after the workshop, Cécile was interviewed on the public radio station France Culture. She explained that in testifying that day, she had stated the facts and assured everybody she had merely defended herself. "But the problem was that my speech sounded too much like that of twenty-one people before me. It blew my mind and I said to myself, *Me too, I'm saying that I gave only two slaps, but I am like them!*" She burst into tears. "I was turned inside out. I spent the whole day telling myself, *I gave two slaps, but it's true that was also violence.* . . . These guys, in their heads, they are the victims, victims of this chick who prevents them from drinking . . . I told myself, *In the end, I am the only one here who feels guilty. I am the only one to admit that if that is so, I have a problem with violence.*" She concluded: "If the justice system condemns me to do this workshop, there must be some meaning to it, but if there is not, that drives me crazy."[55] Equating violent men who systematically consider themselves innocent and a female victim with a tendency to doubt and blame herself and gathering them in the same room—that is indeed enough to "blow your mind."

THE PARABLE OF MANNIFORD McCLAINE

"The one that got away. . . . The biggest heartache of my life was not my husband and the father of my children leaving me. It was never being able to truly land Manniford McClaine."

In the first season of the Amazon Prime series *The Marvelous Mrs. Maisel*, the heroine is entertaining friends at a party to refine her skills as a stand-up comedian and holds them enthralled with the story of how she discovered that the cute captain of the football team at her high school had made front-page headlines when he was arrested for murdering his wife. The punch line of the story is her reaction to his photo on the front page:

> I couldn't believe it. It had to be some other Manniford McClaine. But there he was in the paper, handcuffed, being perp-walked into the station. And I just thought, *My God . . . he still looks* fantastic. . . . I know, my first thought should have been *Dodged that bullet.* "Instead it was, *I don't know. He's single . . . I'm single. . . .*"[56]

The scene is funny, but it pinpoints a situation that is much less amusing: love affairs between murderers and the women who are irresistibly attracted to them. It seems to me this phenomenon has mechanisms similar to what we see at work in situations of conjugal violence. In prison, men whose crimes turned them into media celebrities have their female admirers, and sometimes they honor one by marrying her, to

the disappointment of her rivals. Some are particularly popular thanks to their looks, considered to be a sign of their inherent innocence, and they receive the fan mail of a rock star,
but even those who do not resemble a Greek god have their
groupies. The journalist Isabelle Horlans notes, "Courtroom
chroniclers in the 20th century were already reporting that
Henri Désiré Landru, guillotined in 1922 for eleven murders
[ten women and one man], had received eight hundred marriage proposals among the some four thousand impassioned
letters received during his detention." Charles Manson, the
infamous cult leader, died in 2017 at the age of eighty-three;
three years earlier he had almost married a twenty-six-year-
old fan. In France, Guy Georges, the "killer of East Paris"
arrested in 1998 for the rape and murder of seven women,
"received dozens of letters from women who wanted to replace
his mother or conquer his heart." A law student who fell under his charm when she saw him on television visited him in
prison for several years.[57]

All this might be explained by the cult of celebrity, which is
powerful enough to eclipse any notion of good and evil. But the
inverse is never observed: celebrated female murderers generally
leave men cold, remarks Horlans in her book about women
who love convicted murderers. Thus in Canada the serial
killer Paul Bernardo and his accomplice Karla Homolka (who
were nicknamed "Ken and Barbie") were arrested together in
1993. But Homolka never had fans, whereas Bernardo, found
guilty of forty-three rapes and three murders, "is a celebrity who
gets many requests for visits at the Kingston, Ontario, peniten-
tiary."[58] In other words, most men see a murderess as a person

who has committed terrible acts and so should be kept locked up; she inspires only disgust or indifference. By contrast, some women see a male murderer as a sort of Prince Charming who irresistibly attracts them. Once behind bars, a murderer becomes a "lady-killer," says Sheila Isenberg, who in 1991 authored the first study of the subject (and updated it in 2021). For example the chief of police of a Nebraska town remembers a man who had shot at his wife eight times: "The first week he was in jail, seven women came to visit him . . . [They appeared to] fall madly in love through the little glass window" in the visiting room.[59]

It is tempting to sweep away this disturbing fact by invoking madness. "Crazy people attract crazy people, it's as simple as that," declares the lawyer Éric Dupond-Moretti.[60] But we may also wonder if the killers and their groupies are simply pushing to the limit the usual gender roles that in smaller doses constitute our everyday reality. If virility is linked to strength, to domination, to the exercise of violence, then what could be more virile than an assassin? Thus, the young girls who wrote to the Belgian child rapist and serial killer Marc Dutroux had perhaps integrated *too well* the codes of the surrounding world, without the distance and self-censorship that often comes with adulthood. "The immaturity of these adolescent girls partly explains their attraction to killers, who in their eyes symbolize the height of virility," says the psychologist Philip Jaffé.[61] Isenberg observes, "In our patriarchal culture, murderers are often viewed as more than male: the most macho, strong, violent, and brutal of all men. In a majority of films and television shows, the violent mystique of the murderer—or the cop, spy, undercover agent, etc.—is the erotic centerpiece. . . . Violence itself is eroticized."[62] "He made me feel like a woman," declared Sondra London, the fiancée of Danny Rolling (nicknamed the "the Gainesville Ripper"), who admitted to eight murders.[63]

Most of the groupies or girlfriends proclaim the innocence of the man they love with irrational obstinacy, including when he himself has admitted his crimes. This leads to absurd scenes. In 1989, Shirlee Book married Kenneth Bianchi, who had raped, tortured, and strangled a dozen young women in the Los Angeles hills at the end of the 1970s. In a TV program in which they both appeared, she described her husband as an "affectionate and loving" person, while Bianchi boasted about having "killed those chicks."[64] Among the women in love with men who kill whom Isenberg interviewed, "not a single woman believes that her man really did it." They perceive these men as ordinary human beings who speak, walk, smile, and joke, which they see as proof that they could not have really committed the horrors they are accused of. Nevertheless, according to Isenberg, deep down inside they all *know* these men have killed, but they find this fact extremely erotic.[65]

We might think that these women venerate these men *not despite* the fact that they have killed, but precisely *because* they have killed. In 1979, in Miami, during the third trial of Ted Bundy, convicted of thirty-seven rapes and murders (he had probably committed many more), every day dozens of young women fought over seats in the front row of the courtroom. "I watched the Florida girls who lined up outside the courtroom in Miami, anxious to get a place on the galley bench behind his defense table. They gasped and sighed with delight when Ted turned to look at them," noted Ann Rule, who had been Bundy's friend and colleague for years without suspecting him of his crimes, and who attended the hearings.[66] We cannot avoid the impression that certain women may have internalized widespread misogyny to the point of intoxication, not only forgiving a man for having killed other women, but even finding that supremely seductive—and fantasizing about him killing them, too. It is as if a diffuse misogyny, omnipresent in their environment, has deprived them of the most elementary instinct of self-preservation, leading them to passionately validate what destroys them—or as if they want to try their luck, convinced that he will spare *them*.

Of course, the situation is quite different when there is widespread suspicion that a conviction is due to a judicial mistake, as in the case of Hank Skinner, condemned to death in Texas in 1995. Skinner was supported by the Frenchwoman Sandrine Ageorges-Skinner, who married him, but also by Amnesty International, which backed his request for a new trial. The seductiveness of men who have actually committed crimes but without spilling blood, like the French armed robbers Patrick Brice and Michel Vaujour, is also much more comprehensible. In every case, we find an element of female devotion: Nadine, the wife of Vaujour, helped him escape by helicopter from a Paris prison in 1986, and his subsequent partner, Jamila Hamidi, was also convicted of attempting an identical exploit in 1993. But there is not the same element of fascination as for men who kill—and who quite often kill women. One may suppose that these murders also have a right to redemption or to reintegration into society (in the United States women may campaign for the abolition of the death penalty). But a woman should not be blindly led to offer herself as a sacrifice.

"I FELT LIKE I WAS HIS MOTHER"

Women who admire killers manifest, in an extreme form, the kind of empathy and female abnegation that we observe in countless situations of conjugal violence, which can eclipse the evil that such a man once did (and still might do) to others, or to oneself. They see only the "suffering" and "human qualities" of these murderers, an indulgence that acquires an even more troubling dimension when it comes to criminals who have solely targeted women. These adoring women feel a closer connection with the killers than with their victims. "He knows how to make me forget his terrifying past," said the student who was seduced by Guy Georges.[67] When Mary Bain Pikul fell in love with the father of her daughter's classmate in Manhattan, in 1987, what she remembered about him was not the fact that he was suspected of murdering his wife but "his wit, charm, and intelligence."[68] Similarly, Shirlee Book fell in love with Kenneth Bianchi when she saw "a picture of him looking lonely during his trial."[69] Recalling her meeting in 1995 with Oscar Ray Bolin, sentenced to death in Florida for murdering three women, Rosalie Bolin said, "I felt his isolation, his solitude. He moved me."[70]

Killers in prison powerfully summon up the caregiving compulsion that women are encouraged to develop, as illustrated by the story of Hilary, a nurse in a hospital near Pittsburgh. In her forties and divorced, she met Lucas when he was brought from prison to her hospital after a heart attack. She was moved by the sight of this patient's ankle chained to his bed. She later learned that he was convicted for beating to death (with three accomplices) an old man in the course of a burglary. Before being released, he asked her for her telephone number, but she refused; she later felt she had been a little harsh. Another hospitalization a few months later offered her a second chance. They began a correspondence, and she "couldn't find anything that he was lacking," so she decided she would "stick by him no matter what happened." "I am going to get you out of here," she promised him. Hilary explained to Sheila Isenberg that she always wanted to become a nurse because she "like[s] helping people." She was marked by the model of her mother, who had taken care of a large family. Hilary's first husband, Sid, drank too much; she was aware of that when she married him, but she was certain of being able to save him. This proved hell for her and their four children until the day when she threatened him with a rifle and threw him out. When Lucas was interned in the psychiatric unit after a suicide attempt, she supported and visited him. "I felt . . . like I was his mother. Get him on the straight and narrow, like a mom does to a kid." Hilary worked sixty hours a week, and all she saved was spent to offer Lucas every comfort possible in prison. "I'm the one that buys Lucas his TV, his radio, his clothes, and his goodies from Hickory Farms at Christmas. I'm the one who pays for his phone calls. . . . I've been wanting to get a new washer. But when he calls and says, 'It's so cold and all I have is one blanket.'" [71] Let us consider the hypothesis that a will to control is being expressed through this compulsive caregiving: a prisoner is the perfect object for satisfying the emotional needs of women who present this psychological profile. However, it is still true that their sacrifice has concrete material consequences: it benefits one of the parties and hurts the other. Even if Lucas allows Hilary to realize her fantasy of total mothering, he is enjoying the comforts she is offering him, while she is exhausting herself working for him and condemning herself to a future of poverty.

In the rare cases where women admit the guilt of the man they love, they seem to see him as a challenge. He embodies not only the archetype of the virile man, but also that of a man who is tormented, inscrutable. For months or years, he has led a double life, secretly committing atrocious crimes because of an internal necessity known to him alone. They have the fantasy or ambition to be the one who, thanks to the intensity of the relationship they have formed, will crack his armor. He represents a chance to deliver a sort of supreme performance of femininity. By dint of their compassion, wisdom, patience, and generosity, they hope to be the one who will be able to touch the sensitive soul barricaded behind his traumas and crimes. Society seems to consider this women's proper role.

The faith placed in the compassion, gentleness, and wisdom of women, who are presumed to have almost magical virtues, was flagrantly on display in the trial of Guy Georges in 2001. During the first six days of hearings, Georges categorically denied the rapes and murders he was accused of before cracking: admitting them, crying, and asking for pardon. The testimony of mothers, sisters, and female friends of victims over the preceding days might have pushed him to confess, but the media coverage accentuated this drama. "The Confession Made to Women" was the headline in the magazine *Elle*; the article stated that the judge carefully addressed Georges "without ever being brusque" and his attitude was described as feminine.[72] The principal defense lawyer, Alex Ursulet, was assisted by a female colleague, Frédérique Pons. Ursulet was a Black man (like Georges), and it is possible he hired her at least in part for reasons of image, so that his client would be defended by a white woman. The tactic succeeded so well that he was completely eclipsed by his assistant. When Pons appeared alongside Georges, her face that of a Madonna, her blue eyes and porcelain complexion contrasted spectacularly with the dark skin of the "monster." Their juxtaposition awakened that archaic and racist stereotype that associates white skin with goodness and purity and Black skin with evil. The narrative schema of feminine sensibility triumphing over barbarism seemed irresistible to an audience; the tears that Pons shed in a very tense moment caused a sensation. *Le Parisien* portrayed her as "The woman who made Guy Georges confess" (April 1, 2001). "I had the impression that another being was trying to get out of him," she said after the verdict.[73]

And yet, if one believes the transcripts of the trial, it was while he was answering his male lawyer that Georges, interrogated unrelentingly about his guilt, finally went from "no" to "yes." Even if witness testimony on previous days had prepared the ground, it was the argument made by another man that seems to have won the day. "For your family, your father wherever he is, so that they are able to forgive you, if you have something to do [with the attack], you have to say so," his lawyer begged him. For the first time, the killer then whispered "Yeah" before repeating "Yes" to each victim's name his lawyer uttered.[74] For this, the mother of one of the victims paid homage to the defense lawyer: "In making Guy Georges confess, he proved his dignity."[75] The killer himself mentioned that the testimony of three women had shaken him, before concluding: "There is also my lawyer who did the rest."[76] But apparently the scenario of a Black man appealing to the humanity of another man did not satisfy our prejudices. In the (rather bad) fictional film by Frédéric Tellier about the "killer of East Paris" (*L'affaire SK1*, 2014), Alex Ursulet is not even named, the actor who plays him is simply given a credit as "Guy Georges's lawyer." On the other hand, Frédérique Pons, played by the famous actress Nathalie Baye, is the star, and clearly expresses the fantasy of a thaumaturgic femininity capable of accomplishing miracles. We see her convincing her colleague that they have to push their client to confess: "Nobody has played a proper role with him, neither his parents, nor the Social Work Department,"* she tells him. "In prison, he asked to see a psychiatrist during his first incarceration and he was refused. I want this guy, who is going to spend the end of his life in prison, to see a little bit of light here and there. We have to handle the case differently. We *all* need him to explain himself. I don't want him to be considered solely as a

---

* Specifically, the section that administers to children in foster care.

monster, hated by everybody and not understood. That is my task." To the cop who tells her, "I am the one who hunted this monster for seven years," she responds: "And me, I am the one who is hunting for the man behind the monster."

After the trial, a psychiatrist explained that since Georges had been abandoned by his mother, he did not think he was able to be the object of a woman's attention, "therefore the rapes and murders were committed." Consequently, during the trial these female appeals for him to confess were said to have a particular resonance with him: "Masculine interventions alone would have reinforced his muteness."[77] I do not know if this is valid, but it seems to me that women are placed in danger when they are ascribed this power. About the groupies who rushed to the bedside of the imprisoned killer Luka Rocco Magnotta, Isabelle Horlans writes, "They all want to be the one who will help him get well."[78] This is a risky bet. When an assassin is in prison for life, the consequences of the caring vocations he inspires remain limited, but that is not always the case. Carol Spadoni married Phillip Carl Jablonski while he was in prison for the murder of his wife. As the moment of his release approached in 1990, she confessed her fears to the probation officer, but she was not heeded.[79] Her husband was released and moved in with her in a small Californian town. In 1991, he stabbed her and then raped his mother-in-law before slaying her. He also raped and killed two other women. Back in prison, he put out a classified ad for marriage, in which he described himself as a "gentle giant" and said he was "dreaming of candlelight dinners, romantic walks on the beach, and cuddles in front of the fireplace."[80]

"THE PERFECT BOYFRIEND"

Other elements explain the attraction to a killer, which implicitly convey something about the ordinary lot of innumerable women. All those whom Sheila Isenberg met had had lives punctuated by abuse, sexual aggression, family violence, and (later during their own marriages) conjugal violence. Love and violence were intermingled in their life stories. Some of them admired a man who took action, while they themselves, given what they had suffered in their lives, probably nourished fantasies of murder. Moreover, the relationship with a prisoner was for them paradoxically reassuring, for a man who is confined and under constant surveillance cannot do them any harm. The relationship is usually platonic, and some say they are comforted by being liberated from the imperative of sexual performance. They also appreciate escaping from pressure about their body: "Men sentenced to death don't care about the waistline of their correspondent," says a Frenchwoman who subscribes to an American site specializing in meetings with prisoners.[81] They know they occupy a central place in the life of their fiancé or husband, and since these women are also their life buoy, the prisoners have every interest in accommodating them. The risk of being deceived or betrayed, while not impossible, is much less than with a free man. They know at all times where he is, while being themselves free, with no accounts to give or domestic tasks to perform for a couple. In short, he is "the perfect boyfriend."[82]

All these women manifest an immense thirst for love. We should look again at a disposition to fall in love that is so great it can be activated by the simple image of an unknown person on a television screen—not to mention the fact that this is the image of a killer. It shows how much women are conditioned to dream of love in an obsessional way, to make it the center of their identity and of their existential quest, meanwhile offering great benefits to the men on whom they have set their hearts. Most of the girlfriends of killers have themselves lacked love and attention throughout their lives, so here suddenly is someone who has nothing to do every day but to love and think of them. When she met Oscar Ray Bolin, Rosalie Bolin, who was still called Rosalie Martinez, was married to a famous lawyer and lived with him and their four daughters in a mansion. She left everything to marry Bolin in 1996 (he would be executed in 2016).[83] She shows a TV reporter the letters and cards he had written her almost every day, assuring the audience that they matter much more to her than all the wealth and material comfort that she had given up for him.[84] A documentary on the phenomenon shows another killer, Danny Rolling, being asked by the judge in court whether he has anything to add. Turning to his fiancée, Sondra London, and in his orange jumpsuit and handcuffs, Rolling serenades her in front of the transfixed spectators. This man who broke into the rooms of female students, who raped and stabbed and decapitated them before abandoning their bodies in obscene positions, starts to sing: "I recall the day I first saw you, I reached out to say I love you."[85] It almost seems like a macabre satire of our society, where we are plied with romantic comedies while skeletons knock together in patriarchy's closet.

Moreover, to survive in both their criminal careers and their lives in prison, these killers have developed a great capacity for observation and manipulation; Sheila Isenberg quotes the psychoanalyst Carl Rotenberg, who calls men in prison "the best psychologists in the world." They know how to tell a woman exactly what she wants to hear. This may explain why the word "sensitive" occurs so often when interviewees describe them. Along with their denial of the crimes they have committed, this allows their girlfriend or wife to turn them into blank pages onto which they can project their fantasies. They experience exactly the kind of courtly love described by Denis de Rougemont in reference to the Tristan and Isolde myth: a love that is constantly prevented from being consummated, full of "unsatisfied yearnings," in which the other is a mirage, an ideal figure rather than a real presence. These women are drugged by the many twists and turns in legal appeals, the alternating hopes and disappointments involved in any relationship with a detainee. Like Tristan and Isolde, they are seeking a love that is not made for this lowly world. They want a man who is bigger than life, says Isenberg, who quotes one of them: "We might not even like each other *in the real world*."[86]

Public opinion is generally horrified by the existence of killers' groupies, especially when the killers' crimes have been heavily covered in the media. In the same way, although to a lesser extent, the victims of conjugal violence are often regarded with pitying condescension. These needy women are considered poor, incredulous creatures who suffer from a dreadful lack of judgment. However, it is not they who invented patriarchal culture, nor the association between masculine seduction and violence. They are compelled to reproduce the tropes of sublime and thwarted love that are widespread in society. We constantly praise women in terms that stress their devotion, their abnegation, their concern for others, and implicitly their ability to ignore their own needs. She is "always smiling," has her "heart on her sleeve," is "always there for her children." All these qualities are so inherent in our conception of the feminine that we pronounce these banal words without even thinking about them. Inversely, those who are careful with their generosity, who pay attention to their own needs, who do not feel directly responsible for the well-being of three-quarters of humankind are often perceived as cold and selfish. Therefore, we unwittingly produce women who conform to these expectations.

The world relies too much on female devotion, and too many people abuse it. It's about time that devotion becomes a more common quality. We could begin by valorizing kindness and helpfulness among little boys, too, and by encouraging little girls to pay attention to their own well-being and to defend it, and teach them to become polite and reasonably attentive to others but not *angels*.

The psychologist Philip Jaffé explains the motivations of the admirers of killers: "These women, who wear their heart on their sleeve, have often received a Christian education [and believe that] the person who has committed grave sins may be pardoned."[87] A high percentage of those interviewed by Sheila Isenberg also grew up in Catholicism. Similarly, Marie-Claude, the former victim of conjugal violence quoted previously (the one who had a hard time taking the money due her when she left her husband), remembers that her worried parents had advised her against marrying this man. She did not listen to them: "As a good Catholic, I told myself, 'I will save this boy.'"[88] Still, we may wonder if, in every such case, Catholicism merely aggravated a general disposition linked to how girls are educated, which also exists abundantly in a secular form.

The model of "Beauty and the Beast" lies more or less consciously behind these relationships between a woman who is sweet, devoted, and understanding and a man who is tortured and/or violent, whom she is trying to save. Yet this tale, observes the psychotherapist Robin Norwood, seems to have become a "vehicle for perpetuating the belief that a woman has the power to transform a man if she will only love him devotedly." But this is a misinterpretation of the fairy tale, which is actually about acceptance. In the story Beauty has no desire for the Beast to change: "She did not try to make a prince out of a monster. She did not say, 'I'll be happy when he's not an animal anymore.'" She is *already* happy. He is gentle, full of good qualities, and she loves him exactly as he is. She has no wish to control him, and that is precisely what leaves him free to be transformed into a prince. In short, "Beauty and the Beast" should be taken as a reminder of the fact that we do not have the power to change anybody (at least, not deliberately). There is nothing bad about wanting to be happy, but locating the source of this happiness outside ourselves, in the hands of somebody else, involves evading our capacity and our responsibility to change our own life for the better, Norwood concludes.[89]

LOVE AND DEATH, A DURABLE CLICHÉ

It is rather hypocritical to get indignant about the behavior of victims of conjugal violence or the groupies of killers because our culture constantly presents the harm that a man may do to a woman as proof of love. This is one of the effects of our taste for tragic and impossible passion analyzed by Denis de Rougemont: it supplies a cover for misogynistic violence, it helps legitimize it. The term "crime of passion" (a journalistic term and in no way a legal category) has just started to recede in the press thanks to the work of feminists to promote the term "feminicide." The academics Annik Houel, Patricia Mercader, and Helga Sobota point to this paradox: "Until 1791 'love' was an acknowledged attenuating circumstance, but it disappeared from legal texts when the notion of 'crime of passion' emerged in public opinion." The press, refusing to follow the evolution in the law, effectively decided to perpetuate the indulgence previously found in legislation. It constructed and established the notion of the "crime of passion" throughout the nineteenth century. This enabled a denial of the hazardous nature of the family to women, in an era when propaganda was being deployed precisely around the sweetness of the home. The authors explain that "passion," whether given a positive or negative value, "was perceived as a force against which one could do nothing, which encouraged people to consider this type of crime as inevitable." The distortion by journalists of violence as a testament of love sometimes takes a bizarre turn: discussing a case where a man killed his wife because a divorce was becoming inevitable, then killed himself, a reporter stressed that the murder took place "eleven days before St. Valentine's [Day]" and close to a shop "with a window display of red balloon hearts and the sign 'I love you as strong as that.'" Moreover, a murder followed by a suicide was treated as if it were a matter of a double suicide. "Last Night of Love" ran one headline, and the reporter goes on: "Like the lovers in *Belle du Seigneur*, they both knew that at dawn all would be over."[90]

When Marie Trintignant died in 2003, the press overflowed with use of the terms "love" and "passion": "Love Monster" headlined *Paris match* (August 7, 2003). *Libération* (August 1, 2003) mentioned "those passionate beings who experience feelings of every kind with exacerbated violence," as well as "the ties that hold love and death together." The writer recalled Fanny Ardant's line in François Truffaut's film *La femme d'à côté* (1981) when she kills her lover before committing suicide: "Neither with you or without you." And the article concluded: "This was a film Marie Trintignant especially loved, about a love too strong, an impossible love," thus trying elegantly to justify a murder by the film tastes of the victim. Here again, depriving Trintignant of her own individuality and will, these rationales give the impression that Cantat had executed a plan they made together. In an appalling column by the anarchist playwright and filmmaker Armand Gatti, the filmmaker Hélène Châtelain, and the writer Claude Faber, they wrote: "Now history will remember that Marie and Bertrand are even more linked together—united and inseparable. Although she is dead and he is living."[91] Just a detail.

At the time, the ignorance of her colleagues of both sexes

made Nelly Kaprièlian, another journalist, blow a fuse: "In France, romance excuses everything, including the violence induced by this unconscious desire to symbolically annihilate the other and her voice as soon as she is perceived as the source of suffering—and which has nothing to do with romance or love."[92] But for once the right-wing journalist Valérie Toranian wrote in *Elle* what was necessary (August 11, 2003): "Marie Trintignant did not die as a victim of love and passion. This is an unbearable distortion of reality. . . . This is a woman who was beaten because a man grappling with his demons could resolve his torment only in violence. An atrocious news item. A crime. Dozens of such occur in France each year. And the fact that the protagonists in the drama are famous performers doesn't change anything." Toranian went on: "There is . . . no patent on love for bruisers. Love transcends and disrupts life. Love may sometimes break hearts, but not bodies. Love remains what we have that is best to offer. Not the worst."[93] ("This nightmare he calls love," Krisztina Rády would say on her parents' answering machine seven years later.) After two lines of homage to Trintignant—yes, yes, she was terrific—the writer Bernard Comment, at the time the director of fiction on France Culture radio, spent two columns (in *Les inrockuptibles*) praising Cantat, "this gentle being." In passing, he regretted that "a good editorialist soul [Toranian] was agitating, under the cover of analysis, on behalf of beaten women."[94] Ah, these fine women, always riding their vulgar hobbyhorse, daring to put "a giant" in the same basket as uneducated proletarians.

Annik Houel, Patricia Mercader, and Helga Sobota explain very simply the indulgence of journalists toward those who commit feminicide: these articles are written from the "viewpoint of the male ego." The editors imagine *themselves* as jealous, betrayed, or abandoned. At the time of the Cantat affair, with the waning influence of feminist thought, the culture, fashioned by masculine domination in which we are immersed (and to which certain women adhere while certain men disavow it), could express itself unrestrainedly, without encountering serious protest. In the pseudo-Romantic vision that reigned everywhere, "passionate beings"—to use Antoine de Baecque's expression—were supposed to demonstrate the vastness of their souls by destroying each other (and we know which of the two most often destroys the other), without which the incident would be a wretched story of a bourgeois couple that deserved no attention.

THE EXORBITANT RIGHTS
OF THE TORMENTED ARTIST

In addition to ennobling violence against women in the name of love, this culture of domination promotes the figure of the male artist or writer as a genius who is owed absolute reverence, and whose creative process justifies the worst actions against those close to him but also against anonymous people who come into his orbit. In her graphic novels, Liv Strömquist has told the stories of a number of famous artists who have mistreated and exploited their female companions: Edvard Munch, Pablo Picasso, Jackson Pollock, Ingmar Bergman.[95] During the controversy aroused in France by the praise given to the film director Roman

Polanski, in particular through the awarding of the César for Best
Director in February 2020—despite the multiple accusations of
rape hanging over him—we heard a lot about how we have to
"separate the man from the artist." Apart from the fact that we
may wonder about the feasibility of this separation, the hypocrisy of this idea should be stressed: in our society, the status of
the artist procures exorbitant privileges and legitimates the most
oppressive kinds of behavior. The journalist Nelly Kaprièlian
spoke of Cantat's "pathetic infantilism" during his hearings;[96] in
fact, this behavior revealed a reality long dissimulated under the
performer's aura and prestige.

The author Elizabeth Gilbert has written brilliant pages
about the baneful figure of the tormented artist: "If you are the
Tormented Artist, after all, then you have an excuse for treating
your romantic partners badly, for treating yourself badly, for
treating your children badly, for treating everyone badly. You
are allowed to be demanding, arrogant, rude, cruel, antisocial,
grandiose, explosive, moody, manipulative, irresponsible and/
or selfish. . . . If you behaved this badly as a janitor or a phar-
macist, people would rightfully call you out as a jackass. But
as the Tormented Artist, you get a pass, because you're spe-
cial. Because you're sensitive and creative. Because sometimes
you make pretty things."[97] When the photographer/partner of
Alissa Wenz's narrator makes a scandal during a Paris theater
concert, she stifles the fear that the incident inspires: "I said to
myself, didn't [poets like] Apollinaire or Baudelaire also have
strange behavior in public? Aren't impulses and whims the
mark of extraordinary personalities? I imagined Van Gogh at

that theater, on the arm of his fiancée. Would he not also blow a fuse?"[98]

On the contrary, Gilbert believes that "you can live a creative life and still make an effort to be a basically decent person." She quotes the British psychoanalyst Adam Phillips: "If the art legitimates cruelty, I think the art is not worth having." She is dismayed by the number of artists who refuse to get treatment, to solve their problems, and put those close to them through hell because they confuse their suffering with their creativity. She writes of the writer Raymond Carver, who knew that addiction does not make the artist: "Any artist who is an alcoholic is an artist *despite* their alcoholism, not because of it." Gilbert herself has gone through periods of anguish and depression but she does not wallow in them, she says, because they make her incapable of writing: "Emotional pain makes me the opposite of a deep person; it renders my life narrow and thin and isolated. My suffering takes this whole thrilling and gigantic universe and shrinks it down to the size of my own unhappy head."[99] She chooses to place her life and her work under the sign of love, not suffering. But in the face of this attitude, our dependence on a culture of domination leads us to fear lapsing into sentimentalism or moralism. Our culture tries to present itself as the one and only culture, to make us believe that nothing of value can exist outside it. This is false. Indeed, we could find quite a different set of works that reflect the whole spectrum of human emotions and realities—strong, rich, nuanced, complex, troubling, and funny.

At the time I was writing on conjugal violence fifteen years ago,[100] the memoir by Tarita Teriipaia recounting her life with Marlon Brando had just been published. She remembered how

Brando, after having insistently demanded "a Tahitian child," tried to force her to get an abortion when she became pregnant, because that was no longer convenient for him; how he twice beat her until the blood flowed. He went as far as putting a rifle to her cheek and came close to pulling the trigger. *Paris match*[101] published long extracts under the headline "Love Monster"—the same title they ran for the murder of Marie Trintignant—as did *Elle*[102] under the headline "Mon amour fou avec Brando." For the thirty-five years since I began devouring these magazines, I have been ingesting impressive doses of this romance-infested literature where "love" rhymes with blows, bullying, and oppression.

While I am working on this chapter in the spring of 2020, not much has changed. *Elle* is offering a series on "legendary couples." Two of these couples have sadly familiar stories. First of all, the Hollywood actors Ali MacGraw and Steve McQueen had a "crazy and destructive passion." (Destructive for whom? Guess.) The pull quote is from MacGraw: "I loved the way he breathed danger." They met on a shoot and she got a divorce for him. He shut her up in the house, forbade her to continue acting, and struck her. "Soon, nobody was tolerated at the McQueen home, and Ali was reduced to doing housework and running errands. Her family was frightened by the hematomas that covered her body." After four years she ran away. She would never appear in movies again.

Then there is Miles Davis and the dancer Frances Taylor's story, which is more flamboyant but still puts a young woman through an ordeal. Davis had paranoid crises in which "he ran around the building, butcher's knife in hand, searching every

cupboard and under the bed for an imaginary intruder." Davis
did not strike Taylor, he admired her, but he, too, put an end to
her professional career. For his sake, she even refused a starring
role in *West Side Story* on Broadway. "Nothing was left except
the kitchen for her to express her talent." After the separation,
she would become a hostess at a California restaurant. Both
articles conclude with the protestations of love by the swindled
woman. Ali MacGraw regrets not having been able to see Steve
McQueen before his death, "who despite everything she still
considers the man of her life."[103] And Frances Taylor said of
Miles Davis: "He is still my prince."[104] Nevertheless, other articles in the series portray couples who apparently succeeded in
loving each other without doing more harm than what is caused
by normal emotional fluctuations: for example, the actors
Rooney Mara and Joaquin Phoenix, the artists Niki de Saint
Phalle and Jean Tinguely, the painters David Hockney and Peter Schlesinger. And believe it or not, there is much to tell on
the subject of these "normal" couples, too. But that appears
strange because we have lost the habit of reading about *them*.

So that in the coming decades "legendary" as well as anonymous couples do not perpetuate the same sinister narrative,
perhaps we should follow bell hooks's recommendations and
not think of love as a simple sentiment that permits all sorts of
behavior but as an ensemble of actions. This illumination came
to hooks from the psychiatrist and self-help author M. Scott
Peck, who suggests defining love as "the will to extend one's self
for the purpose of nurturing one's own or another's spiritual
growth," as the act of working both for one's own flourishing

and that of the other.[105] Notes bell hooks, "it becomes clear that we cannot claim to love if we are hurtful and abusive."[106] We cannot take seriously a man who beats his children and his wife, and who at the corner bar proclaims how much he loves them. We cannot say, like that mother to her daughter living with a violent man: "Of course he has a difficult character, but you have to deal with that. The important thing is that he loves you."[107] This new definition of love may be enough to sweep away the mythical "crime of passion." Denis de Rougemont said as much when he analyzed the morbid taste of Westerners for passion: "*To be in love* is not necessarily *to love*. To be in love is a state; to love, an act."[108] Rougemont contrasted passion, where the other is merely a pretext, an illusion, with a love that accepts the other as they are and acts for their well-being.

However, this involves breaking a mechanism that is set up early, when parents who mistreat their children physically and/or psychologically are in effect teaching them the coexistence of love and violence (or violence as an expression of love). Bell hooks remembers her and her siblings' confusion when their father beat them, while telling them he did so "for [their] own good" or "I'm doing this because I love you."[109] She knew it is difficult to accept the definition of love she proposed, since it makes us confront our own shortcomings and failures. It forces us to face the fact we have not known how to love someone else, as well as the fact that others may not have known how to love us. But she is convinced that we ought to have the courage to adopt it and stick to it. "Definitions are vital starting points for the imagination. What we cannot imagine cannot come into being."[110] This definition appears quite simple, but if we put it to work, it would lead many of us—not only the women and men caught in toxic relationships—to some radical reorganizations of our lives.

3

GUARDIANS OF THE TEMPLE

Is Love Women's Business?

never wore my watch . . . He would keep his on." For me, everything is expressed in Annie Ernaux's detail about her rendezvous with her lover ("A") in the 1991 novel *Passion simple*. It lays bare the whole asymmetry in the way in which men and women learn to consider love, what they expect from it, what is at stake for them, and the time and attention they are ready to devote to it. In this case, if A cannot let himself forget the time, it is because he is married and therefore accountable for how he spends it. But the female narrator also has a life apart from their affair, she, too, has obligations—she writes, she teaches, she has two sons—except that in her case passion veers into monomania and triggers an irrational desire for tabula rasa, for flight from the rest of the world. For a year, she says, any activity would seem a means of passing the time between two rendezvous. "I longed for total idleness. I angrily turned down some extra work my boss had asked me to do, almost insulting him over the phone. I felt I had every right to reject the things that prevented me from luxuriating in the sensations and fantasies of my own passion." Now everything that composed her life before her meeting A

appears insipid, impoverished, sad. When the telephone rings
and it is not him, she "loathes" the person who is on the other
end of the line. If he announces that he is coming three or
four days later, she is depressed thinking of all that separates
her from the moment she'll see him, whether her work or even
a meal with friends. When, in a gesture of independence, she
forces herself to go solo on holiday to Florence, she spends the
whole trip imagining herself "in that same train, this time
heading back towards Paris, eight days later." She surmises
that A does not experience their affair in the same way: "He
himself would have been astonished to find out that I never
stopped thinking about him from morning to night." After
their breakup, she agrees to participate in a colloquium in Co-
penhagen only because that would give her the opportunity to
send him a postcard.[1]

Annie Ernaux mentions in passing the cultural environment that fashioned her relation to love; all the representations
that surround her—on television, in magazines, in advertisements "for perfumes or microwaves"—show only one thing: a
woman waiting for a man.[2]

She remembers the "cultural standards governing emotion"
that influenced her, which she calls as decisive in personality
formation as the Oedipus complex: Racine's play *Phèdre*, *Gone
with the Wind*, the songs of Édith Piaf. . . . For my part, if I had
to compose a similar list (although I would like to forget this),
I would cite *Phèdre*, *Gone with the Wind*, *Belle du Seigneur*,
Julien Green's novel *Les pays lointains*, the songs of Dalida*

* An Egyptian-born Italian-naturalized French singer and actress.

("Je suis malade," "J'attendrai," "Parlez moi de lui," "Pour un homme"), and the novel *Passion simple*, which I read when it first appeared in 1991. I was eighteen years old, stuffed with romantic films and novels, and so my dreams were all about love. As an adolescent, I featured on the wall of my bedroom the poster for *Out of Africa*, Sydney Pollack's 1985 film adapted from the Karen Blixen book; in soft-focus I saw a blond Meryl Streep and Robert Redford sitting in a Kenyan field and exchanging languorous looks.

In my love life, I was frightfully unhappy—but that is another story. Or maybe it is *not* another story, or not completely. Among the fascinating variety of reasons that might explain the epic disaster that was my personal life, there is the fact that my absolutist view of love led any man with a more or less healthy mind to flee me. With my slightly exalted nature and my tendency to excessively adopt the cultural messages that surrounded me, to receive them *much too well*, I came to expect *everything* from love. Like Annie Ernaux's, my case illustrates what the sociologist Sonia Dayan-Herzbrun observed in 1982: "The conditions in which most women were raised since early childhood, the discourses they heard or read, the images they saw, made them expect to find someone to love them (a Great Love, a Prince Charming), and this expectation set the tempo of their lives; and thanks to the love of this miraculous man, they always expect to find their identity as a person *and* their identity as a woman."[3] So it is not surprising that Flaubert's Emma Bovary affected me so much.[4] I was a little Bovary, except that my ennui, my impatience, and my romantic daydreams did not spring from the life of a doctor's wife in a provincial village but from my life as a high school student.

Thus the female way of loving, so perfectly illustrated by *Passion simple*, was already intensely familiar to me. Now it appalls me but at the time I found it somewhat sublime. I saw no problem in this downgrading and repudiation of everything that did not concern the beloved being, as she describes. It seemed to me natural (and even enviable) to love a man by hating everything that did not involve him, everything that he had not touched with his grace. I could not understand that it was up to me, to me and nobody else, to put a bit of color into *all* aspects of my life, to think about them, to cultivate them, to take care of them, to tame them, and to love them, instead of waiting for an improbable savior who would make my dreary reality magically disappear. I did not understand that it was incumbent on me to *construct myself* because no film or novel had told me that—or else I did not listen.

Rereading the novel *Belle du Seigneur* today, I can see how feminism has made me much more lucid. I am astonished I was not more irritated at the time, not only by Solal's machismo, by his manipulative and sadistic behavior, but also by the trashy side of Ariane, by her explicitly religious submission (announced in the novel's title: her lover is her "Lord"). Now I am sickened by these rich and idle characters who are lovers only, who have nothing else in their lives. For years, Isolde (Solal's former mistress) prepared for him every day without knowing whether he would visit her; she had taken courses in massage to be more appealing, and when he stopped desiring her (because at age forty-five, of course, she was irredeemably "withered"), she could only die.[5]

Sonia Dayan-Herzbrun details the noxious view of love inculcated in women, the debilitating mixture of glorified suffering and illusions in which they are cradled: "When women sing about love, it is often done in the form of passivity, complaint, waiting ('I will wait, day and night, I will wait for your return'—Dalida)—that can be seen as masochistic pleasure. Thus on the one hand, women are presented with disappointment in love and suffering as our common lot, and on the other, we maintain our dream of happiness in a love so perfect that it is self-sufficient and eternal. These two aspects are contradictory only in appearance, since merely the hope of happiness allows putting up with the current suffering."[*][6]

However, as an adolescent I dreamed not only of love. I was a good student, with a precise and stubborn ambition to become a journalist. It went without saying that later on I would work and I would not be financially dependent on a man. Having grown up in a well-to-do household, I easily accepted this model of independence. And little by little, I found a healthier model of loving. But this romantic and passionate intoxication left its traces—I suppose that the introduction to this book makes that clear. I accept and I claim responsibility for my taste for love, now that it is rid (at least I hope so) of its excesses and errors. I know that it largely results from my socialization as a woman, from my exposure to a certain type of literature, cinema, journalistic prose, etc., but I can call this into question only to a limited

---

* "J'attendrai" is a song by Rina Ketty (1938) covered by Dalida in 1975.

extent. It constitutes a little isle of traditional femininity in a life that otherwise is rather removed from it, and this suits me.

ALIENATION AND WISDOM

In my mind, love *is worth the pain*, it merits our devoting space, time, and attention to it—but it seems this attitude is more widespread among women than men. The sociologist Kevin Diter, who has written about representations of love among children ages six to ten, explained in 2017 to a radio journalist how we learn very early that love is a "girl thing" and "not for boys." "When they [the boys] take an overly close interest in love—they are very aware of it—they risk undermining their reputation and their self-definition as boys"—and hence they could lose their status as dominants. They expose themselves to being treated like "babies," "little girls," "fags." Diter recounts that during his field studies, he was sometimes suspected of pedophilia by certain school principals because it seemed so improbable that a man might be sincerely interested in love and emotions.[7] For males, the impossibility of proclaiming a taste for (and interest in) love persists into adulthood. My friend F remembers a directed study in social psychology he participated in, where he and others were invited to classify by order of importance certain universal values: "I was one of the rare ones (the only one among a dozen young men) to place love as number one, without any hesitation. And I remember the mocking surprise of another student—extroverted, attractive, a figure I envied—for whom friendship came first."

This conditioning to scorn love may create among men a distortion between their lived experience and their thinking. This was precisely the philosopher André Gorz's view when he wrote *Lettre à D.* after fifty-eight years of living with his partner, Dorine. He wanted to repair the error he had committed by underestimating the treasure that was their relationship. Rereading his book *Le traître*, which was supposed "to show how my commitment to you was the decisive turning point that gave me the will to live," he perceived instead that he had belittled her: "Why did I give such a false image of you? . . . Why did I present you as this pitiful creature?"[8] His "virile" socialization—to be precise, the virility specific to French left-wing intellectuals—had equipped him with an interpretive framework for his own life in which it was impossible for love to occupy a central place. For a "serious" man, women and love could only be of negligible importance. Therefore it was just a year before their double suicide that he was able to rectify this prejudice, to acknowledge and recognize fully what he had experienced. This was in total contrast to the other couple whom I mentioned at the beginning of this book: Serge Rezvani never had the least bit of difficulty in living and presenting himself as a lover. On the contrary: he acquired the means of devoting himself to love by retiring to the backwoods with Lula, which he made the central theme of his writing.

So why do women tend to grant such a high price to love? This is what we are going to try to understand in this chapter, but among all the possible reasons, I will start by suggesting one: because we are right to do so! We may overvalue it, but I also believe that men underestimate it. One of the women interviewed by Shere Hite remarks: "I think there is heavy conditioning for men—most are taught that they are not supposed to be affected by falling in love. Many of them hold such things as a job more important. A lot of them are more interested in 'security'—'having a wife,' i.e., somebody at home to count on—than in actually having a love relationship. I think many men don't know *how* to have one. Women, I've noticed, usually want to talk things out more."[9] Perhaps it is my own conditioning that speaks here, but maybe not. When I wrote about typically feminine preoccupations—beauty, fashion, concern for one's appearance[10]—I wanted to stress how they weaken women due to the psychic expense they involve, the insecurity they foster, and the position of dependence in which they place women. But I did *not* want to reinforce the sexist critique of "feminine frivolity." I also wanted to defend the desire for beauty as a legitimate value (as long as one gets rid of its excesses and its destructive aspects), to defend it as the fruit of a culture that is transmitted from generation to generation, which seems worthy enough to challenge dominant values. In any case, I felt myself to be overly influenced by this feminine aesthetic culture and thus unable to denounce it as a whole. I might say exactly the same thing, and admit the same ambivalence, on the subject of love. It, too, is essentially a woman's affair, and it seems to me also the bearer of both alienation and wisdom.

Many women manifest a greater tendency to introspection, to reflecting on themselves—and for heterosexual women, on their relationships with men. Many of us seek answers to questions we pose about life and relationships—amorous, with family, and with friends—from personal development (or self-help) books. This quest earns us immense contempt. Several books have been published in recent years to condemn "self-help" as a whole, as the bearer of "individualism" and "liberalism."[11] Critics contrast it with philosophy, which is so much nobler, supposedly giving man the courage and wisdom to contemplate (without blinking) the horror of his destiny, instead of pushing him toward an extravagant quest for happiness. Of course, you find a bit of everything among these diverse works, all labeled "self-help," just as you find everything offered in diverse therapies. Charlatans proliferate, and many successful writers deliver disastrous advice that ends up confining women to resignation and submission, or that makes individuals feel responsible for social or political problems. (A "pop psych" article in a women's magazine titled "I Cried in the Office, Is That Gross?" offers a spectacular depoliticization of suffering at work.) But not all of them are like this.

Certain feminists, though vigilant about the ideological content of the reading material that passes through their hands, do not look down on self-help books. Bell hooks acknowledged: "I have bought tons of self-help books. Only a very few have really made a difference in my life."[12] In France, the female journalist Victoire Tuaillon also thought that "personal development is not a dirty [concept]."[13] For my part, I had an illuminating experience a few years ago thanks to Melody Beattie's bestseller *Codependent No More.*[14] I bought it because a female friend had recommended it, but I barely read the first few pages before abandoning it. Then, one day, probably because it was the right moment, I suddenly felt the need to read it, and right away. As I was not at home, I bought it in English on my e-reader and read it voraciously during a train trip that seemed fast as lightning. This book changed me, and I could not find what might be politically pernicious in it. By studying the problems encountered by those close to persons suffering from addiction to alcohol and drugs, then by extending her reflections to our relationships, Beattie poses questions and brings essential answers that I had never seen formulated anywhere else.

In France, the antiliberal catechism that battles "individualism" from a position that is somewhat dogmatic neglects one thing: many of us have complicated heritages. We are not nondescript individuals, selfish consumers who are too spoiled, placid, and replete, living in a dream world—or rather, we are not only that. We struggle with the more or less serious problems that fetter us, that make us suffer, that prevent us from loving as we would like, and that are not all attributable to capitalism. Without even mentioning the legacy of victims of violence at home (battering, incest, psychological abuse), the warping in our formation (studied by the Swiss psychoanalyst Alice Miller, what she calls "dark pedagogy") is quite present in all family histories. Sometimes, tragic deaths have shaken our genealogical tree. When bell hooks speaks of "self-love" with friends or acquaintances, she is surprised to see how many are disturbed by this notion, "as though the very idea implies too much narcissism or selfishness."[15] This would be true if self-loathing were not a widespread phenomenon. To not see this, you would have to be still under the command of the puritanism and malevolence toward oneself that have been bequeathed by a long tradition of repressive education. And then, particularly if you are a woman, meaning you have absorbed a daily dose of self-hatred, merely "loving oneself is a punk thing, a revolutionary thing, a radical thing," as the author Judith Duportail correctly hammers home.[16]

We are grappling with configurations that we need to understand and then resolve. And for that, we need help. And seeking help—whether from a friend, a psychoanalyst, or another kind of therapist, or even from a book—always carries a risk of manipulation, since it necessitates trusting and therefore making yourself vulnerable. You have to demonstrate a critical spirit and avoid demagogues and hustlers, but should you completely avoid self-help? Mai Hua's approach as recounted in her film *Les rivières* seems exemplary of the courage and strength with which many women embrace their stories. When she had just divorced, her uncle told her she was part of a "line of cursed women," doomed to be unhappy in love. She decided to go see for herself and filmed a voyage in quest of family genealogy, which transformed her and everybody around her.[17] Similarly, many women in my circle have launched quests or personal revolutions that do not correspond to the condescending cliché of the poor, self-centered, lost girl who is exploited by charlatans. There is perhaps a sort of moral panic in the sweeping condemnations that this searching has aroused.

LEAVING THE SHADOWS AND ANONYMITY

No, women are not necessarily wrong to love as they do, with daring and courage. However, it remains true that the contemporary asymmetry between feminine and masculine attitudes toward love poses many problems, as shown in the sociologist Marie-Carmen Garcia's study of heterosexual and clandestine couples.[18] When both lovers are married to other people, it is most often the women who want to make the new relationship official, while their lovers are hesitant. Women have more difficulty in compartmentalizing their lives. "Unlike what happens with men, whose sexual socializations offer at least two female figures ('the mother' and 'the whore'), women are socialized toward the search for the one and only man who will fill all sexual and emotional functions." They want to be "coherent with themselves, in other words with the norms they have incorporated in the course of their gender socialization." Inversely, notes the sociologist, male lovers manifest a deep attachment to their status as family fathers and make it a point of honor to accept their responsibilities—at least on the surface. Therefore in extramarital relations, the "norms of masculine parenthood" enter into conflict with the "norms of feminine loving," and the latter rarely wins out.[19]

Take, for example, Anne, divorced after four years of a secret and passionate relationship "because she could no longer bear kissing her daughter good night as if nothing had happened." She hoped that her lover, Laurent, would follow her along this path, but he did nothing of the kind. He was far from being as determined as she was, and his passivity exasperated her: "Once he went to see a fortune-teller to know if we were going to live together! As if the decision were not up to him!" Another man, Christophe, explained to Garcia that "I am no longer twenty, I can't do what I want to. As a man, I was taught that it is important to keep your commitments, and you do not leave a woman to whom you are committed. What I do with my penis concerns only me, and also what I do with my heart. But I keep my commitments." Moreover, while single women who are in love with married men may wait for them all their lives, always hoping that he will leave his wife, men manifest an attitude that is less sacrificial. Jean-Jacques maintained a secret relationship with Stéphanie for thirty-four years. She was already married when their affair began and she did not want to leave her husband. One day during the early years of their liaison, Jean-Jacques announced that he had met another woman and he was going to marry her: he did not break off his affair with Stéphanie, but he could not see why he should be deprived of becoming a father and having a family life, too. Stéphanie was "dumbfounded." She would later be extremely surprised when she was the first person he called to announce the birth of his first child.[20]

What function is fulfilled by the conditioning of women to love? Again, even if I do not think that heterosexuality is a patriarchal ruse, it seems to me undeniable that by deluging girls and women with romances, by vaunting the charms and importance of the presence of a man in their lives, they are encouraged to accept their traditional role as caregivers. We also place them in a position of weakness in their emotional life: given that the existence and viability of the relationship is more important to them than to their partner, in the event of disagreement on any subject whatsoever, it is the women who will concede, make compromises, or sacrifice themselves. We educate women so that they will become machines for giving, and men so that they will become machines for receiving.

While confining women to the mental universe of life as a couple, mass culture invites men to dream about the inverse, as Jane Ward notes, by slyly evading the conjugal framework during their free time. Leisure among men sharpens their nostalgia for bachelorhood and for casual sex with younger women—a whole fantasy universe perfectly synthesized in the California mansion of the *Playboy* founder, Hugh Hefner, a hedonistic and luxurious estate peopled with seminaked and flirtatious creatures.[21]

The value women are encouraged to give to love may incite them to practice a form of "dumping *amoureux*," that is to say, offering their love to a man and lowering their requirements for the relationship—their demand for reciprocity in terms of attention, goodwill, personal investment, division of labor, etc.—to compete with other potential female partners, and absorbing the cost to themselves that this involves.* This mechanism procures them a momentary individual advantage, but it harms them in the long term, and it results in weakening heterosexual women as a whole. It allows men to never have to suffer the consequences of their negligent or abusive behavior. Thus, they are never forced to question the assumptions about their place and their rights that have been inculcated in them. They are able to dictate the conditions of the relationship, and if a woman leaves them, they are certain of finding another who will accept their conditions. This is even more true when this psychological position of strength is reinforced by an economic

---

* In economics, "dumping" consists of slashing prices or else minimizing the constraints regarding salaries, social protection, or respect for the environment in order to attract investors.

position of strength—which is common, since men as a whole earn more than women and possess more property.[22] Imagine what our amorous landscape would look like if women remained inflexible on demanding respect for their needs—and if they always had the material means to do so—this is one of the most satisfying fantasies in which I can indulge!

Another explanation often advanced for this stronger and fuller investment in love relations is the desire for maternity. Eva Illouz attributes the greater hurry to get engaged and the "exclusivist sexual strategy" of heterosexual women to the fact that they are "motivated more by a reproductive orientation."[23] But as we have seen, those interviewed by Marie-Carmen Garcia are frequently more ready than men to divorce, and hence to leave the father of their children in order to be able to live openly with their lover: their identity as a lover supersedes their identity as a mother. Similarly, when they have to choose, some women in love with a murderer (as we saw in the previous chapter) abandon their family in order to have this relationship. Moreover, my own case demonstrates that this explanation (the desire for maternity), while partly truthful, is not sufficient: even when I was a starry-eyed girl, I was always determined not to have children.

"Is it legitimate to claim that women desire to marry or to live in a stable couple, only to have children? That is totally implausible," Sonia Dayan-Herzbrun was already claiming in 1982. She offered an interesting competing explanation:

If maternity has long conditioned the recognition of the social existence of women, later on love gave them a right to a history, if not to History. After the era of saints, then of queens, it is as beloveds or as women-in-love that women get spoken about, that their existence is the subject of a story, which appeared with the novel. The novel made women creators and heroines, even if it was at the risk of their lives, since heroines in novels, even if they are not doomed to die like heroines in operas, often end up tragically.

Moreover, the novel is considered a female literary genre—even though some novels deal with men and though some men read novels. So it is not surprising that the novel developed among the bourgeoisie, at the same time as the norm for love-marriage. To love, even while suffering, is to leave the shadows and anonymity, and to have the possibility of identifying with a heroine whose story you have read. The photo-novel took over the social baton from the 'noble' novel and extended its effects to the whole society.[24]

Having already established a parallel between the urge to love and the narrative urge in this book's introduction, I find this thesis rather convincing. Moreover, ethnographic studies of romance literature have shown that female readers appreciate it because it offers them "the fantasy of becoming 'somebody,' in stark contrast to everyday lives characterised by self-denial and taken up with the care of others."[25]

A final explanation arises, no doubt the most massive and essential one: the greater intensity that women invest in love represents the trace of the total dependence that has long been their lot. For centuries, it was only from marriage, their tie to a man, that women could draw social and economic status, even their very identity. This was the principal force fashioning their destinies; even when they were liberated from it, such habits of thinking were not easily erased. Eva Illouz thinks that men are not involved in their sexuality because they have never had to utilize it as a currency of exchange to obtain other resources, material or social: "Women's approach to sexuality . . . is more emotional *because* it is more economic."[26] This dependence remains current, and we should recall the statistics on part-time work: in France, it has tripled in thirty years, and in 2018, it involved 30 percent of women in the labor force, as opposed to 8 percent of men.[27] In addition, in 2011 there were 2.1 million women ages twenty to fifty-nine years old (and not studying) who lived in a couple without having any employment at all.*[28]

HIDDEN DEPENDENCE

Even if on paper women seem to have exactly the same chances as men of ensuring their economic independence, and hence of establishing their amorous relationships on an equal footing, insidious mechanisms prevent them from doing so. A study conducted by Dorothy C. Holland and Margaret A. Eisenhart in the early 1980s startlingly demonstrates this. For several years, the two sociologists followed a group of female middle-class

---

* According to the U.S. Bureau of Labor Statistics, in 2019, 23 percent of U.S. women worked part-time, compared to 17 percent of men, though the percentage of women working part-time "has not changed much over the past five decades."

In addition, heterosexual couples in which only the man worked for pay was 18 percent in 2018, versus 36 percent in 1967 (bls.gov/opub/reports/womens-databook/2020/home.htm).

students in two universities in the southern U.S., one majority Black and the other majority white.[29] Their initial mission was to understand why so few women were becoming scientists or mathematicians, but they were surprised to discover that pre-occupations linked to love devoured a considerable share of the time and energy of female students. All of them were caught in a "peer culture," a sort of parallel and clandestine curriculum that was the only one that really mattered. In this culture—where the presumption of heterosexuality seemed absolute—their value was defined solely by their degree of physical and sexual attractiveness, whereas the value of men depended on their physique *and* on their accomplishments in other domains (intellectual, sports, etc.). How female students evaluated their peers and themselves as a function of these criteria occupied most of their conversations. They tried to increase their capital of seduction through dieting, exercising, going shopping, and trading clothes. All of their outings—to the pool, to parties, or to bars—were motivated by the hope of an amorous encounter. Asked the subject of her major, one of them replied "Men"—and this was barely a wisecrack. Occasionally they cooked for their male friends or cleaned their rooms. Those who paired into a couple began to organize their time around their boy-friend's schedule. They abandoned their own activities to serve fraternities as "sweethearts" and "little sisters" because this was "so important to him"; they grouped all their classes in the first four days of the week to be able to spend long weekends with their boyfriends. They also let their boyfriends make important decisions about their futures. One of them had given up the same major as her boyfriend, who had convinced her that she was "not suited for that field," and so she abandoned it, saying, "He probably knows best . . . He knows me so well."

Faced with this situation, the university abandoned them, the sociologists thought. A female student said that one of her professors, each time he spotted an error in the textbook they were using, declared that it was because a woman wrote it. Another reported that one day while she was standing in front of her classmates, a teacher undressed her with his eyes in an ostensible way. A high school teacher tried to stay in contact with her; he sent her a book by Freud and arranged a meeting to discuss it. Flattered at first, she realized that actually he wanted to become her lover. (When she refused, he accused her of being sexually repressed; if she were a true intellectual, he argued, she would be open-minded and not care that he was married.) From such incidents, these young women drew the conclusion that they were considered incompetent or else simply seen as sexual objects—and they suspected the same would be true in the working world. But this did not affect them much, reported Holland and Eisenhart, since they were so absorbed by the "peer culture" that they paid only distracted attention to their academic courses and career prospects.

Forming a couple appeared to be a life preserver for these young women, their best option. As one married woman put it: "My career goals are for his career more so than mine." Yet they experienced love without great enthusiasm, in a rather pragmatic and disillusioned way. Some even tried to postpone their engagement as long as possible, and when the sociologists came back to them several years later, many of them had divorced. From the start, they were resigned to put up with bad treatment. When one was asked why she remained with her boyfriend despite his behavior toward her, she replied that "it must be love." The only notable difference the sociologists observed between the white and Black students was that the latter, if they married a man of the same skin color, had less hope of realizing their dream of being taken care of by their husband, since at the time Black men were starting to experience unemployment and mass incarceration.

No, we cannot easily get rid of the model of economic dependence—nor of all the other types of dependence this entails and that exceed it. In 1981 the American feminist essayist Colette Dowling explained this aspiration to be *taken care of* at all levels, on an expectation that an external intervention will deliver us from all our responsibilities toward ourselves. She called it the "Cinderella Complex."[30] And in fact it would be surprising if all the stories of a Prince Charming women had been fed since early childhood left no trace. Their upbringing and education plant within girls a "hidden dependency," Dowling asserts. Hence if we want to gain our freedom, we have to add to the concrete struggles for work equality an effort at internal emancipation. If we sense this tendency in ourselves it has to be honestly recognized; we have to dare to be "courageously vulnerable." "The first thing women have to recognize is the degree to which fear rules their lives," writes Dowling. She quotes the New York artist Miriam Schapiro, who said she had "spent her whole life with the feeling that an unprotected child lives inside her" and that only painting allowed her to assert herself and become more alive.

Even mentioning this problem carries certain risks. Some people rush to conclude that if women do not take their full place in the worlds of work, or politics, or art, it is because of their own inhibitions, their persistent taste for a timid and withdrawn position, and not because of the sexism they suffer—and/or the refusal of their partners to perform household or child-rearing tasks. However, I think that these archaic forces that work on us are real; they must be put on the table. It is her own trajectory that brought Dowling to these reflections. As a freelance writer, she alone had to provide for her three children after her divorce; her ex-husband had frequent stays in a psychiatric hospital. She was well out of the marriage, but "a secret, unconscious part of [her] was waiting to be bailed out again." After four years, she did meet another man, also a writer, and in 1975 they left New York to live in a large country house.

Then her life changed. For the first months she let herself be absorbed by domestic duties: she kept the house and garden, made the fires, prepared sumptuous meals. The rare times she sat down in her own office, she confined herself to "riffling through papers." She had rediscovered a world close to that of her childhood, "a world of cherry pies and bed quilts and freshly ironed summer dresses." In the evening, she typed her partner's manuscripts. "I had slipped back—*lounged* back, really, as into a large tub of tepid water—because it was easier. Because tending flower beds and organizing shopping and being a good—and provided-for—'partner' is less anxiety-provoking than being out there in the adult world fending for oneself."[31]

So Dowling slipped back comfortably into this traditional role. Later she also realized that she feared losing her femininity by returning to the professional arena. Nevertheless, she ended up blaming her companion, even detesting him for having more social ease and confidence than she did. It was he who finally slammed his fist on the table: this is not what we agreed on, he told her. There was never a question of his paying all the bills. He refused to take care of her, and that made her terribly angry at first. She resented him for all the household tasks that she performed (she does not say if he assumed his share of the domestic labor when she had balanced the household finances, which is a shame). Then she reflected. She gradually became aware of her reflexes, her obscure aspirations, her fears. She drew upon them for an article titled "Beyond Liberation: Confessions of a Dependent Woman," which was published in *New York* magazine in June 1981 and caused an immense stir: "Each day the mailman would arrive with a new batch of letters and I would take them out back to a little gazebo behind the house to read them and cry."[32]

THE IRRESISTIBLE ROLE OF THE HELPLESS WOMAN

Colette Dowling was born in 1938. Might dependence be solely the problem of women who, like her, waged feminist battles in the 1970s? I am not so sure. Such figures continue to haunt our imaginary lives. A dozen years ago, I wrote (just for pleasure, with no intention of publishing it) a novel in which a thirtysomething writer stays on the property of a rich fortysomething patron in the guise of a writing residency. Both are comfortable together without anything happening between them. Then at the end of the stay, he makes her an offer: she can keep her apartment on the property as well as her monthly allowance, on the condition that she accept an unusual personal arrangement. Sometime after finishing this novel, I heard talk of the enormous success of a book that supposedly illustrated a tendency toward "mommy porn." Reading the plot summary—a seductive young billionaire proposes a sexual pact to a female student—I thought, *Oh, boy.* Without knowing it, I had written an intellectual version of *Fifty Shades of Grey!*[33] (Ah, yes, you dream of being Simone de Beauvoir and you wake up as an understudy to E. L. James!) Thus, at the start of this twenty-first century, the fantasy of a man able to shelter you forever from need, while making you discover new sexual horizons (Marie-Carmen Garcia's "all-in-one" man)[34]—a man, in short, who brings you both security *and* excitement, was still powerful enough to push at least two women simultaneously to novelize this fantasy. One of them, if she had been asked, would define herself as a feminist—while the other created a worldwide hit in *Fifty Shades of Grey*. (In 1990, Garry Marshall's mythic film *Pretty Woman*, in which a prostitute [Julia Roberts] crosses paths with a rich and seductive businessman [Richard Gere] who propels her into a universe of luxury while also bringing her happiness in love, owed its success to almost the same narrative mechanism.)

Taking a retrospective look at my years as part of a couple, I might first believe that dependence, though present in my fantasies, was absent from my lived experience. We were both journalists, I was earning a living, I was writing books. . . . But then

I remember that for a rather long period when I was a freelancer, my companion paid the whole rent. Later, I would gladly have done the same for him if that had been necessary, but the occasion never arose, and I am not sure this was by chance. Above all, he had my emotional dependence, and I only measured its scope much later. I was anxious and unsure of myself, but I had stumbled on the most generous man in the world, who reassured and encouraged me constantly. I drew precious and undeniable benefits from his gratifying view of me, from his astute advice, and from the confidence he inspired in me. But I got into the habit of constantly turning to him, of sharing my smallest doubts so that he would comfort me. We settled into our respective roles that in the long term did not do us any good, either as individuals or as a couple. After our separation, I had a love affair with a man who, for all sorts of reasons, had very little time to devote to me. I went from one extreme to the other, and the shock was rude. But even apart from this new relationship, the fact of now living alone forced me to confront my dependence, to remedy it, to learn autonomy. And frankly, it was about time. (When I set about writing the book *In Defense of Witches*, I confided in a friend my fear of not completing it without my ex-companion, who had sustained me during the writing of my previous long-form essays, at my side. When the book's French sales exceeded 100,000 copies, this friend shot me a sarcastic quip: "Okay, now are you convinced that you're capable of writing a book on your own?")

Unconsciously, I had probably slid into the role of the deprived woman, without resources, all the more easily because this attitude "has always been regarded, and is still regarded today, as an admirable and even glamorous feminine attribute," to use Penelope Russianoff's words. I discovered this American psychotherapist by seeing her cameo in Paul Mazursky's film *An Unmarried Woman* (1978), which I mentioned in the *Witches* book. The heroine goes to consult her after her breakup with her husband. I had been struck by her presence and by her atypical beauty, without knowing she was actually a therapist and that a few years after appearing in this film, she devoted a book to the question of the affective dependence of women that she was constantly confronting in her practice.[35] She recounts a scene from her childhood: One day a bat entered the house where she was living with her parents and her sister. Since her father was outside, her mother called him for help. He chased the terrified creature while they shivered and trembled. "Our hero vanquished the bat. And my mother was so grateful! And my sister and I, following our mother's example, fell all over him, too, gushing our praise and admiration." Yet she knew that if her father had been absent, her mother would have been quite able to get rid of the animal on her own. "She learned at an early age, and I learned from her, and even my youngest female patients learned from their adult female role models, to play to a male audience very differently than to a female audience or to themselves alone."[36] It was quite probable that I, too, had incorporated the idea that imitating weakness and powerlessness—at the risk of cultivating *real* weakness and powerlessness—was an appropriate way of manifesting love to a man—and of receiving it.

In Elisa Rojas's novel *Mister T. et moi*, the narrator's friend gives her this advice for seducing the man she has fallen in love with:[37]

> "There are many men, in fact, what they want . . . is that you play . . . the kitten."
> "The WHAT?"
> "The kitten!"
> "But what does that mean? You have to meow?"
> "It means the defenseless but slightly mischievous girl, one who needs them."

Elisa is stunned:

> "I have to lie? But I don't know how to do that! I am incapable of that and what's more, I really don't want to. It would be false advertising. I am not 'a fragile little thing' who needs help. T. knows that. And what kind of man can you catch with that? Guys who like to torture animals?"

I admit it: unlike Elisa Rojas's narrator, I have played the kitten!

But there is an important proviso: to a certain extent, we *all* depend, women and men, on others. It is not a matter of claiming that the ultimate goal is not needing anybody. The suffering caused by the disappearance of the beloved being from our lives, whether this disappearance is provoked by a breakup[38] or by death, is on a par with the happiness this person has brought us. The closeness with which two lives may be intertwined, the richness represented by an amorous relationship—or a friendship or a blood tie—is a miracle to be cherished. During a reading in Brussels in 2019, a young woman admitted to me her perplexity about the notion of female independence that I developed in *Witches*; she had no desire to be alone, she told me. But there is a world between withdrawing to a desert island and thinking that one "is nothing without a man." However, this is the conviction that Russianoff detected among most of her patients, even when they tried to protect themselves from it. One of them said with a sigh that if she met the ideal man she would not need psychotherapy. Others who were married had adopted the centers of interest and leisure pursuits of their husbands, and no longer even went out without them. Thus, winning independence does not mean doing without relationships (unless that is what you wish), but rather finding the correct place from which one can go out and form relationships.

PUTTING ONESELF IN ORDER

At the time I was reconquering my own independence, I realized that I was mixing things up. I anxiously wondered what would happen to me if I suffered a major blow: a disease or a bereavement. But at the time, I was in good shape, like all the people I loved. If I found myself in distress, I had people to turn to, starting with my former partner, as I was able to verify in the summer of 2020, on the occasion of a postpandemic panic attack. While waiting for confinement to end, I was mostly capable of taking care of myself. I was not a deprived little thing. I could overcome on my own any daily vexation.

We can strive as much as possible to extend the areas of our life where we are autonomous, on a practical or psychological level, without taking anything away from the irreplaceable shock of the romantic encounter.

In his book *We: Understanding the Psychology of Romantic Love* (1985), the psychoanalyst Robert A. Johnson, a disciple of Carl Jung, took up Denis de Rougemont's ideas about passion. For him, passion is the only place in our life where we can still express a religious or spiritual impulse. "Romantic love is the single greatest energy system in the Western psyche. In our culture it has supplanted religion as the arena in which men and women seek meaning, transcendence, wholeness, and ecstasy."[39] This is a rather convincing thesis when we think of how frequent it is for women in love with a murderer or a violent man to have a Christian upbringing, including heroines in novels: Emma Bovary and Ariane, who in *Belle du Seigneur* reads Psalms and replaces God's name with her love Solal's. But transposing a religious impulse into one's emotional life amounts not only to enclosing oneself in an attitude of blind and resigned submission but also to asking the impossible of the person one claims to love. For Johnson, we ought to repatriate this impulse to the sole place where it can best express itself: inside oneself. We ought to be bent on nurturing our own internal lives by engaging in creative or spiritual activities. Only then might we envisage our amorous relationships very differently.

The change we need is illustrated by Johnson in the form of a dream reported by a thirtysomething patient. The young man recounts: "I am carrying the bell that once belonged to the Virgin Mary to the great basilica which was built centuries ago to house it when it was found. The shape of the bell was known, and a niche has been prepared over the altar, exactly the correct size to fit the bell. A priest had been on duty at all times for several centuries to accept the bell when it would be returned. I walk into the basilica, down the long aisle, and present the bell to the waiting priest. Together we lift it up and hang it from the hook in its niche. The bell fits its place perfectly." For Johnson, we can see this tale as a symbolic description of the gesture of reparation by which the Western model of passion described by him and by Denis de Rougemont, the result of a badly placed impulse, may at last stop ravaging our lives. We can see it as the resolution of this dependence that pushes so many women to wait for *salvation* from a *miraculous* man.

Becoming independent signifies restoring order inside oneself, and not in renouncing any sexual or love life—far from it. There may be one exceptional case: when we maintain either sustained or episodic relationships with men not out of real desire, but out of addiction to their gaze, out of conformity to "what is done," or out of fear of being alone. Some people think it is indispensable to learn to do without this completely, to come back to sexuality later when you have built a base of autonomy. In *Revolution from Within*, Gloria Steinem mentions a female musician she knows named Tina, who had the habit of dropping everything she was doing as soon as a man manifested interest in her. She ended up taking a radical measure: "For five years she composed, traveled, lived alone, saw friends, but refused all invitations from eligible men. She fixed up her own house, took vacations to new places, and taught songwriting. She lived a full life—but one that did not include sex or romance. It was hard for the first two years, Tina said, and very frightening. Without seeing herself through a man's eyes, she wasn't sure she existed at all. But gradually, she began to take pleasure in waking up alone, talking to her cat, leaving parties when she felt like it. For the first time, she felt her 'center' moving away from men and into some new locus within herself." After five years, she met a man very different from those she had previously attracted or was attracted to, and she married him.[40]

Others take a still greater distance from the habits of thinking inculcated in them. Among the women interviewed by Évelyne Le Garrec in the 1970s was Flora, a thirty-eight-year-old journalist who said: "I discovered something: that one could easily do without a man. Perhaps because I am getting older. . . . And I have always done well without them, but I had an education that said: you have to fuck, you have to fuck."[41] In Sophie Fontanel's novel *L'envie*, which recounts a deliberate period of sexual abstinence, the narrator hears a doctor on the radio asserting that "the more an individual makes love, the better s/he becomes in all domains": "And I burst out laughing."[42] The injunction to have some kind of sexual activity may be valid for both men and women, but among the latter, it becomes all the more pressing since regular contact with a male body represents a sort of sanctification. It is taken to be a token of both social status and physical equilibrium, which is not always synonymous with pleasure. In the course of her divorce, Marielle, a twenty-seven-year-old textile worker in Roubaix, met a married man and became his mistress. But she insists that if ever he spoke of leaving his wife, she would oppose this out of sympathy for the wife. And she added: "Plus I do not love him, I don't even take any pleasure from having sexual relations with him, and the days when I cannot, I am really content."[43] Similarly, a patient of Penelope Russianoff's called Jane likened sex with partners to satisfy her "sexual needs" to going to the dentist: "I don't really like to do it. But I *have* to do it, you know. Keeps me healthy."

One day, while Jane was recuperating from a bad case of the flu, she reflected on her situation. "I thought about what all my sexual experiences were adding up to—and the answer was nothing."[44] Not even momentary gratification, most of the time. Essentially, she got more from watching television. So she imposed months of abstinence: "I was really celibate—and I discovered that I did not become ill or crazy as a result. My vagina did not rust." Sophie Fontanel, too, rejects this prejudice that the absence of sexual contact provokes an irreversible physical withering. She describes the period immediately following her decision to stop making love, which was taken during a winter holiday in the fresh air of the mountains: "Once the benefits of the mountain wore off, not only did my face maintain the healthy complexion from my vacation, but my radiance was accentuated. I found I was starting to shine in photos. What encounter could transfigure me like this? What rendezvous was I going to with eyes brimming with confidence and the luminous skin of someone getting out of prison?"[45] What if the secret of physical blossoming is neither to fuck or not to fuck, but to do what suits us? Jane added: "Now, when I go out, it's because I want to, not because I assume I need to. I do it out of choice, not desperation. And when I sleep with a man, I get more out of it—because I'm doing it out of real desire, not . . . to assuage loneliness" or to feel validated.[46]

Perhaps "validation" is the key word. In an episode of her podcast *Sexe Club* devoted to the "culture of sex without engagement," Samia Miskina goes back to a period when she had multiple adventures: "I told myself that I adored going from one relationship to another, that I felt free. This was not completely false, since I really took pleasure in the majority of these relations. But in hindsight, I realized that in each encounter I was seeking a validation. That of men, of course; one that proved to me that I was pretty, desirable, fuckable. Each time I came home accompanied, it was a small victory."[47]

If men also suffer from the pressure of having "to fuck," I do not believe their identity is molded by the gaze of women like the identity of women is by the gaze of men. Penelope Russianoff was often stupefied to find that only sex with a man had a rightful place in her patients' eyes. They were embarrassed when she spoke about masturbation; they could not let themselves indulge in it since they would see it as a degradation. For my part, I recognize myself in the voluptuous autonomy described by Sophie Fontanel: "When was I happier than during the first months of respite? I took baths in lavender milk. The Japanese sell a perfumed powder, it turns the water white. By pouring the contents of the sachet into the bathtub, by delighting in this creaminess, then plunging into it, I had the impression that the gods were smiling down on me."[48] One unshakable fact is that the overwhelming happiness of having sex is inaccessible to us in the absence of a partner. But this does not mean that our whole capacity for pleasure should be locked up or conditional upon a masculine presence. Many other activities may be sources of intense pleasure. For me: writing, reading, being absorbed in fiction, walking, eating, swimming, dancing, fantasizing, covering myself with creams and oils. . . . I am ambivalent about my friends who have lots of sexual adventures. On the one hand, I envy their audacity. But on the other, I remain perplexed when I see them spend their energy, suffer from major disagreements with their partners, and sometimes be very hurt in relations with men who do not even please them that much. (I don't mind running the risk of being hurt, but it has to be for the sake of someone who is worth the pain.) I sometimes wonder what portion of real desire and what portion of a need for validation are contained in their intense sexual activity. Another result is that I preserve my serenity better than they do. One day, one of them asked me to read a breakup message sent to her by a man so I could give my opinion. She also asked another of her friends. I told her naively that I found the message rather touching, while the other woman responded, "What a jerk!" Which inspired my friend to conclude: "You are less angry than we are."

OTHER WOMEN: LAST RESORT OR RIVALS?

Among the traces left in women's psyches by centuries of total dependence on men, there is also a certain type of relation with other women. During their study in two American universities in the 1980s, which we looked at earlier in this chapter, Dorothy

C. Holland and Margaret A. Eisenhart noticed that female peers
had only a "peripheral" existence for these students. Female friends
had the sole function of acting as a support group in a young
woman's search for a fiancé. When they went out as a group, it
was always in the hope of meeting "someone interesting"—i.e.,
a man. Only the magic of a masculine presence might save their
day or their evening from the mediocrity and the misery in
which they were stagnating. Once when they had organized a
party, one of them regretted that guys had not come; when a
few turned up, she shouted: "Now the excitement begins." Not
many of them envisaged that a relationship with another woman
might have value in itself, outside the help she supplied in the
enterprise to find love.[49] One of Penelope Russianoff's single
young patients abstained from going out with friends—in any
case, she had never formed female friendships. She seemed
afraid that their presence would dissuade a man from coming
up to talk to her, that it would prevent him from noticing her
among the other women. She also dreaded offering a pathetic
image: "People do sometimes regard two women together or a
group of three or four women together as kind of spinster types.
And even if you're the most popular thing in your secretarial
pool, and you know this, you can't help but feel as if people are
pitying you, looking at you strangely, when you're in exclusively
female company. And what if the man of your dreams is among
the people pitying you? He might notice you from across the
room, but he thinks, since you're with all these women, that
there must be something wrong with you."[50]

    When other women are not considered negligible or as de-
meaning company (with all the self-hatred this implies), they

can appear as a threat. Ascribed by misogynists to the natural pettiness of women, rivalry in fact is born directly from their history, from the subordination to which they have always been reduced. It comes from the era—probably not much changed—when our whole destiny depended on our capacity to be *chosen*, to the exclusion of all other women, by a power both absolute and capricious (this is still the regime under which actresses live). More generally, the stage play of female rivalry and the power this confers on men is a constant in Western culture. In his famous BBC documentary series in 1972, *Ways of Seeing*, the art critic John Berger showed how in European painting the prime theme of the Judgment of Paris (depicted by Lucas Cranach the Elder and by Rubens, who made several versions) perpetuated the tradition of men looking at women and deciding among them according to their tastes. In mythology, the Trojan prince is invited by the goddesses Aphrodite, Athena, and Hera to choose the most beautiful among them and present to her the "apple of discord." Paris chooses Aphrodite, who promises him the love of the most beautiful woman in the world. This is Helen (the wife of Menelaus), whom he will kidnap, unleashing the Trojan War. "Beauty in this context is bound to become competitive," Berger observes. "The Judgement of Paris is transformed into the beauty contest."[51] (Four or five centuries later, the reality TV show *The Bachelor*, in which a single man is invited to choose a companion among more than two dozen candidates who are successively eliminated, reproduces the same scenario.) Ironically, this episode of *Ways of Seeing* concludes with a discussion between Berger and a small group of women (among them his partner at the time, Anya Bostock Berger), whom he asks to react to what has just been said about the tradition of the female nude. I can't stop myself from wondering if these women felt in competition with each other to retain the attention, by their charm and the pertinence of their statements, of this handsome and charismatic man.

This heritage, as well as the anxiety that we constantly feel on the subject of ourselves, of our value, of our attractiveness, may even produce destructive behavior. I have sometimes met women who seem to live their relations with half of humankind in the mode of "her or me," as if there were not enough space for all of us. When I was faced with these women, I would feel annihilated, reduced to a small pot of insignificant ashes. Especially the first few times, because I did not understand what had happened. At first I assumed that my suffering derived simply because I didn't measure up, before understanding that other women, equally beautiful and brilliant, were far from giving me the same feeling of being crushed. Since then, when I am confronted with this veiled hostility, which is sometimes dressed up as smoothness or flattery, all sorts of alarm bells sound. I try hard to keep my distance from such a woman, but now I know her behavior is coming from deep insecurity. I know that this destructiveness arises because she has the impression of defending herself from an existential threat; I know this because I, too, feel this insecurity. Most of the time, I adore witnessing the talent and success of other women: they make me happy, inspire me, stimulate me. But sometimes the old anguish of being eclipsed, the fear that others' best qualities cancel my own, returns in force.

The American writer Jenny Tinghui Zhang remembers the

first time one of her friends, age eleven or twelve, made her doubt herself by making disdainful comments about her body, and the frequency with which this experience was repeated over the following years. She had to wait until her entry into professional life, in a tech sector dominated by men, to find herself surrounded by women who stuck together. She says she then experienced "a muscular coalition of support and solidarity" from the benevolent company of other women. "This glow comes to me regularly now. Like after the election [of Donald Trump], when I made eye contact with another young woman at CVS and we both gave each other a quick, sad smile. . . . Or simply getting complimented on my outfit, hair, or earrings by a stranger on the street. These moments of feminamity are not superficial. For me, they are radical moments of understanding and empowerment. Veiled in compliments is the same message over and over again: Keep going."[52] The sorority is a reality, and a very lovely reality. But it can also be precluded or made more difficult by the persistent fear of seeing yourself made invisible, supplanted, relegated, by the terror of discovering yourself to be banal, with nothing to distinguish you—"infinitely forgettable," as Jane Birkin wrote[53]—by the logic of "her or me."

As a woman, you are pushed to have a pitiless view of yourself and others, hypercritical—in fact, hateful—as if it were a matter of constantly measuring the competition, ceaselessly reevaluating your own place within a great rivalry for masculine attention (or just for attention), with a mixture of anxiety and hostility. This conditioning may undermine our finest impulses of solidarity. Among the musical interludes of the series *Crazy Ex-Girlfriend*, there is one in which Valencia Perez, the haughty yoga instructor with the perfect body, picks up a guitar and, in the middle of the street, plays a hymn to sorority that is rather improbable coming from her: "Women Gotta Stick Together." Female passersby join in, but each time an enthusiastic dancer comes along, Valencia cools her ardor by integrating into her song a perfidious comment about her: "Women have the power, the power to make a change / Like this girl should pluck her eyebrows."[54]

To have a chance of overcoming this inherited distrust of other women, we have to confront it honestly, realizing that it is not our generosity or personal elegance that is at issue (or not only that!). The problem arises in every domain of our lives: love, professional, political activism. Whatever we do, apparently, we still perceive ourselves as the goddesses in the Judgment of Paris, or like the girls that the mistress of a brothel lines up in front of the client so he can choose. Male rivalry also exists, but it seems to me to arise from a felt legitimacy, from the assurance of it being within men's rights to demand whatever attention or preeminence is available. Theirs does not rest on the same fundamental insecurity. And above all, it is not fed from outside in the same way. To pit women against each other, sometimes without being aware of this, is a reflex, an irresistible temptation, among both women and men. In 2020, Gloria Steinem and Eleanor Smeal, another militant feminist of her generation, stood up against what they found to be a biased view of the story of modern feminism presented in the series *Mrs. America*. This TV miniseries aimed to reconstruct the battle that took place in the 1970s around the Equal Rights Amendment (ERA), designed to inscribe the principle of equality of the sexes into the United States Constitution. Steinem (played in the series by Rose Byrne), Smeal, and other feminists were fighting to get the amendment adopted by all the states, while a militant conservative, Phyllis Schlafly (Cate Blanchett), mobilized Republican housewives against it. By presenting the two camps in this way, the series reduced this battle to a "catfight," charged Smeal and Steinem in a joint op-ed, whereas according to polls, a large majority of American women had always been favorable to the ERA. They reproached the series for ignoring the intense and decisive activities of multiple lobbies opposed to the amendment, in particular the insurance industry, which, if the ERA were passed, would have been forced to "stop charging women more for less coverage." Schlafly and her followers had served only as "cover" for the interests of these powerful economic sectors, they said. And they wondered, "Would a national legislative failure of a civil rights movement be attributed to rivalry between the followers of Martin Luther King Jr. and the followers of Malcolm X? Somehow, we don't think so."[55]

In the winter of 2021 on Instagram Rupi Kaur commented on a poem in her collection *Home Body* that dealt with female rivalry,[56] explaining that it had been inspired by the "scarcity mentality," meaning the mentality of people who see life like a cake: they believe that if someone takes a large slice, this means that there will be less for others, which is "bullshit." During tours to promote her books, many young women told her they have been educated to think like that. Now they want to get rid of the idea that there is "only room for one woman at the table." They refuse to be set against each other, to think that the success of another deprives them of something. Several times, she says, an audience member has stood up and cried something like: "When one of us rises, we all rise!" And then the whole room bursts into applause.[57]

This is good, but it is undoubtedly more difficult to reach the end of the "scarcity mentality" in the realm of love, where most often it is indeed a matter of effectively occupying a unique place. However, when the beloved man chooses another, perhaps we should try at least to live through the bouts of sadness that assail us without calling our very being into question. I remember my alarm when I read *The Idiot* by Dostoyevsky: two men in love with the same woman are ready to kill each other because of this rivalry, though at the same time they love each other like brothers. Who would have thought it possible to make people cry over the tragic story of two women torn between their lifelong friendship and their love for the same man? For such a case to be possible, one would have to have a very strong and solid sense of one's identity, one's own value, and the certainty of one's sovereignty on all levels. All these things women have little chance of possessing, but we can try to cultivate and conquer them.

AND MASCULINE DEPENDENCE?

"Women have, indeed, come a long way—socially, sexually, and, to a lesser extent, economically," writes Penelope Russianoff. "Emotionally, however, they still have a long way to go."[58] The emotional dependence from which they suffer seems invasive to her because it extends to all sectors of life. Meanwhile men feel themselves to be legitimate in the job market and those of the upper classes feel entitled to enter any career. However, Russianoff stresses it would be wrong to deduce from this that men do not suffer from emotional dependence: "Men are dependent, too. My male patients are often miserable over bad relationships (or having *no* relationships). I've consulted with enough bachelors to know that the carefree playboy is pretty much a myth. There are playboys, all right, but I've seldom met one who was totally free of the very same cares that plague single women. These so-called 'most wanted men' rush home from work and straight to the phone to make a date. God forbid they should spend the evening alone! And I've treated many a widower, anxious to get married to fill the unfaceable void in his life."[59] This dependence goes unnoticed because it is denied; if admitted, it would offend the masculine ego. In *Lettre à D.*, André Gorz expressed his remorse for having written in one of his books about a female character inspired by Dorine, who "would have destroyed herself" if her hero (he) had left her, whereas it was *he* who had more need of *her*: "So why do I seem so sure that our separation would be more unbearable for you than for me? To avoid having to admit the opposite?"[60] Liv Strömquist has devoted some hilarious pages to this mixture of blindness and smugness, in which she shows how the boasting of certain reactionary American male comics, who repeat how women are difficult and clinging, who proclaim their allergy to intimacy, their disdain for emotions, etc., and the cultural attitude that this boasting reflects and amplifies, in fact masks a deep need for the presence of women and the emotional security that they bring. She summarizes this mystification by imagining the exchanges between one of these archetypal men and the woman who shares his life:

"How do you want to celebrate Valentine's Day?" she asks him.

"But I don't want to celebrate Valentine's Day," he answers. "I detest it. I detest love. I detest sentiments. I detest women. I detest everything that interests women. But for pity's sake, remain at my side anyway! If not I will collapse like a house of cards!"[61]

Meanwhile, the blogger Emma dramatizes a scene where a man sitting in the living room rants: "I am fed up with her wanting flowers! Or when she wants us to eat at the table to 'discuss something' instead of watching a series on TV." So Emma draws arrows to show the places in the living room that testify to the feminine attention from which this man benefits, that ensure his well-being without his even realizing it. His clothes: "T-shirt bought on sale because the others were full of holes." The glass he holds in his hand: "Preferred beer, advance-cooled in the fridge." On the coffee table in a diffuser: "Essential oil against spring allergies."[62]

Women can so often pass for capricious and tyrannical creatures, making exorbitant emotional demands, and men for solid and autonomous beings with cool heads, because the emotional needs of the latter, contrary to those of the former, are taken care of and fulfilled in a zealous but invisible manner. When a woman is cataloged as overly demanding, often she has done no more than demand reciprocity in the attentions she lavishes. We saw in the previous chapter to what extent men's emotions are the major business of women, of men themselves, and of the whole society. For something whose existence they sometimes deny, or that they pretend to master perfectly, men's emotions truly take up a lot of cultural space. In 2016, the author Erin Rodgers turned the term "gold digger" about-face: usually used to designate women in search of a rich man, she suggested it also be applied to men "who look for a woman who will do tons of emotional labour for them."[63] Notes the journalist Melanie Hamlett, "While [women] read countless self-help books, listen to podcasts, seek out career advisors, turn to female friends for advice and support, or spend a small fortune on therapists to deal with old wounds and current problems, the men in their lives simply rely on them."[64] It seems that women are both sought after and yet despised for their emotional competence. Most often, it is also they who take the initiative in a discussion, or suggest couples therapy, or make the appointment for couples therapy. Ruth, a British woman questioned in the 1990s, at age thirty-six: "It's always been me looking after the relationship. I sometimes like envisage it like a little garden, you know? I'm the one who does all the gardening and the men come out and sit in it [laughter]. . . . They sit in it, and I'm pulling the weeds up, pruning the roses."[65]

The most elementary emotional needs of women are stigmatized, presented as outrageous and unreasonable. The term "*attachiante*" (a portmanteau of *attachant* (endearing) and *chiant* (a pain in the ass)), which many French women use to describe themselves on dating sites,[66] indicates that they have themselves integrated this stereotype. Rereading her conversations on Tinder, when she asked for her history on the site in 2017, Judith Duportail understood that, faced with the men she had met thanks to the app, it was impossible for her "to dare to show my vulnerability, or dare to speak of emotions, or dare to express my needs." "I was too afraid of seeming tiresome. I wanted to appear a cool girl. It was a kind of obsession. . . . But I think that the cool girl is a concept directly inherited from patriarchy to muzzle our needs and our requirements which are quite legitimate, which are not hysterical things. The cool girl is the beautiful girl, who remains fuckable, who laughs at everything, even the worst humiliations. And I think that this kind of totem that we are pushed to attain restricts our freedom. It even disrespects us."[67]

In her book *Outdated*, the feminist writer Samhita Mukhopadhyay attacks the stigma of the "Desperate Girl." She deplores the fact that most feminists have internalized this stereotype: "We will do anything we can—including betraying our feelings and instincts—not to be her. Needy, desperate, and nagging are all labels slapped on women when they have needs or demands in a relationship," she writes. "It's based on sexist and retrograde ideas that women are inherently more emotional and therefore must always be managed by men."[68] She says these crippling representations have the effect of encouraging men to neglect the desires of their partners, while dissuading the latter from expressing them. *Don't Be That Girl* is the title of the book by a "dating guru," a doctor who advised *The Bachelor*. The subtitle is "A Guide to Finding the Confident, *Rational* Girl Within" (my emphasis), which pinpoints the hatred of emotions underpinning the enterprise. The author enumerates all the types of girl you "shouldn't be": Desperate Girl, of course, but also "Agenda Girl," "Yes Girl," "Drama Queen Girl," Bitter Girl," "Insecure

Girl," "Working Girl."[69] The list leads you to conclude that the only possible salvation lies in not being a girl *at all*.

The result of all that is a situation likely to put knots in your brain: when a woman tries to get rid of her tendency toward emotional dependence, she cannot always know if she is behaving like an autonomous adult or letting herself be treated like a doormat. "Have you ever let the guy you're dating off the hook for something he did that upset you because you were invested in being the 'casual, strong, independent, not needy' girl?" asks Mukhopadhyay. She also confides: "I remember telling my best friend for the umpteenth time that it was okay, despite a series of neglectful moves on behalf of her then 'almost sorta maybe' boyfriend, to still love him and be with him. After all, I rationalized, she didn't want a relationship in the traditional sense, so this 'here today, gone tomorrow' relationship seemed just fine. The truth was that there was nothing fine about it. Nothing about feeling unsatisfied, unhappy, neglected, or insecure is ever fine."

These days, the dominant feminist attitude consists of appropriating what was historically "men's approach to sexuality," as Eva Illouz remarks, demanding the ability to separate sex and love and to defy the stigma of the slut. But here again, this demand might be used to justify forms of abuse. It is sometimes difficult to determine if the model of emotional detachment is a feminist conquest, or else a way of conforming to masculine expectations. For some men, it seems to serve as a cover for realizing their desire, which we have already encountered in previous chapters, for a woman who renders a service and shuts her mouth. One of those questioned by Illouz, a forty-nine-year-old Parisian professor of finance named Ambroise, described the difference between the ordinary and the ideal woman: "After you have had sex with a woman, she never leaves in the middle of the night; forget it. That would be too good; no, she will stay till the morning, she wants to cuddle, have breakfast. Gosh. The ideal woman is the one who leaves in the middle of the night. She leaves on the table a goodbye note, saying it was great, without her phone number. That's the ideal woman."[70]

To make matters worse, in line with that delicious and well-known rule that women are stigmatized for a certain type of behavior but *also* for the inverse behavior, you risk being despised when you practice your sexuality freely, with a minimum of emotional involvement, but *also* when you are "overly" sentimental. You bring on stereotypes of the devouring woman—clinging, a nuisance—when you take it into your head to feel emotions. Women's stronger investment in love is perceived as the manifestation of a vapid and shameful sentimentality. Perhaps we should defend *both* the right to separate sex and love *and* the right to not censure our sentiments? Samhita Mukhopadhyay also questions the exemplary nature of so-called "masculine" sexual behavior (once again, I am not claiming that this is the effective behavior of *all* men): "After all, does having sex like a man make you a 'man,' or someone deliriously detached from your emotions and therefore unable to participate in one of life's greatest physical pleasures?" And if men can be presented by some reactionary self-help writers as "simple" beings (whereas women, of course, are "complicated"), is this not because men are calmly conscious of the fact "that patriarchy benefits them"?[71]

At the end of 2017, after having been a Tinder subscriber for two years, Sara-Vittoria El Saadawi wrote an article expressing her impression of having been "strangely mistreated." She recounts her encounters with men, some of whom had insisted on having sex with her immediately, despite her hesitations and her wish to take her time, and who then used her to satisfy their own fantasies, while being unconcerned about hers. Lisa Wade also remarks, "Men have more orgasms than women in hookup culture, then, because the culture doesn't promote reciprocity. It's specifically designed for men's orgasm."[72] Given that her pleasure counted for so little, El Saadawi regretted not having gotten paid, since "after my sweet favors, I ought to ask for 500 euros from all these horrible guys!" And when she dared to show the slightest attachment, they unceremoniously rebuffed her: "It is cold competition because it is so admirably normal these days to feel nothing at all. You have to hide that it gives you pleasure, and remain in an ice-cold state and consider the partner, male or female, as an object for your satisfaction and nothing else. . . . That is the right pose to adopt. To fall in love, to suffer, to be monogamous—all that is silly, archaic, feminine!" Not only did El Saadawi run up against an absolute ban on any affect, but some men manifested an annoying tendency to confuse "not getting involved" with "acting like a pig." One of them amused himself by derisively imitating her groans of pleasure. Another, after having lowered her skirt, considered her hips too wide and her buttocks too well-rounded for his taste, and so he planted her there, half naked on her bed, and put her legs around his neck.[73] In my circle, a young woman told me about one of her lovers who, without being "involved" with her, is concerned about her pleasure, treats her with respect, offers her breakfast when morning comes, and appreciates her conversation. This kind of man does exist. But I am not sure that he is in the majority.

MALE FORTRESSES AND FEMALE COUNTERFEITS

We should examine these different relations to emotions and intimacy that men and women usually develop—as many psychological and sociological studies attest—as well as the mystery of this split.[74] During a study in the United Kingdom in the 1990s, Wendy Langford did in-depth interviews with fifteen heterosexual women (from the working or middle classes) about their love lives.[75] She perceived that many of them followed the same path. The first meeting and falling in love were experienced by the two partners as a "revolution." Under the spell of falling in love, each seemed liberated from the limitations imposed by gender conditioning: the women proved to be daring, independent, confident, capable of moving mountains, while the men did not fear opening up, showing themselves as vulnerable, or speaking about their emotions—"[He is] 'different' from other men," marveled their lovers. However, even if both lovers experienced intense happiness and a spectacular personal evolution during this period, quite often the eternal felicity that they thought they were promised did not occur. The miracle proved to be terribly fragile. The woman felt she had grown wings, that she did not need anybody, that she was able to do everything on her own, but she owed this sentiment, paradoxically, to the rewarding gaze of a man. Admiring her intrepid personality, this man soon saw that she still made emotional demands on him. Then he freaked out and shut down completely. The gender conditioning from which they had both been delivered during that initial honeymoon phase fell heavily back on their shoulders. The "revolution" of love, with its great "unleashing of repressed energies," was followed by a "counter-revolution."

When the couple did not break up, a routine was established that lacked any sharing or communicating. The woman, not wanting to give up on the happiness she had known, persisted in asking the man for the intimacy he gave her at the start: "I know there's a deeper, more loving man" inside, said Kate. But the more she insisted, the more he panicked and barricaded himself in his fortress. This silent man is not the same as the stormy man we saw in the previous chapter (although in some cases he can end up being violent, too), but he still causes great suffering. Through his retreat and silence, he exercises formidable power. His destabilized lover then questions herself. She tries to rectify her personality so as to obtain once more the approval that made her so happy. Langford writes that she "self-objectifies," meaning that she tries to see herself from the outside, from *his* point of view, in order to understand what she is doing wrong. Her insecurities, which the love affair had silenced, are reactivated and even reinforced. Paradoxically, in the hope of finding again the precious recognition of her individuality that this man had offered her, she becomes her own counterfeit and disowns her individuality. She silences feelings or desires that she fears might displease her lover. She reduces herself to silence. She also exhausts herself trying to decode his attitudes, to interpret the smallest sign that he gives her, to understand his dispositions; she discusses these things with her friends (usually female), sometimes for hours. She loses herself in conjectures, to the point of forgetting about herself.

Trying to counterbalance the deep sadness and frustration that this situation causes her—some women fall into depression—she finds refuge in mothering: she manages all household logistics, cares for children (when there are any), organizes daily affairs, the household budget, leisure, vacations. Talking to Langford, some profess a bitter and even vengeful pleasure in feeling themselves so competent and independent. They describe with disdain the stupidity of their companion, his infantilism: "I think of myself as having three children, three people to look after. It is just that one goes to work and the other two don't," says Diane. They sometimes even conclude that it is they who hold the power within the couple—which seems dubious since their spouses usually mistreat them emotionally while benefiting from the innumerable services they render. Thus, this feeling of power is merely a derisory consolation for what one of these women describes as "having your personality squashed." Even having sex feels to them like "one aspect of their maternal duties," one more domestic task. Langford summarizes: "Once love seemed like a shared project with shared goals, but now the heroine finds herself deciding what the hero should have in his sandwiches, while he shows more interest in his computer."[76]

This type of life together—where the spouses merely rub shoulders, bristling with resentment, each locked in a gender role—appears to be very widespread.

Why does this "counter-revolution" occur? Langford borrows the language of psychoanalysis to explain it. When the two partners fall in love, she says, each sees in the other an idealized parent, who repairs everything bad that occurred in childhood, thus offering to restore the other to a "narcissistic perfection." The woman encounters the figure of a perfect father, who grants her desires and recognizes her as his equal. Meanwhile, the man encounters the figure of the perfect mother, whose apparent independence and self-sufficiency reassure him. It seems that she is going to give him all that he desires without bombarding him with demands he might not be able to satisfy, which would make him feel deficient. He will not be forced to defend himself against the fantasy threat of drowning in a "boundless and insatiable" femininity. The recognition he shows the beloved woman depends paradoxically on her correspondence to his unconscious ideal ("Good Mummy"), but as soon as he conjures up "Bad Mummy," he withdraws it. He starts to respond with "reticence and silence," reintegrating "a rigid and frustrating masculinity."[77]

What strikes me is that the mechanisms described by Langford in 1999 exactly correspond to those raised twenty years later by Carol Gilligan and Naomi Snider in *Why Does Patriarchy Persist?* The writers explore how patriarchy fashions our private lives: it contains not only a political dimension, with its discriminations and violations of private life, but also a psychological one. Even if we are feminists or (for men) pro-feminist, totally in favor of equality, we remain prisoners of certain unconscious schemas of thought. In particular, we do not see how girls and boys growing up inflict a self-amputation, suffer a sort of rite of passage that marks their allegiance to patriarchy. They follow "a culturally scripted journey toward female selflessness and masculine detachment."[78] "Patriarchy harms both men and women by forcing men to act as if they don't have or need relationships and women to act as if they don't have or need a self."[79] Masculine detachment and feminine self-censorship: here we find again the attitudes observed by Wendy Langford in couples wrestling with the "counter-revolution," meaning the redoubling of their respective gender conditionings, which love at first sight had temporarily dissolved.

These self-amputations cause great suffering, write Gilligan and Snider, since men need as much as women to form deep and satisfying relations with someone else, and women need as much as men the power to be authentically themselves and to express themselves without self-censorship. Why, then, do we not revolt? Why does patriarchy continue to impose its law on all women and all men? They suggest this is because by "requiring a sacrifice of love for the sake of hierarchy . . . patriarchy steels us against the vulnerability of loving and by doing so, becomes a defense against loss." It is both "a source of lost connection and a defense against further loss."[80] Our fidelity to patriarchy sabotages our love lives, and we suffer from it, but we fear we will suffer even more if we deliver ourselves to love without holding back.

Boys learn to define themselves in opposition to all that is feminine. They learn that to be a man means to dissimulate one's emotions and to mime independence, indifference, detachment. Meanwhile girls are confronted with an impossible dilemma: either express their thoughts and thereby become "bad company," or else counterfeit a suitable personality in order to be accepted and socially integrated. In effect, society forces them to choose between "having a voice or having relationships." Finally, "femininity comes to be associated with pseudo-relationships (and the silencing of self) and masculinity with pseudo-independence (and the shielding of relational desires and sensitivities)—two sides of the same coin."[81] In passing, this also shows why detachment is an attitude so valorized in contemporary sexual and love relations: "Detachment is mistaken for maturity precisely because it mirrors the pseudo-independence of manhood, which in patriarchy is synonymous with being fully human,"[82] observes Snider. The self-amputation required of boys by patriarchal law has become the supreme value, which should be scrutinized by both men and women.

Gilligan and Snider invite us to struggle actively against the effects of patriarchy deep within us, instead of going back to the love affair and expecting it to deliver us from that conditioning in a temporary and illusory way. They invite us to turn love into a *permanent revolution*. The sacrifices imposed by the patriarchal order are not ineluctable, they claim. This order is subverted each time a man dares to reveal his feelings and each time a woman dares to see and say what she knows deep down. For example, when a father, marveling at the frankness and spontaneity of his eleven-year-old daughter, states: "I don't want her ever to lose that," Gilligan answers, "Then you're involved in social change."[83] The coauthors write that you have to understand that if patriarchy lives and prospers inside us, then "political change depends on psychological transformation, and vice versa."[84]

"BECAUSE YOU'RE ALIVE"

We may see this transformation at work in the British TV series *Sex Education*.[85] At the Moordale Secondary School, girls and boys are discovering themselves and experiencing the surprises of love; by overcoming fear, shame, and taboos, they are able to overcome patriarchal authority, incarnated by their principal, Michael Groff, a hard and withdrawn man. His son, Adam Groff, also being educated at the school, is doubly subject to his authority. At the beginning of the series, Adam (the character's name is symbolically charged) appears to be an archetype of uncouth virility: a tall, inexpressive clod, with almost no intellectual and emotional capacity, but said to be endowed with an enormous penis, who spends his time bullying and extorting the other students. His father, who terrifies him, forces him onto the straight and narrow, and constantly threatens to send him to a military school. When Adam discovers his bisexuality, at first he is paralyzed; he is incapable of living openly with the mutual attraction that ties him to his eventual lover Eric. It is his mother, Maureen, who shows him the way to emancipation by asking Principal Groff for a divorce after years of putting up with his coldness. She explains to her son that when you love someone there is a tiny part of yourself that is scared you might one day lose them, and his father is so afraid of this he has stopped feeling anything at all. She instructs her son that he has to allow himself to feel love, even if it causes pain, "because you're alive."

These words have a spectacular impact on her son. He puts her advice into practice, and an impressive physical transformation results: for the first time, Adam's face, which up to now has been a sad mask, starts to shine and express joy. It is as if, by being invited to embrace the "vulnerability of loving"[86]—in the words of Gilligan and Snider—his mother has delivered him from the bad patriarchal fate. When he meets his father again, Adam casually asks him: "All right, Dad?" He has just declared his crush on Eric in front of the whole school. His fear and submission have evaporated, and his hatred along with them.

While waiting for that moment, many men remain detached from their emotions. And the saddest thing is that we often eroticize their coldness and silence, finding them mysterious and deep; we think being withdrawn is a virile and attractive trait. This is what one of my friends and I nicknamed the "Don Draper effect." During a conversation, we tried to discern what made the hero of the *Mad Men* series so seductive, and we reached this conclusion: the attitude of these men is so frustrating that the slightest openness on their part, the least authentic exchange, timid and ephemeral as it might be, is experienced as an overwhelming epiphany. A guy mumbles three slightly personal words and you are convulsed with emotion, impressed by this instance of sublime communion. In fact, some of the most striking scenes in *Mad Men* are those in which this hero, barricaded behind his secrets, drops his armor and gives a glimpse of his feelings, his vulnerability, his soul. He rarely opens up to his successive wives, Betty and Megan, who are spectacularly beautiful trophy wives with whom he maintains conventional (and oppressive) relations, but instead confides in other women: his collaborator Peggy Olson* and Anna Draper, the widow of the man whose identity he has usurped. However, while this mechanism might yield splendid television moments, in real life it encourages women to endure psychological abuse for six months, or ten years, in the hope—generally in vain—that one day the miracle will be reproduced and eventually become the new normal. We see better how this situation is untenable if we transpose emotional scarcity for other needs: of course, when we are suffering from hunger, a crust of stale bread might seem like a crazy feast; when we are dying of thirst, a mouthful of stagnant water might seem marvelously fresh. However, should we condemn ourselves to such a sad and poor diet? Can we really make it a principle of living to deprive ourselves of food that is as various as it is fabulous, of the thousand delicious beverages that exist on earth?

Moreover, most of the time women with an emotionally closed-off partner express deep despair. When Shere Hite did her study of 4,500 women in the 1970s, 98 percent of them who were in a relationship with a man wished for "more verbal closeness" with him; they wanted him to speak to them more "about [his] own personal thoughts, feelings, plans, and ques-

---

* Particularly in the magisterial episode "The Suitcase" (season 4, episode 7).

tions, and to ask them about theirs." Some said they never felt
so alone as in the course of their marriage; others cried about
it at night lying alongside their sleeping spouse.[87] It is doubtful
that things have radically changed in the last fifty years (nor that
they are very different on the European side of the Atlantic). In
February 2021, in a heartfelt letter in the "Ask Polly" column of
the website *The Cut*, a thirtysomething British woman shared
her feelings after a breakup. In their circle, she said, everybody
thought that her ex-partner and she were the ideal couple. And
yet, her desire for intimacy had always been frustrated. "I . . .
believe that being in deep, sustained relation with another person
is one of the big wonders and joys of being alive." She thought
that "Do[ing] the Work," trying to understand yourself, was one
of the most fascinating and most urgent aspects of being alive.
He, on the other hand, did not understand what she wanted from
him and found her complicating things for no reason. Around
her, she saw a number of other couples in which the woman
hoped to get from her avoidant partner the same emotional and
reflexive investment as her own—in vain. She finally decided to
live only with a man who has been through therapy.[88]

In her response, the column's moderator, Heather Havrilesky, begins by noticing that in our "disjointed, individualistic,
workaholic culture," the foundations of human happiness are
personal and financial success, with all the rest being considered a waste of time. Even therapy, she remarks, is often envisaged as a means of making yourself a more effective animal
rather than doing the work of "exploring past traumas, understanding your own shadow, cultivating an inner life, and excavating your shame; you're seeking out new mysteries and new

layers all the time." Rather than only date a man who has been in therapy—a rather narrow criterion, which does not take into account the fact that not everybody has the means to do so—she advises her reader to ask, "Is this man curious and open to learning new things—about me, about himself, about his past, about my past, about the world?" You can tell when somebody has this curiosity, she says: "People like that ask open-ended questions and listen to the answers. They're attracted to the workings of your mind, thrilled by the big ideas you throw into the mix, excited by the process of excavation itself."[89]

But Polly also invites the young woman to refrain from hasty and definitive judgments. She warns her against a simplistic vision that puts men in two quite distinct categories: on one side, those who are "totally avoidant/unavailable" and, on the other, those who are "completely available, open, sensitive, feelings-embracing." For her part she likes a blend of the two types: "I like people who are conflicted but curious, who lead with their intellect but who are also trying to evolve emotionally in spite of not knowing what the fuck they're doing on that front most of the time." She concludes: "So part of what you're looking for is actually *bravery*: someone who's curious, engaged, interested in ideas, and unafraid of the unknown. Are men like this common? Definitely not, but they do exist. Should you lower your standards or cast a wider net simply because men like this are rare? I don't think so."[90]

Here I should also cite bell hooks's remark in *Communion*: in affairs of the heart, women are often arrogant because they are made to believe "that we will instinctively know how to give and receive love."[91] The idea that women should work *still more* on their capacity to love, while they already do that so much more than men, irritates me greatly. But I have to admit that hooks has good arguments, starting with this one: it is difficult to love when you detest your body—which, due to their education, is the case with a great number of women.

If you are getting the impression that mutual love is an unattainable utopia, I should specify that intimacy and sharing within heterosexual couples do exist. Among the women who answered Shere Hite's questions, some were very happy: "We go through cycles of talking about intimate matters. Very intense. I don't think either of us can live with the intensity full-time, so we don't do it all the time. We went through extensive and intense therapy together, bared our souls. It was passionate, loving, gay, joyous, freeing. Everything it should have been," said one. Another said each day she enjoyed "horizontals" with her partner: they lie down next to each other, embracing, contemplating, exchanging confidences. A third: "He always asks how I am, wants to know little details of my day, tells me what happened to him at work, we trade funny stories. I especially like it when he comes and sits and talks to me while I am taking a long bath. There I can unwind and think out loud about whatever's on my mind. We keep each other up to date that way."[92]

KNOWING HOW TO GIVE UP

There remains a question to be asked about the women Wendy Langford interviewed: we saw that some were extremely unhappy in their coupledom, although they did not live under a regime of terror like the victims of conjugal violence, nor did they depend financially on their partner: Why didn't they leave? Langford cites the case of Sarah, twenty-eight, in a couple with Wayne, twenty-six. Sarah knows that Wayne has affairs with other women. She takes maniacal care with her appearance, does all the household work, attends soccer matches with her partner although she hates all that—in the hope that he will finally get involved in the relationship. Just after falling in love with him, she felt herself invincible; now she is breaking down. She is a victim of what Langford calls the "security paradox"; once we have reached existential security and have developed a powerful feeling of our singularity thanks to a particular person, we are almost certainly going to continue seeking these gratifications from the same relationship, even when it "*undermines* [our] self-confidence, and reinforces painful contradictions" in our life. The more women's self-esteem is wounded by their relationship in a couple, the more they depend on the regard and recognition of their partner—a phenomenon that reaches its paroxysm among victims of violence. Due to a lack of confidence in their own resources, they consider it legitimate to give up their "autonomy and subjectivity" in exchange for a form of emotional security. This logic ends up forming a psychological prison around them. Sooner or later, though, all of them must face this painful truth: if, by falling in love, they found themselves being faithful to this new personality, they must now separate from the person who was the agent of their liberation. The best way of remaining faithful to their dream of love is to give it up. Which Sarah admits when she declares about Wayne:

"I feel the only way I will ever get him to give me any kind of respect is to dump him."[93]

Having been sensitized to the charms of love from earliest childhood does make a large share of our self-esteem depend on the presence of a man in our life, which may also compound the difficulty of leaving, or letting go of the affair when you have to. This education makes us more fragile not only in the course of a relationship but also near its end.

In the autumn of 2019, the man I loved put an end to our relationship—for the second time. He could not find a place in his life for a love story. But he did not seem to want us to stop seeing each other or being close, which in the beginning I accepted, as I had already accepted it after our first breakup. This implied keeping quiet about how hurt I felt, dealing alone with my disappointment and sadness. This also prevented me from turning the page and thus kept alive my hopes that this love story would resume. But it seemed necessary that I move on with my life. Initially I feared I would fall into a sort of black hole if I didn't see him anymore. However, after a few weeks, I realized that this eventuality no longer inspired the same panic. I distanced myself and, against all expectations, I felt very good. I was *in accord with myself*; I was doing justice to myself. And later, even when moments of sadness and missing him arose, I did not regret my decision. I translated into action the fact that I *deserved better*—better than such a frustrating story (after a few dazzling months, we had experienced our own "counter-revolution"). I merited someone who truly wanted me, who was ready to make a place for me in his life. I already realized that early in the relationship, but it remained a purely theoretical and inconsistent knowledge, stripped of any weight, until this time I *felt it*. The benefits of distance now became something tangible, though previously I always ended up sacrificing them, because they seemed paltry in relation to the pleasure of renewing the tie, even in a platonic mode. From then on, I understood that consideration for myself should have its rightful place. I was like a shipwrecked person swimming at night who is surprised to find an unexpected shore.

During this period, I had a dream. I was coming out of the metro at Place Maubert in Paris, returning from somewhere, and I was getting ready to go home on foot when I bumped into an old friend with whom I was out of touch. I was surprised to dream of him, since I had not thought of him for a long time. He announced his intention of walking me back home and this annoyed me. This man seemed to love me too much for my taste. I knew how he could be clinging, unstable, unpredictable. I was almost afraid he was being aggressive or would insist on entering my home, and I asked myself what I would do then to summon help; since he was a friend, nobody would take me seriously. I tried a feint by telling him that in fact I had to go in the opposite direction, but to my great consternation, he changed direction along with me. And I told myself that I was unlucky to run into him by chance. The dream stopped there. But it remained in my memory with particular clarity, and so I submitted it to a friend who interpreted dreams, thinking: *Good luck with that one, darling*. She began by making me notice that I was getting out of the metro: once again, I was on my way, in movement (in fact, in dreams I had at the time, there was always some mode of transport: an electric scooter, a Vespa, a bus . . .). Then she reminded me that all the characters that appear in our dreams are parts of ourselves. They incarnate forces that evolve on the stage of our psyche. She asked me what I would say to him if I were faced with him again. I thought and answered: "That I had been afraid of him, that I was not sure I could trust him." And suddenly I had a revelation: it seemed to me that through this dream I had been in the presence of that part of myself that had brought me to cut off contact with my former lover and that doing so made me feel good, which brought me to savor the thought that I was doing myself justice thanks to this new capacity to not want to maintain the relationship at all costs. I had been surprised by these new tendencies; I had not understood where they came from, and I wondered if I could trust them, if they were not going to bring me to ruin and unhappiness, like that friend who surged up at the metro exit.

In her graphic novel *The Reddest Rose*, Liv Strömquist lashes out at the discourse that stigmatizes women because they "love too much," because their love is inappropriate, too invasive. She defends the idea that you should be able to love without restraint, without worrying about the reciprocity of your feelings, quite simply because loving "is cool": it is the secret of happiness and of the meaning of life. She criticizes the conception of love as an investment on which you should expect a return. She attacks "today's ideal, which says that the way to love is to protect the self and to ensure 'fairness' in the relationship—make sure you don't 'give' more love than you 'get' from the other person." She cites two examples of women who proved faithful to their feelings of love in the face of all opposition: Lady Caroline

Lamb, who at the start of the nineteenth century continued to pursue Lord Byron with her impassioned declarations after their rupture, and Princess Parvati, who in Hindu mythology was confronted with the indifference of the god Shiva and so exiled herself for several years to a forest, until her beloved put her love to the test and finally rewarded her for her fidelity. The moral of the latter story, writes Strömquist, is that "the way to love is total uncompromising devotion."[94]

This position awakened the internal conflict between my feminist convictions and my mystical and absolutist view of love. After I weighed things, I came to profoundly disagree with Strömquist's thesis in these pages. First of all, there is a difference between the two stories she tells: while Parvati withdrew to a desert, Lady Caroline increased the scenes she made over Byron. Strömquist is glad that this behavior was "much more annoying for Lord Byron" than if "Caroline had, in a responsible and self-respecting way, simply quit loving him once she realized her love wasn't reciprocated." A woman who comes to terms with things, she says, and can be left without suffering any negative consequences, is "every egotistical bastard's Dream: to tinker with another person's excruciatingly strong emotions." Except that Lady Caroline's behavior corresponds to the definition of harassment, which is still a problem. Maybe a man who breaks things off is indeed "an egotistical bastard" . . . but maybe not. And even when he is, an adult is meant to accept the other person's sovereign decision when that person does not wish to pursue the relationship. It appears to me hypocritical to demand that men stop spoiling the lives of their former lovers while allowing women to act in the same manner toward their ex-lovers (even if women rarely threaten the physical integrity or the lives of their ex-partners).

I do not regret having at first rebelled against the rupture of a romance that had intoxicated myself and my lover, that made us feel so intensely alive. But nor do I regret having let it go. It takes two to tango; that is the whole beauty of the thing. This does not necessarily mean the unloved woman should "stifle her own feelings of love 'in a minute,'" as Liv Strömquist seems to think. In fact, taking into account the different educations of men and women, it is almost inevitable that many heterosexual women find themselves with a surplus of love. But at least you can reflect on what to do with that surplus. And continuing to throw it at the head of someone who no longer responds is not necessarily the best solution. You cannot love for two. You cannot breathe into the other your own desire to see the love affair continue. You cannot always be the one who recovers the relationship that the other has thrown far away, like the faithful dog who tirelessly brings back the ball to its master. You have to clear the necessary space for the expression of the other's will, accepting the risk that this might mean the death of the relationship—that the ball will remain forever abandoned in a thicket.

It seems difficult to sweep away the matter of self-respect. Criticizing the application of capitalist rationality in love relationships results in legitimizing and dangerously strengthening the masochistic tendencies inculcated in women. Ridiculing the concern for "self-preservation," saying to her readers that the "way to love is total, uncompromising devotion"—i.e., what our whole culture whispers to very young girls at the risk of

delivering them bound hand and foot to abusive partners—
seems criminal to me. Yes, it is true that society teaches us to
be addicted to love, before it goes on to ridicule us for that.
Here, as elsewhere, the patriarchy's attitude toward women can
be summarized as "Heads I win, tails you lose." But we will not
get out of this by simply reinforcing our dependence on love,
which is no less a real problem.

In August 2018, Sophie Fontanel posted on Instagram a
photo of the house where she spent her vacations, accompanied
by these words: "I dreamed of this today, in a state of total repose
I am unaccustomed to, dozing in front of the two doors you
see here: I was thinking of my love life—especially of a recent
story. And suddenly I understood things. Until very recently,
my preference was to wear myself out dealing with closed (or
barely open) hearts. I now discovered I was no longer interested
in my habit of bashing my hope and the best of myself against
walls. I felt bizarre: finally I had gotten rid of my locksmith's
soul. Perhaps it will be my own key that a man will find from
now on; I saw the absurdity of my old and recurrent battles. You
throw yourself into a conquest, deep down, because you doubt
yourself. You persuade yourself that if you don't do the work,
nothing will be accomplished. Laziness had just taught me a
formidable lesson. You learn at any age. It's like a miracle."[95]

For my part, it is possible that very soon I will change my
tendencies, that I will abandon my fine resolutions and again
choose to pursue some kind of relationship independent of
the satisfaction it might bring me—I can never decide firmly
between these two attitudes. But if this should happen, at least
I will not revert to my previous trajectory—all those means of

locomotion in my dreams are not there for nothing. At least I will have touched this feeling with my finger. I will have reached that shore. I will have taken an additional step toward understanding this: loving love, really loving it, also implies learning not to stick to it doggedly. And I will know how to resume my path, even while stumbling.

4

THE GREAT DISPOSSESSION

Becoming Erotic Subjects

For two years, the Japanese artist Keiryû Asakura worked on creating the ultimate sex doll, able to offer to the touch the illusion of a living human body. "Like a young dissected cadaver, this body reproduces life-size that of a flayed woman," wrote the blogger Agnès Giard,[1] reviewing this project by a modern Pygmalion.* "Her eyeballs seem to burst out of their sockets. Her femurs seem to have been scraped with a knife. The flesh on her hands seems to leak bits of bone." The doll is endowed with "an extractible vulva like you can find these days in sex-shops. It is inserted into a cavity between her thighs." The artist explains that he "needed to find a distraction for his libido without harming anybody and without having to invest in a relationship." Back in 2004, Giard had devoted an article to Japanese companies that were commercializing "love-dolls" made of silicon to serve as both wives and sexual partners. The bachelors who bought and installed them in their homes sometimes took

---

* In Greek mythology, the sculptor Pygmalion fell in love with his statue Galatea, who was brought to life by the goddess Aphrodite.

them to a restaurant or on vacation and created photo albums to immortalize their life "as a couple." The creator of one of these companies explained: "The dolls should not smile. They should have a vacant air so their owner can project his fantasies on them. They should offer no resistance and easily adopt roles and personalities. The dolls should reflect back our dreams as in a mirror. They should also have infantile faces, since buyers 'want women with a novice and inexperienced look.'"[2]

Giard admits that Asakura's project "might seem macabre," but no, she reassures us, "this is not about necrophilia. On the contrary, it's about creating life." I have a hard time sharing her enthusiasm. In fact, her article is chilling, perhaps because at the time I read it, I was researching this book and constantly running up against the obstinate refusal of some men to accept women as beings endowed with their own personalities. Perhaps also because it is always men who try to "create life." Curiously, we never hear of a female Japanese artist deciding to fabricate the ultimate masculine doll in her cave because she is sick of real men and does not want to "invest herself in a relationship"! Women generally accept masculine subjectivity; they are even curious and inquisitive about it. There are less good reasons for this openness of their minds: being dominated forces you to take an interest in the dominant's psyche. Thus, in many companies, employees spend a considerable amount of time observing their boss, wondering about his attitudes and moods, speculating on the mysteries of his personality—whereas the inverse is not true. We have also seen how the whole society adopts men's point of view, spontaneously puts itself in their place, and above all is concerned—almost solely—with their desires and their emotions, which causes among women a permanent decentering of themselves. This also implies that, in a heterosexual relationship, the stress is on the fantasies and desires of men, on their viewpoint, while women are supposed to correspond to this projection and to satisfy male expectations.

This division of roles is solidly anchored. In 1972, three years before the feminist film theorist Laura Mulvey famously analyzed the male gaze,[3] John Berger in *Ways of Seeing* showed how the female nude exemplified this relationship in painting. The protagonist of a painting does not figure in the frame; it is the spectator, inevitably envisaged as a man. "Everything is addressed to him. Everything must appear to be the result of his being there. It is for him that the figures have assumed their nudity." Berger juxtaposes Ingres's *Grande Odalisque*, in which a nude concubine looks at the spectator over a bare shoulder, and a model looking back at the camera lens for a men's magazine, in order to stress the similarity of their attitudes. "It is an expression of responding with calculated charm to the man whom she knows is looking at her, although she doesn't know him." (In 1989, the Guerrilla Girls, a group of feminist artists, would create a poster on which the head of the *Grande Odalisque* is replaced by the head of a growling gorilla, with this caption: "Do women have to be naked to get into the Met. Museum? Less than 5% of the artists in the Modern Art Sections are women, but 85% of the nudes are female.") Often the only male presence in paintings of female nudes is that of a chubby cupid, who is not a very serious rival for the spectator. However, even when the woman is represented in the company of a lover, as in *Bacchus, Ceres, and Cupid* by Hans von Aachen, attention is not drawn to the lover, notes Berger, but to the man who stands in front of the canvas, "her true lover." In *An Allegory with Venus and Cupid* by Bronzino, Venus does kiss Cupid, but "the way her body is arranged has nothing to do with that kissing;" it is twisted in order to be better offered to the voyeurism of this invisible spectator/owner. The gaze of this spectator appears as a magnetic force that pulls her toward it. "The picture is made to appeal to *his* sexuality; it has nothing to do with *her* sexuality."[4]

This all-powerful nature of male subjectivity and the male gaze has the consequence that women learn to see themselves as a spectacle offered to men and to the world in general. "A woman is always accompanied (except when quite alone, perhaps even then) by her own image of herself," says Berger. "While she is walking across a room or weeping at the death of her father, she cannot avoid envisaging herself walking or weeping." He reaches this famous conclusion that will be quoted in innumerable feminist works: "Men look at women; women watch themselves being looked at." This voyeurism determines not only the relations between men and women, but also the relation of women with themselves. In 1980, the feminist essay writer Anne-Marie Dardigna studied several works of French erotic literature in *Les châteaux d'Éros*.[5] The only gaze that the heroines of these novels have of their bodies is one that "confirms them as objects"; when such a heroine "thinks of her body, of her clothes, her makeup, it is as a function of what men will see; she sees herself as seen through the male gaze."[6] Thus when Rebecca, the heroine of *La motocyclette* by André-Pieyre de Mandiargues, alone in front of her mirror, slowly takes off her biker's outfit, under which she is naked, the author writes: "And she was imagining what he saw, he with marsh-colored eyes, and of the pleasure he took in this kind of stripping."[7]

The whole female being is fashioned by this relationship, by this permanent consciousness of being seen, which may prevent a woman from having access to her own desires, sensations, and sentiments. "The experience that the teenage girl has of her body makes her feel alienated from this body," states Manon Garcia, taking up the pioneering analyses of Simone de Beauvoir on this subject. "When a girl experiences street harassment or sexualized comments on her changing body she is forced to discover herself as an object before she can fully live in this new body."[8] Barbara L. Fredrickson and Tomi-Ann Roberts confirm this observation: "[At puberty] for perhaps the first time . . . an adolescent girl recognizes that she will be seen and evaluated by others *as a body*, and not as herself." In a 1997 article, these American researchers offered a detailed exploration of objectification and its effects on women's mental health.[9] Among their findings: while men are most often represented in art and in the media with a focus on facial features, "women tend to be portrayed with an emphasis on the body," and even more so if they are Black women. "Indeed it is not uncommon for magazine photographs to portray dismembered women, eliminating their heads altogether, focusing exclusively on their bodies or body parts."[10] (Advertising for the French brand of lingerie Aubade, with the significant slogan "Lessons in seduction," offers a perfect example of this practice.) Objectification, write Fredrickson and Roberts, "functions to socialize girls and women to, at some level, treat *themselves* as objects to be looked at and evaluated"—not without reason, since appreciation of their physique has more consequences for their professional and love lives than it has for men.[11] An example: I mentioned in my book *Beauté fatale* that sometimes breast augmentation may deprive breasts of their sensitivity to caresses.[12] The operation involves privileging the visual result (for others), at the risk of sacrificing one's own sensations and one's pleasure. Today, this tendency is accelerated by the possibility of presenting oneself on dating applications, on Instagram or other platforms, in the hope of arousing desire and/or monetizing one's publications. A British journalist looked into the Brazilian butt lift (BBL), the cosmetic surgery that is the world's fastest-growing operation and also the one with the highest mortality rate. A patient explained to her that after retouching their photos on dating apps, her friends no longer dared to go on any dates, since the gap with reality was too great: "If you've had a BBL, it's like you've already edited your body in real life, so you don't have to edit your pictures." Conceiving of yourself in two dimensions, as an assemblage of pixels, obliges you to deny being flesh and bone, with your capacities for pleasure and pain. (This patient says that during the weeks following the operation, when someone brushed against the areas of her body from which the fat was taken to be reinjected in her buttocks, she cried out in pain.)[13] An image can feel nothing; it has no sensations, or regards, or thoughts, or desires.

LOOSENING THE VICE

Two very different events have contributed to loosening this type of relationship women have to themselves. Starting in the autumn of 2017 the #MeToo movement exposed sexual violence in a massive and international way; it created a cultural context in which it is more difficult now to objectify women as blithely as before. Its consequences are incalculable, but here I want to pause over one ripple: in January 2018, the French *Marie Claire* noted that two lingerie brands had made the unusual choice to show clothed women in their advertising.[14] One campaign used a fully dressed writer, a fencer, and an artist: these women were chosen for their personalities, their passions and talents, not for their perfect appearance—impersonal and interchangeable, treated as objects. The ad campaign "showed individuals with impressive careers rather than as languid flesh," the journalist concluded. The other campaign had been mounted by the photographer Mario Testino, who said he wanted "to capture what these women feel when wearing this lingerie under their clothes"—in short, the emphasis was put on their sensations and not (or not only) on the spectacle they were offering. "It is women's *creativity* we are being sold, their power to act. A female subject whose inner life is shown, not her body. Woman as an expressionless clothes-horse—that is a code of the past," commented the semiologist Mariette Darrigrand.[5] Of course, there is nothing revolutionary here: it is still a matter of selling lingerie and therefore showing images of desirable women according to rather conventional criteria (remember that Testino was himself accused of sexual harassment and abuse by several male models).* But note the inter-

---

* The actor Tina Fey also recounts that in 2011 when Testino was photographing her he told her: "Lift your chin, darling, you are not eighteen." She adds, "I'm pretty sure he says that to models who are nineteen" ("Miss Bossypants" in *Vogue*, April 22, 2011).

esting distance from the brutal objectification produced by ad campaigns like Aubade's.

The second event that for some women unleashed a liberation from the tyrannical (and often interiorized) male gaze was the global confinement in the spring of 2020 due to the Covid-19 pandemic. Suddenly extracted from the ordinary social environment that riddles them with judgmental looks, women were recentered on their own perceptions. Some used that period to cultivate a more natural image of themselves, doing without makeup and hair coloring.[16] "People who . . . proclaim that they cannot leave the house without makeup are now finding themselves very much *not* leaving the house," wrote the journalist Aniya Das. "In return, they are rewarded not only with the money saved on numerous hair and makeup products, but with accumulated time each day."[17] Many women also took advantage of comfortable clothing, which let their body breathe more than their ordinary outfits (abandoning bras especially), and adopted joggers. "Apparently the first thing most women got rid of were tight jeans and skirts that kept riding up," noted the journalist Myriam Levain.[18]

This movement unleashed a flood of memes and tweets showing the hairy monsters, repulsive and unrecognizable, that women were supposedly becoming during confinement (we saw a lot of Chewbacca, the hirsute Wookiee from *Star Wars*). The men who produced them, observed Camille Froidevaux-Metterie, were manifesting their rancor at being deprived of "available" female bodies: "For the most violent (like harassers, indecent exposure guys, or rapists), their prey had disappeared. For others, it was bodies to look at and lust over that were vanishing. Insults and mockery were the remaining means to keep women's bodies in the position of object. In degrading itself, this object might become detestable. The reality is that it escaped them!"[19] In media promoting the fashion and beauty industries there was panic. "You are not supposed to look like shit when you are at home," the *Madmoizelle* site hammered into its readers (March 17, 2020). To reintroduce the external gaze into women's lives, mass media banked on women's ultimate ties with the world: social networks and videoconferencing. "Posting your day's look [on Instagram] allows you to continue to exist in the eyes of others," suggested *Madame Figaro* (April 2, 2020). *Elle* offered "five tips to be on top on Zoom, Teams, Skype, etc." (March 27, 2020), while *Femme actuelle* warned against "three mistakes that uglify you during a video conversation" (March 24, 2020). The despair was such that even harassed and exploited delivery people were used to reestablish the male gaze: "The idea is to be rather eccentric so that your pizza delivery person is surprised!" (*Madmoizelle*). Threatening injunctions to "hold the line" appeared. The confined female reader was supposedly lazy, and so was encouraged to fill this free time with various beauty practices.

With total hypocrisy, *Madmoizelle* explained that being alone at home was the occasion "to try out something audacious," to "understand what suits you, what is your style . . . in short, to learn to know yourself better, without having to suffer the opinions and critiques of others, whether in the public space or among your friends." So you had to replace the male gaze with continuing to envisage yourself from the *outside*, by increasingly trying on clothes in front of the mirror. In their 1997 article on the objectification of women, Barbara L. Fredrickson and Tomi-Ann Roberts stress that its notable effect is to compromise the possibility of women experiencing total absorption in a physical or intellectual activity, "when a person's body or mind is stretched to its limits in a voluntary effort to accomplish something difficult and worthwhile,"[20] those rare moments when "we feel we are truly living, uncontrolled by others, creative and joyful."[21] The more frequent these moments, the more our quality of life increases. To achieve this peak state, you have to be able to lose consciousness of yourself, which is impossible when you are constantly reminded to worry about your appearance.

Among the women experiencing confinement, some recognized their ambivalence, or else proclaimed their attachment—forced or voluntary—to certain clothing, accessories, or beauty practices. The attributes and gestures of femininity are so diverse in their implications, in the degree of noxiousness or pleasure they may procure, that we cannot put them all in the same bag. The essential thing is that this margin of freedom, this escape from immediate external constraints, was offered to a great number of women, whatever the use they chose to make of it. "Certainly putting on a face mask or doing one's nails at home are small pleasures like others, which these days have the effect of a welcome pause. But at the end of two weeks being shut up at home, we are just starting to know whether we are doing it for ourselves or for others," remarked Myriam Levain.[22] Concluded Camille Froidevaux-Metterie, "In every case we are relieved of the weight of external summons, free to present us to ourselves (since we no longer need to present to others) as we wish. Our bodies might indeed, for a while, truly belong to us."[23]

Aesthetics *versus* comfort: most of the time, this is how the terms of the debate are posed. The alternative presented to women is either to offer the appearance that culture requires of them (and this may be at the cost of the greatest suffering) or to favor their well-being by flouting external judgments. And in fact, it is important to decouple the value—social, professional, amorous—of women from their appearance, to authorize them to live without being pretty to look at. The TV series *The Queen's Gambit* concerns a young American chess champion, Beth Harmon, who is wrestling with her addictions to alcohol and pills. On Twitter in the autumn of 2020, a female viewer criticized the idea that the screenwriters seemed to have of a woman who was a complete wreck. Passed out on her sofa, Beth Harmon is in fact shown to us as a sexy baby doll, makeup on, with shaved legs, and impeccably blow-dried hair.[24]

Nevertheless, I wonder if, in addition to getting rid of the tyranny of beauty, there was not also a questioning of our very notion of beauty, the assumptions that determine it. We should now cultivate the beauty that is ours as subjects, attract attention to it, demand that it be recognized. While I was working on this chapter in early 2021, I happened to have a new pair of ankle boots. They were flat, warm, waterproof, incredibly light, and absolutely comfortable (and vegan, if you please). They held the foot well, but my toes had all the space they could dream of, and they wriggled with joy. At each step, I hugged the ground completely, before detaching myself with delicious ease. These shoes transformed my daily walks—which, with lockdowns and remote working, had assumed a particular importance—into moments of ecstasy. They gave me the impression of flying, of moving on a cloud.[25] I also find them very pretty: I shamelessly admire them in the mirror before going out. But I am well aware that this opinion would not be shared by all. It is the Swiss country girl in me who finds them pretty, rather than the Parisian woman I supposedly have become after more than twenty years. (To be a woman in Paris involves considerable pressure. To take up the image of Laurent Sciamma, it's like being a "pizza-maker in Naples.") These shoes are not delicate ones made for feet that never seem to sweat, redden, or swell. And yet, adopting the perspective of "deep heterosexuality" theorized by Jane Ward, which I mentioned in my introduction, I would very much like for a man to be capable of finding these ankle boots pretty, too. I would like him when he saw them, instead of grimacing in irritation at my refusal to produce an image of conventional femininity, to be capable of imagining how agreeable it is to me to walk in them—or perhaps notice the ease of my steps—and find them pretty because he shares in my pleasure, because he approves of the extra vitality they give me, because he is happy for my toes. We could try to invent an aesthetic that relies on identification rather than on objectification, which celebrates the well-being of women, rather than the shackling and standardization of their bodies (this is daring, I know).

HISTORY OF A SILENCING

To be objectified implies not only being reduced to an image but also being reduced to silence, to having no hold over the

discourses held about you (or on any subject), having no voice
in the making of one's stories and representations. At the start of
2018, I finished the writing of *Witches* by mentioning the breach
opened by the #MeToo movement—which had risen to prom-
inence three months earlier—in the masculine control of the
story. Since then, this contestation has only been amplified. Its
most significant French illustration was perhaps the publication
of the book by Vanessa Springora *Le consentement*, in which she
recounts her adolescent years spent in the claws of the much older
writer Gabriel Matzneff.[26] Having been transformed by the pedo-
phile "writer" into an anonymous, flirtatious, and interchangeable
figure of girlhood who was devoted to serving his fantasies and
those of his readers, she now turned the tables on the discourse
by appearing with her own name, voice, words, experience, and
point of view. She described her trauma and dryly pulverized the
sterling image that Matzneff had constructed in book after book of
himself as a sublime lover, a subversive adventurer. His enterprise
had benefited from the complicity of the Parisian literary milieu:
for example, the TV host Bernard Pivot in 1990 referred in a light
tone to the "stable of young [female] lovers" of Matzneff, his stu-
dio guest, whom he characterized as a "collector of starry-eyed
girls." In writing her own account, Springora reminds us that these
"young lovers" and "starry-eyed girls" are *people*.

Her book showed how the "dispossession" inflicted on
her also methodically deprived her of speech. For example,
Matzneff insisted on writing for her an essay she would submit
to her French teachers, thereby stealing her voice from her. She
says that he had never been interested in her diary or encouraged her to write anything: he was protecting his monopoly,

his power as a famous writer. He did encourage her to write him letters, as he did with his other pubescent lovers, and he would publish extracts from them in his books. "These weren't words of contemporary young women, but universal and timeless terms taken from the epistolary literature of love. G. whispered them to us by stealth, breathing them onto our very tongues." She had the impression of "instinctively conforming to what you might call a 'technical specification.'"[27] Meanwhile, Matzneff's own journal, which an editor published at regular intervals, became a disciplinary instrument designed to shut her up: "At the first hint of a reproach, he would rush to uncap his pen: 'You shall see what you shall see, my pretty one! What a portrait I'm going to sketch of you in my little black book!'"[28] Little by little, he shut her up inside "a prison made of words." When Springora finally managed to escape him, reading his journal account of their "breakup" triggered an anxiety crisis so violent that only a shot of Valium brought it to a halt. Later on, each new publication in which Matzneff recalled their relationship had the effect on her of "a blade plunged into a wound that had never scarred over."[29] One day in the street, she started to doubt her own existence; it seemed "my body was made of paper, ink flowed through my veins."[30] In the hospital, she was told she had just had a "psychotic episode, with a phase of depersonalization." She replied: "You mean all this is true? I'm not . . . *fiction*?"[31] Long before she made public her version of the story, a "talking cure" with a psychoanalyst saved her, as if each word that came from deep within gradually gave her back her reality as a subject.

At the end of her book, Springora recalls her stupefaction

upon discovering that Matzneff had gifted his manuscripts and correspondence to the Institute for Contemporary Publishing Archives. Henceforth, if she wanted to reread her own letters, she would have to make an official request and invent some kind of pretext. This seizure of Springora's words and experiences corresponds to the one experienced by the writer and model Emily Ratajkowski. In 2020, in a chilling article, the American model made an inventory of all the times that men, familiar or unknown, had stolen her image from her.[32] She notes in particular the "portraits" produced by the artist Richard Prince, which consisted simply of giant prints of her own Instagram photos, including photos of her that had appeared on magazine covers that she had posted on the social network. Everybody in her circle, including her boyfriend at the time, believed that Prince was doing her a great honor. Now if she wanted to buy back her own image, originally published on her own Instagram account, it would cost her $80,000. Moreover, before making his prints, Prince had commented on her Instagram posts from his own account. Under one of the two photos, which represented a naked Ratajkowski, he wondered: "Were you built in a science lab by teenage boys?"[33] In short, he was inviting her to wonder if she were not a pure fantasy, a pure masculine creation, as Matzneff had managed to make Springora believe (until her psychotic crisis) that she was a "fiction," with no other existence than the one he gave her.

Although it is particularly flagrant in the case of Springora, due to the criminal imbalance between the two protagonists in terms of age and power, this imprisonment of women in the words of men, and this appropriation of their speech, appears to be somewhat universal. The dominant laws of our amorous and sexual universe are reproduced in the château to which O, the heroine of the erotic novel by Pauline Réage *Histoire d'O* (1954), is brought. Residents are told "not to look a man in the face or speak to him," whether master or valet. "The only times you will open your mouth here in the presence of a man will be to cry out or to caress."[34] Created by Réage to please her lover, the editor Jean Paulhan, who wrote the preface to the novel, O "comes to fit the exact hollow in the masculine *imaginaire*," observes Anne-Marie Dardigna in her study of erotic literature.[35]

Writing at the end of a decade, the 1970s, marked by significant feminist activism, Dardigna remembers the terror manifested by many men, ten or fifteen years earlier, when women started to talk about their desires, their fantasies, and their vision of sexuality: they became "petrified into a stunned silence." She commented on "the terror of silent reprobation felt by women through their whole body so that they cannot speak."[36] The woman who tries to criticize the dominant view of eroticism, or who dares to make herself the subject of a love story, is perceived as a threat that is taken care of through ridicule, by turning her into a grotesque creature. When in 1992 Annie Ernaux published *Passion simple*, the story of a torrid love affair she had when she was fifty with a man ten years younger than her,* "the masculine critique was particularly frightful," she remembers. "I was even dubbed 'Madame

---

* In the 2020 film adaptation directed by Danielle Arbid, the age discrepancy is maintained but with a ten-year shift: the actress is forty and the actor thirty-one.

Ovary.' A male writer would never suffer this kind of criticism! Men have the right to write about passion without such push-back, but not women. They should remain in their place and be loved (or not)!"[37]

Almost fifteen years later, we were able to verify that this analysis holds true, upon the publication of the two volumes of the graphic novel *Fraise et chocolat*, in which Aurélia Aurita enthusiastically recounts the impulsive start of her sex life with her partner at the time, the author and editor Frédéric Boilet.[38] The forums on the ActuaBD website, dedicated to comics and graphic novels, still have the hostile reactions from the publication of the complete edition in 2014. "A masterpiece of masturbatory narcissism," one reader says. To which another disdainfully replies: "At the same time, not enough of the body in the drawings so it could really benefit from that."[39] One senses the irritation at the intrusion of a woman into a solidly masculine genre—and its machismo. "Can we seriously call this a BD [graphic novel]," asked a reader; "Aurélia Aurita speaks of sex without coyness, but that is not truly exciting," decreed another. "We have to shut our eyes or else be very imaginative. But this should please feminists who do not like the classic image of woman as represented by men." Another picked up the thread: "I agree with you. Except that true feminists, real ones and not upscale feminists, won't waste their time reading this kind of thing. And it is completely out-of-date." In short: the author is vain and navel-gazing (women, right?), she lacks "modesty," she draws badly, and in any case, her work is not exciting. "A woman talking about pleasure and sex always encounters hostile reactions, in 2014 as in 2006," snapped a female poster,

who concluded: "Still, we are speaking about BDs, every author of which has notebooks full of naked girls and regularly
publishes books containing sex. It's demoralizing . . . to always
read so much hypocrisy and bad faith."[40] At the time, the French
daily paper *Libération* introduced Frédéric Boilet by saying he
was known for having been "the object of the sexual bulimia of
Aurélia Aurita in *Fraise et chocolat*," a surprising formulation that
pathologizes the author and makes her into a vaguely menacing
creature, as if, in both graphic novels, the spirit of initiative and
the sexual appetite were not equitably shared."[41]

THE WOMAN WHO FANTASIZES IS A MONSTER

In 1973, Nancy Friday published *My Secret Garden*, in which
anonymous American women discuss their fantasies and how
they feature in their sex lives.[42] In the prologue, she relates how
the book was received, in contrast to how her fantasies were
received when she took the risk of confiding them to men over
the course of her life. First came a scene with a lover; they understood each other well, so when he asked one evening in bed,
"Tell me what you are thinking about," she answered without
any self-censorship. His reaction stupefied her: "He got out
of bed, put on his pants and went home." Thinking it over
later, she realized that actually she had only ever participated
in *his* fantasies. Burned by the experience, she kept quiet with
subsequent lovers until she met the man who would become
her husband; she risked once again revealing what was on her
mind. "His look of amused admiration came as a reprieve; I

realized how much he loved me, and in loving me, loved any-thing that gave me more abundant life." Before rediscovering her self-confidence, she put into the novel she was writing a chapter devoted to the erotic reveries of her heroine. But her editor was disgusted. This would make her character appear to be a monster, he told her. "If she's so crazy about this guy she's with, if he's such a great fuck, then why's she thinking about all these other crazy things . . . why isn't she thinking about him?"[43]

Friday would often run up against the feeling of treachery and panic felt by some men when they discover that their part-ner has fantasies. One of them even responded to her appeal to hear from other women by saying that he was writing to her on behalf of his wife who had let him know that she had absolutely no fantasies whatsoever—and he signed the letter in *her* name! This deeply irritated Friday: "A man can have an orgasm while his wife's thinking about the grocery list. Is this preferable?"[44] The more open-minded couples, however, could receive a providential improvement in their own sex lives by opening up about their fantasies. One woman vouches for this: "My husband knows of [my fantasies] and fully approves; I sometimes think he even relies on it, say, when he's tired. It's as though he were saying, 'Come on, baby, remember how it was, get us up there.'" She observes that her fantasies produce "more erotic session[s]" for both her partner and herself, which in turn supply material for new fantasies: "My fantasies are money in the bank."*

---

* The reaction of someone reading the manuscript of this book: "Aha! I must not have the same bank as she does!"

Friday knew she might have responded to her editor in many ways. She would have wanted to ask why the desires and fantasies of men were widespread without anybody finding this deviant or disturbing: "When Henry Miller, D. H. Lawrence and Norman Mailer—to say nothing of Genet—put their fantasies on paper, they are recognized for what they can be: art." But she said nothing: "My editor's insinuation, like my former lover's rejection, hit me where I was most sensitive: in that area where women, knowing the least about each other's true sexual selves, are most vulnerable." Her project—to collect female fantasies by means of interviews with her friends and letters received in response to classified ads in the press—aimed to put an end to this mutual ignorance, to stop women from feeling guilty. *My Secret Garden* confirms that when women are guaranteed total anonymity they will indeed offer the scenarios that most efficiently bring them to orgasm, whether alone or with a partner. Here we are far from the soothing representations of a romantic and sentimental sexuality: there are double and triple penetrations, there are dogs, there are donkeys. . . . This leads us to assume that most of the time, female fantasies are the victim not only of male censorship but also of self-censorship by women themselves, out of concern for self-preservation. When you are confronted your whole life with the risk of sexual violence, you do not wish to give the slightest pretext for "girls love that" discourses—as if the fantasy could be confused with reality, or as if trashy fantasies mean that you are at the disposal of the first scumbag who comes along.

But it remains true that in French erotic literature of the twentieth century, women have been largely deprived of speech about their experience of love and sex. The analysis of the deep roots of this literature—Pierre Klossowski, Alain Robbe-Grillet, Georges Bataille, and a few others—in Anne-Marie Dardigna's *Les châteaux d'Éros* produces the same kind of comfort as the abrupt and salutary demystification in *Le consentement*. Like Vanessa Springora with Matzneff, Dardigna annihilates in a few murderous phrases literature that pretends to be so intimidating as to be unassailable. She strips bare their deep conservatism; the way in which, while wanting to be transgressive, these novels remain prisoners of Catholic morality and its obsession with sin; the conventional and false nature of their ramblings about love and death; their dread of the female body and sex organs, which denote an uncontrollable and overwhelming nature that it is up to the civilizing male to curb; their "inflexible rejection of women" that reduces them to a currency of exchange among men; finally, their base in a privileged and reactionary high society. In the United States, Kate Millett did the same critical work at the end of the 1960s, analyzing with pitiless acuity a few scenes chosen from novels by Henry Miller and Norman Mailer.[45] This kind of work should be pursued because it shows how often what we learn to consider as "heterosexual sex" is in reality sex by and for men; we cannot distinguish the difference. This confusion is fed by both the cultural and economic subordination of women, who end up disappearing into the background—and this comes to seem natural. There is something absurd in the supposed split between a feminism called "pro-sex" and an "abolitionist" or "radical" kind of feminism. Rather than "sex" or "no sex," shouldn't the decisive question be, *Sex for whom?* Faced with any sexual situation involving women and men, we should consider whether it exists to serve the desires, fantasies, and pleasure of its *male* protagonists or also, on an equal footing, the desires, fantasies, and pleasure of its *female* protagonists. Nor should sex for women merely consist in a "pleasure in giving pleasure" that has been inherited from customary female abnegation.[46] The results of such questioning would probably be a little depressing.

HARRISON AND ME

But what would erotic freedom look like? Is it even possible to have desires we are sure belong to *us* when we have been plunged our whole lives into a world governed by masculine domination? As a kid, lacking any notion of what adults could be doing with each other, I was like a little factory of fantasies, and these fantasies already involved the clear superiority of boys, along with a vaguely masochistic aspect. When I think back on it, this is what fascinated me: Where did that aspect come from? I knew nothing of life, I had just arrived on this planet, but I had already incorporated certain great laws of my environment. Similarly, around the age of six or seven, in my small attic room in the family home that served as a games room, my friend J and I adored playing the same scenario over and over again: I pretended to be a woman who left home to go out walking, while he was a sort of wolf-man waiting for me, crouched behind a tree. I had barely taken a few steps "outside" when he threw himself on me (on top of cushions) to "devour" me. I found this game that associated the masculine with predation to be intensely satisfying.

In adolescence, this taste was confirmed. I was fascinated

by the type of virility incarnated by the actor Harrison Ford, in both *Star Wars* and *Indiana Jones*. The scene in *The Empire Strikes Back* in which Han Solo surprises Princess Leia while she is repairing something in a corner of the spaceship, when he makes her reluctantly admit that he pleases her, before he kisses her despite her rebuffs, appeared to me as the height of romance and eroticism. I loved this idea of a man who sees you clearly and who takes the initiative to bring you closer, which probably reveals to what extent I was paralyzed at the prospect of having to formulate (or accept) my desires, or be obliged to take some kind of initiative myself—here again appears the dream of being taken charge of by a providential man that I examined in the previous chapter. In his youth, the blogger Jonathan McIntosh also watched Ford's films "dozens of times," strongly identifying with the characters he played. In a 2017 YouTube video, he examined the schema used in several of the actor's "seduction scenes."[47] Ignoring the perfunctory protestations of female characters, the hero gradually circumscribes them, invades their personal space—until, cornered, they give way to him. The sequence in *The Empire Strikes Back* is echoed in *Indiana Jones and the Temple of Doom*, when Willie (Kate Capshaw) tells him she has had enough and is not going back to Delhi with him, and turns away furiously, and the adventurer brings her back to him with his whip and kisses her. In both cases, the kiss is interrupted by a comic intrusion—by C-3PO in *Star Wars* and by an elephant spraying the couple in *Indiana Jones*.

This schema is obviously not reserved to characters played by Ford, even if the scriptwriters used (and abused) it in his case:

McIntosh also shows a scene from the James Bond film *Spectre* in which Bond (Daniel Craig), after having shattered a glass of liquor as the implacable sign of virile determination, advances slowly toward a retreating Lucia Sciarra (Monica Bellucci) while explaining how he was right to kill her husband; when she is backed up against a mirror, he kisses her. Through these films and many others, millions of female spectators, including me, learned to associate brutal force and the threat of seduction, while millions of male spectators, including Jonathan McIntosh, learned that a woman's "no" was merely a "yes" that could not be admitted, that their anger and protests were always feigned and their imprecations just invitations to come on more strongly. In short, my erotic *imaginaire*—and maybe yours, too—is founded on a culture of rape.

The writer and performer Wendy Delorme believes that our fantasies begin by "inception": she is referring to the film of that name made by Christopher Nolan (2010), whose hero "is charged with implanting ideas in the subconscious of a subject in such a way that the subject thinks s/he had these ideas on his/her own."[48] In a 2013 article, Delorme traces the origins of an erotic image that came to her at the age of twelve. Sleeping naked in her bed, she imagined a Master, a man with an indistinct face standing on the threshold of her bedroom, who approaches slowly. "I visualized myself attached on my bed, covered with a fine cloth that he lifts softly by sliding it over by body. I quiver and find myself unable to imagine farther because at that age I did not know what happens, concretely, 'next.'" It was only thirty years later, coming by chance on a

TV rebroadcast of *Angélique, Marquise des Anges*,* which must have marked her childhood, that she suddenly understood where this fantasy came from: this "Master" was inspired by Angélique's husband. She now became aware that in the course of the film, the heroine is "sexually assaulted every twenty minutes by various attackers." And that, here again, these rapes are shown as the realization of her deep desire: "Each time a man is on the point of taking her by force, she is shown defending herself with the gestures of a dragonfly, before succumbing with pink cheeks, eyelids lowered, and fainting in a posture that so resembles erotic abandon that it is very troubling." Delorme describes the power of this "sea of literary and media productions," which "forge our erotic imaginations even before we know what a consensual and desired sexual relation might be."[49]

That our fantasies might be fashioned early on by cultural influences does not mean, though, that they are engraved in marble. Upon first reading, *Histoire d'O* entranced me.** I reexamined it after reading Anne-Marie Dardigna's analysis in her book *Les châteaux d'Éros*, and the enchantment disappeared. O's sacrificial mysticism, with its strong residue of Catholicism, repelled me. (Anne Desclos, the real name of Réage, reckons she

---

* A 1964 historical romance film about a woman forced to abandon her lover in order to marry a nobleman.

** In Pauline Réage's erotic novel (1954), a young woman, O, is brought by her lover, René, to a château, where, like other captives, she is placed at the disposal of all the men present and regularly whipped. When they go back to Paris, René "gives" her to his friend, an older Englishman called Sir Stephen. Behind the pseudonym of Pauline Réage hides Dominique Aury, the secretary of *La nouvelle revue française*, a literary journal, who had written this story for her lover, Jean Paulhan, himself the director of that journal.

would have made an "excellent nun.")[50] Eleven years before she wrote *Histoire d'O* under her penname, she had published an anthology of French religious poetry. O's childish femininity disgusted me, and the devotion that men inspired in her now appeared ridiculous. I was embarrassed that she was suffering so much, that it was almost never a matter of her own pleasure, and that she felt "disgusted" by the very idea of masturbating. I never understood the charm of the whip, but this time, it frankly revolted me. ("There's nothing like devotional books to give you a good idea of what torture is all about," said Réage.)[51] I never liked the fact that O becomes an object of exchange between the two men who share her "as no doubt in days gone by, when they were young, they had shared a trip, a boat, a horse," nor the idea that "what each of them would look for in her would be the other's mark, the trace of the other's passage."[52] I could not find the sublime beauty in the annihilation of her personality, which culminates in her physical annihilation. I was struck by the reactionary atmosphere in which the tale is bathed, by its lugubrious tone. I was not astonished to learn that Réage had a "suppressed military vocation."[53] Nor that for her the body had "something made to be reduced, to be mastered, commanded."[54] In short, the reading pact was broken.

With the *Histoire d'O*, as with *Belle du Seigneur*, rereading it after ten, fifteen, or twenty years served as a marker of my evolution. The risk, though, was of catapulting myself into a fantasy no-man's-land: I am no longer so easily entertained, I no longer consume anything whatsoever, but I have difficulty finding ecstasy in trading old for something new. Although I sincerely admire her approach, the feminist pornography of Erika Lust often arouses in me only polite titillation. In *Les chemins de désir*, Claire Richard recounts running up against the same realization: "Yet, in theory, I am completely in favor. I fight for women's reappropriation of their body, I am pro-sex, I admire Ovidie, I am a fan of Annie Sprinkle, I've read Wendy Delorme. But feminist porno does not appeal to me. I have tried, but I am conditioned. I get wet over mainstream porn. It's like you can be in favor of sustainable agriculture and secretly adore Burger King's Triple Whopper!"[55] One of her friends suggests a possible explanation: "Porn is associated with transgression, that's what makes it so attractive. But if it is aligned with your convictions, it's no longer transgressive."[56]

Is transgression an indispensable part of fantasy? Nancy Friday offers a wider definition: "I think that a lot of female fantasy is a psychic need for a more complete exploration of everything that was kept from them as girls, of everything that conceivably could be thought sexual." When she masturbates, one of Friday's interviewees, Mary Jane, usually dreams that she is walking alone on a beach, that she takes off all her clothes and goes swimming in the sea, before lying naked in the sun and feeling the breeze caressing her skin; sometimes the scene shifts to a mountain waterfall.[57] Voilà, that's all. So in some cases, the transgressive element may be . . . rather thin. What is certain is that fantasy involves letting your imagination run wild, allowing your mind to form all kinds of images and scenarios responding to an obscure and profound necessity by erasing any moral consideration. And then it can contain a large portion of transgression.

Except that there are a thousand possible forms of transgression, and we can choose those that suit us. Thus I came upon a film by Erika Lust that truly captivated me: *Safe Word*, a sadomasochist miniseries whose heroine fully exists, with her personality, desires, and point of view. She is shown in her daily routine, in her professional life; she is searching for active pleasure; the story is told from her perspective, and the pornographic scenes are focused above all on her pleasure.[58] In other words, I can have my dose of transgression without identifying with an ectoplasmic neophyte like O. Even if we are seeking transgression, something in what we read or watch has to appeal, in one way or another—even if in the most twisted way—to a notion of *pleasure*. And these predilections may vary, as witnessed by the evolution that caused my susceptibility to the world of Pauline Réage to disappear.

O, OR A STORY OF PIRATING

I am not rejecting a fantasy of being reduced to total power-lessness. In *Histoire d'O*, I still recognize its attraction. Rather, everything that surrounds the story in this novel I can no longer bear. Reexamining it today, I understand that what especially exasperated me, more than anything I have already mentioned, is the way that Jean Paulhan pirated the book. His preface has every sign of marking territory, as if he were deliberately pissing around his mistress's work. He is moved by a detail in the story: "The day when René abandons O to still further torments, she still manages to have enough presence of mind to notice that her lover's slippers are frayed, and notes she will have to buy him another pair." Paulhan marvels: "To me such a thought seems almost unimaginable. It is something a man would never have thought of, or at least would never have dared express." His preface is called "*Le bonheur dans l'esclavage*"; he delights in this ultimate masculine combo: domestic slavery mingled with sexual slavery. We should salute this major contribution to erotic literature: women's mental competence even amid whips and chains, brave little darlings. I also grind my teeth rereading another famous extract from Paulhan's prose (featured on the cover of my edition, eclipsing the voice of the female author). He exults: "At last a woman who admits it! Who admits what? Something that women have always refused till now to admit (and today more than ever before). Something that men have always reproached them with: that they never cease obeying their nature, the call of their blood, that everything in them, even their minds, is sex. That they have constantly to be nourished, constantly washed and made up, constantly beaten. That all they need is a good master, one who is not too lax or kind." And farther along: "Women at least are fated to resemble, throughout their lives, the children we once were."[59] Argh.

The novel is instrumentalized, first by Paulhan to trumpet his anti-feminist generalizations, then by the whole cultural and media milieu. When the film adaptation by Just Jaeckin came out in 1975 (he had previously directed *Emmanuelle*), the magazine *L'express* put *Histoire d'O* on its cover: the actress Corinne Cléry, bare-breasted, with hands over her head, and a caption quoting Paulhan's words: "Finally a woman who admits . . ." and this clarification: "By Jean Paulhan of the Académie Française."[60] Naked and silent women offered to the audience's concupiscence and men of the French Academy: in a France full of feminist effervescence (and during International Women's Year), here is how each finds its correct place. In the magazine's inside pages, another extract from this deplorable preface was highlighted: "Everything happens as though there exists in the world a mysterious equilibrium of violence, for which we have lost all taste, and even our understanding of the term. And, personally, I am not displeased that it is a woman who has found them again." Activists in the MLF (Women's Liberation Movement) descended on the offices of *L'express* with the cry: "No money off our bodies!" and "The police protect rape."[61]

But Pauline Réage cannot be held directly responsible for the political use made of her work. In a 1988 interview, she considered that the preface "did not correspond that much to the book," tacitly admitting: "The angle he had taken pleased him. Too bad it created a bigger scandal than the novel."[62] She herself had not written to be published and had "not imagined for a second that this would be possible." She stated, "The publication was because he [Paulhan] wanted it to be published, it was all the same to me." *Histoire d'O* was not a novel, but a "letter," she insisted, intended only for her lover: "The story of Scheherazade, more or less."[63] We may understand her exaltation during those summer nights when she was writing in the solitude of her bedroom (Paulhan was married, she was divorced) and sending him in the morning one chapter after another. She made a lovely tale of this: "The days lingered on forever, and the morning light penetrated at unwonted hours to the dusty black curtains of passive resistance, the last remaining vestiges of the war. But beneath the little lamp still lighted at the head of the bed, the hand holding the pencil raced over the paper without the least concern for the hour or the light. The girl was writing the way you speak in the dark to the person you love when you've held back the words of love too long and they flow at last. For the first time in her life she was writing without hesitation, without stopping, rewriting, or discarding, she was writing the way one breathes, the way one dreams."[64]

In truth, with this tale she was trying to respond to Paulhan's expectations. "One day a girl in love said to the man she loved: 'I could also write the kind of stories you like . . .'"[65] He salutes the success of this enterprise; as he puts it: "In her own way, O expresses a virile ideal. Virile, or at least masculine."[66] But it would be wrong to say that this novel is entirely alienated from Réage. These are still *her* fantasies, and long-standing ones (going back to when she was fourteen or fifteen, she said), which she is dramatizing: "Let's say that it was a way of expressing a certain number of childhood and adolescent fantasies that persisted in my later life; all I was trying to do was to tell the stories that I had so often told myself, for fun and pleasure, as I was falling asleep."[67] The Roissy château to which O is brought is inspired by the subterranean space under her family home that she had imagined as a child. In effect, O is passive and silent, merely repeating the words that her lover dictates (or murmurs). But it is Réage who is speaking. She built this story, chose every word for it. Despite everything that it can be accused of, *Histoire d'O* is the expression of a woman's vital drive, of her love and desire for a man. Life is short and the urgency of living, of loving, of climaxing obliges us to deal with our *imaginaire* such as it is, even if it is laden with all the jumble of a conservative education.

Moreover, Anne Desclos, only officially confirmed at age eighty-six to be Pauline Réage in 1994 in the *New Yorker*,[68] had never publicly taken anti-feminist positions. She did not like the Women's Liberation Movement but said she had always been a "feminist." Questioned in 1975 about the statement by Paulhan (who died in 1968) that *Histoire d'O* proves that "everything is sex" among women, "even their minds," she replied (with a certain insolence): "One could say the same thing about men." She added, "Even men who accept that on an intellectual plane [women are human beings, too] tend to forget it and revert as soon as love or eroticism comes into play. They revert to the cliché of women as sex objects or erotic objects. Women almost never reciprocate and conceive of men in the same way, and if ever they do, men are so offended they never forgive the poor woman."[69]

Her case shows that a woman, even when she writes an international bestseller, is muzzled, crushed, and underestimated by her contemporaries. There were very few interviews with Réage; and yet in one made in 1988 (and published by Gallimard in 1999, a year after her death), the interviewer asked her almost exclusively about Paulhan—who was certainly an important publisher but who never published a notable work—and about all the other Great Men she had mixed with during her life, since for twenty-five years she had been the only woman on Gallimard's review panel. She was invited to share her expertise on subjects such as "it was said that Jean Paulhan always spoke standing up" (in effect, the world wants to know everything) and on the owner Gaston Gallimard: "Who was Gaston deep down?" Out of 117 pages, only thirteen are devoted to *Histoire d'O*.[70] It is easy to attribute to Réage a "vocation" for being "clandestine": she had an interest in that, the poor thing! As if she had been left any choice! (Although concealing yourself behind a pseudonym must have had its charms: like hearing Albert Camus decree in front of her that it was impossible that *Histoire d'O* was written by a woman!)[71]

A POISON . . . OR AN ANTIDOTE?

It is not certain that men's fantasies are more authentically their own, which might also annoy and upset them. But at least their fantasies being infused with masculine domination does not involve the same element of masochism as it does for women. They are not confronted with this disagreeable sentiment that a part of themselves—the most intimate, the most secret, that which relates to their quest for pleasure and fulfillment—must make itself the accomplice of an order that oppresses them. The "strange voice" that enters the head of the writer Claire Richard summarizes this turmoil: "How can you be a feminist and yet get excited by stories in which women are treated like dogs? How can you read Christine Delphy [a French feminist] and yet fantasize that you are being treated like a whore? But what is wrong with you? You must reread Monique Wittig—and fast as you can!"[72] Meanwhile, faced with the same alarming dissociation, Wendy Delorme refuses absolutely to be ashamed or to let herself be blamed for having undergone conditioning. After describing a scene in which she imagines herself at the center of a gang bang, she concludes: "I have no feeling of guilt. Without this fantasy, I might spend more than twenty minutes in coming, maybe I would not come at all, I don't know." She adds that even if she is aware of what gives her an orgasm, "this is a symptom that the world is fucked up, that centuries of oppression cannot be erased in sixty years of feminism: that I am incapable of fantasizing outside the mental cage that was constructed for my body by people other than myself."[73]

But having solved this matter does not resolve everything. Agreed, it is not our fault, but is it serious? Is it something with which you can live or should you try to change? And does it have consequences or not? Does it do us harm that we are unaware of? In 1983 the Australian-British feminist Lynne Segal, irritated at hearing sexual liberation discussed only in terms of anatomical knowledge (even if she admits its importance), wrote that "it does not feel like personal liberation to be able to orgasm to intensely masochistic fantasies." And stop telling her not to worry because in any case, fantasies evolve over time. "But change over time is exactly what masochistic sexual fantasies usually do *not* do. They usually survive, often despite the pursuit of autonomy and strength in our everyday lives." She herself feels angry about them and "the disconnection which occurs with lovers who, at least recently, are most caring, gentle and as extensively physically stimulating as I could wish." Her fear is not that these fantasies encourage real submission (she does not believe so), but that they "make your sexual partner irrelevant, reducing sex to masturbation."[74]

Others think that we can calmly accept this apparent contradiction between our convictions and our imaginary aspirations.

Between 2010 and 2012, the writer Cheryl Strayed (author of *Wild*) anonymously maintained a love-advice column ("Dear Sugar") on a friend's literary site. There she responded to all kinds of dilemmas submitted by likewise anonymous correspondents, both women and men. These exchanges were gathered into a book.[75] One of these letters, sent by a thirty-four-year-old heterosexual woman who defined herself as "strong, independent, 'normal,' feminist-minded," is titled: "Icky Thoughts Turn Me On." Its author explains that her fantasies relate to incest, the idea of being taken brutally, of being forced to submit. She is all the more shamed by this because her father, who died in a car accident when she was eight, was "mildly sexually abusive" to her. She is asking "Sugar" what she should do: "Should I give way to my sick thoughts or should I fight them off?" She adds that she detests unbalanced power relationships "outside the bedroom," that sadomasochism does not interest her, and that the only form of domination she would like to experiment with in bed is "exclusively psychological/conversational."

In her response, Strayed begins by reassuring the correspondent of her normalcy. Then she advises her not to underestimate the effect of family history and says that she should enter some kind of therapy to explore it. This would also allow her to discover whether her fantasies are connected to it; she herself does think there could be a connection, but that does not mean that the letter writer desires (or would have desired) to be raped by anybody: "It means, perhaps, that you lost something or were wounded in a place that your sexual longings are maybe—and only maybe!—attempting to recover and repair." She invites her to not be afraid of that: "The deal with sexual fantasy is that it's *pretend*. And when a fantasy is acted out, it's done so between and among *consenting adults*. There's a world of difference between being raped and asking someone to rip your clothes off and fuck you." She hammers home: "You are the agent of power in your sex life, even if what you want is to relinquish your power and agency while you're having sex. You can take that power back at any moment."[76]

An interesting path opens up in this idea that the scenarios that appear compromising and humiliating to us actually come to our aid, that they have a therapeutic function, the function of resolution. Nancy Friday considers that "we win in all of our fantasies." Including in fantasies of rape: "Yes, even those involving the so-called rapist, that *deus ex machina* that we roll in to catapult us past a lifetime of women's rules against sex."[77] It frees us of guilt about our desire, as I wrote above. Moreover, most of the time, the fantasy is a totally unrealistic vision of rape: you imagine yourself forced at the beginning, and later on not only consenting but ecstatic. As implausible as these scenarios may be, and as problematic as their omnipresence is in the cultural representations that surround us, at least they do not call upon *real* masochism. Although some of the women who testified in *My Secret Garden* had fantasies featuring the worst torments, this does not imply any desire for those fantasies to become reality. "I hate what is happening to me in my fantasies, but it is inextricably involved with my very real pleasure," said one of them.[78]

Perhaps when women swear that they have no desire whatsoever to be tortured, or raped, that they hold onto their physical and psychic integrity, that moreover they are independent, feminists, etc., we might actually believe them. Maybe we might actually believe ourselves. Since our fantasies take shape in moments when we are trying to attain maximum well-being, we might think that they aim to smooth out the difficulties presented to us by any possible means. And if they incorporate masochistic elements, maybe they are not a poison that is infiltrating us but rather an antidote to that poison? They have great plasticity, they appear at the snap of our fingers and disappear just as quickly if they do not satisfy us, they are pragmatic, they pull out all the stops. We might suppose they mix all sorts of heterogeneous elements that melt into each other: some borrowed from situations we would really like to experience, plus the stratagems that authorize the liberation of our desires of which Nancy Friday speaks, still others that arise from incantations to ward off these desires or from compensation. Every day, in effect, even the least feminist of women must spend considerable energy, consciously or not, on defending herself against masculine domination, compromising with it and/or fighting against it—if only by being vigilant when she walks the streets alone at night, for example, and in all sorts of other circumstances. We might suppose that this is exhausting, and that it creates a tension that occasionally requires a resolution.

At times, whether we are committed feminists or we reject this term, perhaps we need to become in our thoughts the cute little sows that roll joyously in the muck of masculine domination, because all the rest of the time, it is too exhausting to try to avoid being splattered. The fantasy of being subject to one or several men, the acceptance of (and even the demand for) the degrading adjectives thrown in our face, the active search in imagination for the violence with which we are constantly threatened—all may aim to neutralize this domination, to subvert it. The fact that we often imagine taking pleasure in this violence (which can only occur in the fantasy world) might imply that, from now on, nothing bad can happen to us. Our minds may use this ruse to persuade us that we are sheltered, that we are invincible.

With this hypothesis in mind, I reread from a totally different perspective the observations that I reported above. "Read Christine Delphy" and "dream we are treated like a whore" would not imply any contradiction but would simply represent two different and complementary outlets in the face of sexism, two psychic tools that we use in alternation. This might also be why masochistic fantasies "do not evolve," even when we become more free and autonomous, as Lynne Segal remarked. If they do not disappear, it is because masculine domination itself has not disappeared, and therefore we still need these fantasies. This might also explain why lesbians sometimes have fantasies of heterosexual submission, as Wendy Delorme testifies. Similarly, feminist porn does not completely convince us, because it lacks this function of warding off the fear and tension inspired by patriarchy in daily life. Maybe this is what Claire Richard's friend tried to say when she remarked that it was not "transgressive" enough.

This does not imply that we ought, for our own psychic relief, to gorge on videos in which other women are exploited and abused in completely real ways (what a horror). For that, *hentai*, Japanese animated pornography—which Richard also mentions[79]—is interesting, because fantasies pass directly from one brain to another without necessitating the sacrifice of real women. And their emancipation from any kind of realism opens infinite possibilities, which may prove liberating: it is simply implausible that you would take pleasure in being raped, but is *no more* plausible than being kidnapped in space by a monster with tentacles. If you need confirmation that in *hentai* all is pure fiction, you have it from me! I am by no means calling for a multiplication of violent pornographic images; but these images exist because masculine domination exists. And as long as this is the case, it is possible for some women to subvert domination in order to make defensive use of it.

I do not know if this hypothesis about the function of certain fantasies is correct. But other explanations seem to me to present too many affinities with the good old prejudices about women for us to trust them. They seem to betray our deep duplicity, our basic masochism. As for the idea that we are poisoned by the cultural productions that surround us (the "inception" described by Wendy Delorme), shouldn't we suppose that, in the moments when our brain is trying to give us maximum pleasure, to make us achieve the fullest peace, it would be capable of defending us against this kind of undesirable infiltration? Shouldn't we have confidence in our brain, even if it sometimes uses processes that we find a bit . . . troubling?

The scene in *The Empire Strikes Back* when Han Solo surprises Princess Leia may have struck me so forcefully because of my mind's vulnerability to rape culture. But perhaps I was also relieved at seeing an on-screen depiction of a threatening attitude that was not a *true* threat but rather the actions of a handsome man, desirable and basically well-intentioned, who is one of the "good guys." The woman, too, wanted the embrace, and the scene ends on a comic note that confirms its inoffensive and touching nature. Perhaps in watching this scene I was not learning to associate a threat with a seduction, as I wrote above; instead I was relieved to see a threat being revealed as a seduction, and consequently being defused. I might have needed this. When I first saw the film, I already knew what a real threat was. At age thirteen, one day I was dragged during recess along ten meters of a school hallway by three older students who proclaimed they were going to rape me in the bathroom. For weeks afterward, I gazed with repulsion at the sweater I was wearing that day on the shelf of my closet—an H&M turquoise sweater—and I believe that I never wore it again. Even if I never consciously linked this episode with my fantasies of love, is it possible they could remain completely disconnected? Agreed: this scene in *The Empire Strikes Back* is not terrific. With respect to the representations of heterosexual relations in culture, we can—and should—do better. But if my brain used it to reassure and console me, I should not be annoyed but rather grateful.

Moreover, although scenes embued with rape culture that we see or read in all sorts of fiction affect us enormously (especially when we are young), and may be incorporated into our reveries, are they truly at the *origin* of our fantasies of submission? As I have said, it seems that my own began very early on, in fact in kindergarten. At the time, I did not know how to read and I did not yet watch television. Should we deduce that I was already subject to masculine domination and that I might already feel the need for a resolution to the psychic tension it creates? Well, now that I think about it, yes. I remember in particular that a little boy in my class told me his father was a policeman, that he had a rifle and that he was going to come to my house to kill me. I was convinced this was true and that nobody could protect me; I was terrified. I burst into sobs, and when I got home, I trembled with fear the whole evening. Is it possible that my fantasies that put boys in a position of power had something to do with this kind of fright, and that the game in which J threw himself on me to devour me had the similar goal of allowing me to tame the perceived threat by mastering it—and by making it, precisely, a *game*—which might explain the intense satisfaction it brought me?

If this analysis is correct, we can see Jean Paulhan's mistake when he saw *Histoire d'O* as an admission of the slavish nature of women. Pauline Réage was not admitting anything of the kind—apart from, indirectly, that phallocrats of the Paulhan kind made her sweat. (She said she realized very late, after having received an indignant letter from a reader reproaching her for depicting men as bastards, that her novel could have been a way of taking vengeance on the masculine race.)[80] So we may suppose that she, too, had a strong need to resolve the tension created by the experience of domination. By transforming the intimate imaginary production of his mistress into a public object in a widely distributed book, by taking it literally to make anti-feminist use of it to feed the great machine of daily sexism, Paulhan might have been both a manipulator and the victim of an enormous misunderstanding. Similarly, in "rape" scenarios in which we start by defending ourselves and end up getting off on it, our brain allows us to lift sexual prohibitions, but their sense and function change completely when that scenario is incorporated into any cultural work. It does give credence to the idea that when a woman says "No," she is thinking *Yes*.

There are not only the voices that are silenced, or buried, or discredited, there are also the ones that are subverted, or utilized, or betrayed, or that are covered by others speaking louder. Am I mistaken in thinking that this is what Paulhan did with Réage? Or is it my own interpretation that betrays her? I don't know, so I quote her:

> All those untold generations of women who out of decency or fear or modesty have failed to speak out without exception have a secret universe of the mind . . . one that is not necessarily O's—in fact, O's may well make them shake their heads in horror. Till now they have held their tongues but that time is past: from now on they'll speak out.[81]

Let's hope that they will be ever more numerous and speak ever louder. And that their voices will finally take their place in the definition of what we call love.

NOTES

Introduction

1. *A Lady Comes to Her Lover's House in a Rainstorm*, ca. 1830, opaque watercolor and gold on paper, 24.5 x 15.7 cm, San Diego Museum of Art.
2. Alain Badiou, with Nicolas Truong, *Eloge de l'amour* (Paris: Flammarion, 2009). In English: *In Praise of Love*, trans. Peter Bush (London: Serpent's Tail, 2012).
3. Annie Ernaux, *Passion simple* (Paris: Gallimard, 1991), 65. In English: *Simple Passion*, trans. Tanya Leslie (New York: Seven Stories Press, 2011).
4. Féminicides Par Compagnons ou Ex collective, https://www.feminicides.fr.
5. Cristina Nehring, *A Vindication of Love: Reclaiming Romance for the Twenty-First Century* (New York: HarperCollins, 2009), introduction.
6. Wendy Langford, *Revolutions of the Heart: Gender, Power and the Delusions of Love* (London: Routledge, 1999), summary and conclusions.
7. Nehring, *Vindication of Love*, chapter 5.
8. Victoire Tuaillon, *Le cœur sur la lable* (Paris: Binge Audio Éditions, 2021). See also Tuaillon's podcast of the same name.
9. Amandine Dhée, *À mains nues* (Lille: La Contre Allée, 2020), 103.
10. Liv Strömquist, *Les sentiments du Prince Charles; I'm Every Woman*; and *La Rose la plus rouge s'épanouit* (Paris: Rackham, 2012, 2018, and 2019, respectively). In English: *Fruit of Knowledge: The Vulva vs. the Patriarchy*, trans. Melissa Bowers; *The Reddest Rose: Romantic Love from the Ancient Greeks to Reality TV*, trans. Melissa Bowers (Seattle, WA: Fantagraphics, 2018 and 2023, respectively).
11. Fanny Arlandis, "Joumana Haddad: 'L'écriture a allégé le poids de mon identité,'" *Télérama*, October 6, 2019.
12. bell hooks, *Communion: The Female Search for Love* (New York: William Morrow, 2002), 58.
13. hooks, *Communion*, 72–73.

14. Mona Chollet, *Sorcières: La puissance invaincue des femmes* (Paris: Zones, 2018). In English: *In Defense of Witches,* trans. Sophie Lewis (New York: St. Martin's Press, 2022).

15. Nehring, *Vindication of Love.*

16. bell hooks, *All About Love: New Visions* (New York: William Morrow, 2000), introduction.

17. hooks, *All About Love,* introduction.

18. Patricia Mercader, Annik Houel, and Helga Sobota, "L'asymétrie des comportements amoureux: Violences et passions dans le crime dit passionnel," *Sociétés contemporaines* 55, no. 3 (2004).

19. In March 1971 on RTL the host Menie Grégoire presented a live show "Homosexuality, This Painful Problem." A homosexual group made this the occasion for their first public protest.

20. Alice Coffin, *Le génie lesbian* (Paris: Grasset, 2020).

21. Quoted in Jane Ward, *The Tragedy of Heterosexuality* (New York: NYU Press, 2020), 12.

22. Emmanuèle de Lesseps, "Hétérosexualité et féminisme," *Questions féministes,* no. 7 (1980).

23. Adrienne Rich, "Compulsory Heterosexuality and Lesbian Existence" in *Blood, Bread, and Poetry: Selected Prose 1979–1985* (New York: Norton Paperback, 1996).

24. Annick Cojean, "Virginie Despentes: 'Cette *histoire de féminité, c'est de l'arnaque,*'" *Le Monde,* July 9, 2017.

25. Ward, *Tragedy of Heterosexuality,* 2.

26. Ward, *Tragedy of Heterosexuality,* chapter 4.

27. Ward, *Tragedy of Heterosexuality,* 142–43.

28. Laurent Sciamma, *Bonhomme,* script extract sent to author.

29. Ward, *Tragedy of Heterosexuality,* 161.

30. Ward, *Tragedy of Heterosexuality,* 22, 172.

31. Ward, *Tragedy of Heterosexuality,* 155.

32. On this subject see Mélanie Gourarier, *Alpha mâle: Séduire les femmes pour s'apprécier entre hommes,* La couleur des idées (Paris: Seuil, 2017).

33. Gourarier, *Alpha mâle,* 273.

34. De Lesseps, "Heterosexualité et féminisme."

35. Coffin, *Le génie lesbien.*

36. De Lesseps, "Heterosexualité et féminisme."

Prologue

1. bell hooks, *All About Love: New Visions* (New York: William Morrow, 2000), introduction.
2. André Gorz, *Lettre à D.: Histoire d'un amour* (Paris: Galilée, 2006), 72. In English: *Letter to D: A Love Story*, trans. Julie Rose (London: Polity, 2020).
3. Benoîte Groult and Paul Guimard, *Journal amoureux, 1951–1953* (Paris: Stock, 2021), 231, 264.
4. Michel Leiris's book was translated as *Manhood: A Journey from Childhood into the Fierce Order of Virility*, trans. Richard Howard (Chicago: University of Chicago Press, 1992). Anne-Marie Dardigna, *Les châteaux d'Éros, ou les infortunes du sexe des femmes* (Paris: Maspero, 1980).
5. Denis de Rougemont, *Love in the Western World*, trans. Montgomery Belgion (Princeton, NJ: Princeton University Press, 1940), 23–24.
6. De Rougemont, *Love in the Western World*, 285.
7. De Rougemont, *Love in the Western World*, 322.
8. Albert Cohen, *Belle du Seigneur* (Paris: Gallimard, 1968). In English: *Her Lover (Belle du Seigneur)*, trans. David Coward (New York: Penguin Classic, 2005).
9. De Rougemont, *Love in the Western World*, 234.
10. Cohen, *Belle du Seigneur*, 793.
11. *Radioscopie*, France Inter, April 2, 1980.
12. Dardigna, *Les châteaux d'Éros*.
13. Eva Illouz, *La fin de l'amour. Enquête sur un désarroi contemporain* (Paris: Seuil, 2020), 123. In English: *The End of Love: A Sociology of Negative Relations* (London: Polity, 2021).
14. Clément Arbrun, "Pourquoi les femmes souffrent du 'caca-shaming,'" *Terrafemina*, September 20, 2019.
15. Nick Haslam, *Psychology in the Bathroom* (London: Palgrave, 2012).
16. Natasha Hinde, "Tinder Date Goes Horrendously Wrong When Woman Tries to Throw Poo Out of Window," *HuffPost (UK)*, September 6, 2017.
17. Sandra Lorenzo, "The Now Famous 'Tinder Poop Incident' Had a Happy Ending," *HuffPost*, September 13, 2017.
18. "Fariha Róisín, Writer," *Into the Gloss*, July 10, 2019, https://intothegloss.com.
19. Cohen, *Belle du Seigneur*, chapter 34.
20. *Radioscopie*, France Inter, April 1, 1980.
21. On this subject, see Dossie Easton and Janet W. Hardy, *The Ethical*

Slut: A Guide to Infinite Sexual Possibilities (Emeryville, CA: Greenery Press, 1997).

22. Cristina Nehring, *A Vindication of Love: Reclaiming Romance for the Twenty-First Century* (New York: HarperCollins, 2009), 125. For a more critical view, see Julie Beauzac, "Frida Kahlo, au-delà du mythe 2/2," February 26, 2020, in *Vénus s'épilait elle la chatte?*, podcast, 36:37, www.venuslepodcast.com.

23. Quoted in Jane Ward, *The Tragedy of Heterosexuality* (New York: NYU Press, 2020), 141.

24. De Rougemont, *Love in the Western World*, 309.

25. Judith Duportail, *L'amour sous algorithme* (Paris: Éditions Goutte d'Or, 2019).

26. De Rougemont, *Love in the Western World*, 303.

27. Mona Chollet, "Éloigner les hommes et les femmes," in the chapter "L'hypnose du bonheur familial," *Chez soi: Une odyssée de l'espace domestique* (Paris: La Découverte, 2015).

28. Marlène Duretz, "Les nostalgiques du confinement rechignent à quitter leur cocon," *Le Monde*, May 12, 2020.

29. *L'énigme Rezvani*, dir. Gloria Campana (Paris: MC4 Production, 2003).

30. Serge Rezvani, *Le roman d'une maison* (Arles, France: Actes Sud, 2001), 96.

31. Séverine Auffret, *Des blessures et des jeux: Manuel d'imagination libre* (Arles, France: Actes Sud, 2003).

32. Gorz, *Lettre à D.*, 106.

33. Mona Chollet, "Comme si ta vocation était de me conforter dans la mienne," *La méridienne*, December 28, 2017, www.la-meridienne.info.

34. Nehring, *Vindication of Love*, chapter 4.

35. Grace Dent, "Gwyneth Paltrow Is Right—Living Apart from My Partner Is Like Having My Cake and Eating It," *Guardian*, June 22, 2019.

36. Nancy Huston, *Journal de la création* (Arles, France: Actes Sud, 1990), 166.

37. Quoted in Nehring, *Vindication of Love*, chapter 4.

38. Illouz, *La fin de l'amour*, 39.

39. Julia Sklar, "When Living Apart Keeps You Together," *Curbed*, February 12, 2020, www.curbed.com.

40. Voltairine de Cleyre, *The Voltairine de Cleyre Reader*, ed. A. J. Brigati (Chico, CA: AK Press, 2004), 40, 51, 59.

41. De Cleyre, *Voltairine de Cleyre Reader*, 47, 58.

42. Évelyne Le Garrec, *Un lit à soi: Itinéraires de femmes* (Paris: Seuil, 1979), 19.

43. Gisèle Halimi, *Le programme commun des femmes* (Paris: Grasset, 1978).

44. Le Garrec, *Un lit à soi*, 17.

45. Sklar, "When Living Apart Keeps You Together."

46. Chollet, chapters "Métamorphoses de la boniche" and "L'hypnose du bonheur familial" in *Chez soi* and *Sorcières: La puissance invaincue des femmes* (Paris: Zones, 2018); in English: *In Defense of Witches*, trans. Sophie Lewis (New York: St. Martin's Press, 2022), 71.

47. Coline Charpentier (@taspensea), Instagram, March 5, 2021.

48. Marie-Carmen Garcia, *Amours clandestines: Sociologie de l'extraconjugalité durable* (Lyon, France: Presses Universitaires de Lyon, 2016).

49. *J'en ai marre des mecs*, France Inter, March 11, 2020, https://www.radiofrance.fr/franceinter/podcasts/alors-voila/j-en-ai-marre-des-mecs-mais-marre-marre-marre-5083439.

50. Coline Charpentier (@taspensea), Instagram, November 24, 2020, https://www.instagram.com/p/CH_ASXVAzvi.

1: Making Yourself Less Noticeable to Be Loved?

1. "Non, Nicolas Sarkozy n'a pas été retouché pour apparaître plus grand," *Paris match*, July 4, 2019, parismatch.com.

2. Pauline Thurier, "Pourquoi la une de *Paris match* avec Nicolas Sarkozy et Carla Bruni pose problème," *Les inrockuptibles*, July 5, 2019, lesinrocks.com.

3. Catharine MacKinnon, *Toward a Feminist Theory of State* (Cambridge, MA: Harvard University Press, 1989), 113.

4. Manon Garcia, *We Are Not Born Submissive: How Patriarchy Shapes Women's Lives* (Princeton, NJ: Princeton University Press, 2021), 37–38.

5. Katrin Bennhold, "Keeping Romance Alive in the Age of Female Empowerment," *New York Times*, November 30, 2010.

6. Nicolas Herpin, "La taille des hommes: Son incidence sur la vie en couple et la carrière professionnelle," *Économie et statistique* 361 (June 2003).

7. Daphnée Leportois, "Pourquoi on voit si peu de couples où l'homme est plus petit que la femme," *Slate (France)*, August 23, 2019.

8. Leportois, "Pourquoi on voit si peu de couples."

9. *Pourquoi les femmes sont-elles plus petites que les hommes?*, dir. Véronique Kleiner (Paris: Point du Jour, 2013).

10. Priscille Touraille, *Hommes grands, femmes petites: Une évolution*

coûteuse. Les régimes de genre comme force sélective de l'adaptation biologique (Paris: Éditions de la Maison des Sciences de l'Homme, 2008).

11. Kleiner, *Pourquoi.*

12. Mona Chollet, "Femmes et nourriture, un rendez-vous toujours manqué," in *Beauté Fatale: Les nouveaux visages d'une aliénation féminine* (Paris: La Découverte, 2012, 2015).

13. Quoted in Peggy Sastre, "Si les femmes sont plus petites que les hommes, ce n'est pas à cause du steak," *Slate (France)*, December 22, 2017. See also Philippe Huneman, "Sur une polémique concernant une hypothèse relative au dimorphisme sexuel de la stature chez les humains," Medium, May 3, 2020, philippe-huneman.medium.com.

14. Chollet, *Beauté Fatale.*

15. Mona Chollet, "The Dizzy Heights" chapter in *Sorcières: La puissance invaincue des femmes* (Paris: Zones, 2018). In English: *In Defense of Witches*, trans. Sophie Lewis (New York: St. Martin's Press, 2022).

16. Noémie Renard, "L'impuissance comme idéal de beauté des femmes," *Sexisme et sciences humains*, January 2, 2016, antisexisme.net.

17. Poppy Noor, "What Is 'Sexy Baby Voice'? We Spoke to a Sociologist to Find Out More," *Guardian*, February 26, 2020.

18. Laélia Véron, "La voix neutre n'existe pas," April 7, 2020, in *Parler comme jamais*, podcast, 42:00, Binge Audio.

19. Catherine Schwaab, "Anna Mouglalis: Le jour où 'je décide de garder ma voix . . . et trouve ma voie,'" *Paris match*, November 6, 2019.

20. Marie Piat, "Photos: Ces stars féminines trop musclées!," *Public*, October 27, 2013, public.fr.

21. Géraldine Sarratia, "Paul B. Preciado: 'Ma masculinité dissidente est aussi délirante que la masculinité normale,'" *Le goût de M*, May 22, 2020, lemonde.fr.

22. Alice Zeniter, *Je suis une fille sans histoire* (Paris: L'Arche, 2021). The Balzac quote is from *Splendeurs et misères des courtisanes.*

23. Ben Rothenberg, "Tennis's Top Women Balance Body Image with Ambition," *New York Times*, July 10, 2015.

24. Gloria Steinem, "The Strongest Woman in the World," in *Moving Beyond Words: Age, Rage, Sex, Power, Money, Muscles: Breaking the Boundaries of Gender* (New York: Simon and Schuster, 1994).

25. *Pumping Iron II: The Women*, dir. George Butler (Holderness, NH: White Mountain Films, 1985).

26. Steinem, "Strongest Woman in the World," 106.

27. Mathieu Palain, "Franck et sa femme," February 12, 2020, in *Des hommes violents*, podcast, 28:00, Radio France Culture.

28. In France, men earn on average a salary 22.8 percent higher than that of women. See "Les inégalités de salaires entre les femmes et les hommes: État des lieux," Observatoire des Inégalités, March 25, 2019, inegalites.fr.

29. Sendhil Mullainathan, "The Hidden Taxes on Women," *New York Times*, March 2, 2018.

30. Lauren Provost, "Le divorce: la malédiction de l'Oscar, selon une étude canadienne," *HuffPost*, February 27, 2021.

31. Olle Folke and Johanna Rickne, "Top Jobs Lead to Divorce for Women, but Not for Men," *LSE Business Review*, July 11, 2019, blogs.lse.ac.uk.

32. Raymond Fisman et al., "Gender Differences in Mate Selection: Evidence from a Speed Dating Experiment," *Quarterly Journal of Economics* 121, no. 2 (February 2006).

33. bell hooks, *Communion: The Female Search for Love* (New York: William Morrow, 2002), 143–44.

34. bell hooks, *Communion*, 152–53.

35. bell hooks, *Communion*, 154

36. bell hooks, *Communion*, 155.

37. Eva Illouz, *La fin de l'amour: Enquête sur un désarroi contemporain* (Paris: Seuil, 2020), 120. In English: *The End of Love: A Sociology of Negative Relations* (London: Polity, 2021).

38. Illouz, *La fin de l'amour*, 105–6

39. "The Day Keanu Reeves Protected Winona Ryder on the Set of *Dracula*," *Vanity Fair*, June 23, 2020.

40. Titiou Lecoq, *Slate x Titiou* (newsletter), June 26, 2020.

41. *C à vous*, aired March 8, 2019, on France 5.

42. Jean Duncombe and Dennis Marsden, "Love and Intimacy: The Gender Division of Emotion and 'Emotion Work': A Neglected Aspect of Sociological Discussion of Heterosexual Relationships," *Sociology*. 27, no. 2 (1993).

43. Jane Birkin, *Munkey Diaries, 1957–1982* (London, W&N, 2020); *Post-scriptum: Le journal intime de Jane Birkin, 1982–2013* (Paris: Fayard, 2019). All the following quotations are taken from these two books.

44. Pierre Loti, *Madame Chrysanthème* (1887; Paris: Flammarion, 1900). In English: *Madame Chrysantheme*, trans. Laura Ensor (New York: Dutton, 1897), 7–8.

45. Loti, *Madame Chrysanthème*, 46.

46. Loti, *Madame Chrysanthème*, 216.

47. Michel Brix notes that Kuchuk Hanem "lived in (Esna), in Upper Egypt, on the west bank of the Nile. The Egyptian government had relegated prostitutes to Esna—which at the time made this spot a 'tourist attraction,' as one would say today" (Michel Brix, "Flaubert et Kuchuk Hanem: Un sonnet retrouvé," Centre Flaubert, flaubert.univ-rouen.fr).

48. Gustave Flaubert to Louise Colet, March 13, 1850, in *The Letters of Gustave Flaubert: 1830–1857*, trans. Francis Steegmuller (Cambridge: Belknap Press, 1980).

49. Edward W. Said, *Orientalism*, 1978, Kindle edition, 2014.

50. Gustave Flaubert to Louise Colet, March 27, 1853, in *The Letters of Gustave Flaubert: 1830–1857*, trans. Francis Steegmuller (Cambridge: Belknap Press, 1980).

51. Elisa Camiscioli and Christelle Taraud, "Économie politique de la sexualité coloniale et raciale," in *Sexualités, identités & corps colonisés*, ed. Gilles Boëtsch et al. (Paris: CNRS Éditions, 2019).

52. Serge Tcherkézoff, "La construction du corps sexualisé de la Polynésienne," in *Sexualités, identités & corps colonisés*.

53. Jean-François Staszak, "Paul Gauguin," in, *Sexe, race & colonies: la domination des corps du XVe siècle à nos jours*, ed. Pascal Blanchard et al. (Paris: La Découverte, 2018).

54. Léo Pajon, "*Gauguin—Voyage de Tahiti*: La pédophilie est moins grave sous les tropiques," *Jeune Afrique*, September 21, 2017.

55. Tarita Tériipaia, with Lionel Duroy, *Marlon Brando: Mon amour, ma déchirure* (Paris: XO Éditions, 2005).

56. Rokhaya Diallo and Grace Ly, "La geisha, la panthère, et la gazelle," October 9, 2018, in *Kiffe ta race*, podcast, 36:00, Binge Audio.

57. Diallo and Ly, "La geisha."

58. Catherine Durand, "Grace Ly: 'Je ne laisse plus rien passer,'" *Marie Claire*, April 2021.

59. Franchesca Ramsey, "The Weird History of Asian Sex Stereotypes," *Decoded*, MTV Impact, May 25, 2016, YouTube video, 6:13.

60. Jean-François Staszak and Christelle Taraud, "Les nouveaux territoires de la sexualité postcoloniale," in *Sexualités, identités & corps colonisés*.

61. Clément Pouré, "La Yellow Fever n'est rien d'autre qu'un fétichisme raciste," *Vice*, July 5, 2008.
62. Julien Brygo, "Profession, domestique," *Le Monde diplomatique*, September 2021.
63. Robin Zheng, "Why Yellow Fever Isn't Flattering: A Case Against Racial Fetishes," *Journal of the American Philosophical Association* 2, no. 3 (2016).
64. Zheng, "Why Yellow Fever Isn't Flattering."
65. Pauline Verduzier, "Le problème avec les hommes qui n'aiment que les femmes Asiatiques," *Slate (France)*, January 19, 2019.
66. Marion Bottero, "Le fantasme de la femme thaïlandaise et la crise occidentale de la masculinité," *Moussons* 29 (2017).
67. "Vincent Cassel: 'Les hommes? On n'est un peu que notre bite . . . ,'" *Closer*, February 9, 2011.
68. Valentin Etancelin, "Après les César, ce message de Vincent Cassel passe très mal," *HuffPost*, March 3, 2020.
69. Dalia Gebrial, "Decolonising Desire: The Politics of Love," Verso (blog), February 13, 2017, versobooks.com.
70. Zheng, "Why Yellow Fever Isn't Flattering."
71. Grace Ly, "Je suis une femme asiatique et j'en peux plus des hommes qui ne sortent qu'avec des Asiatiques," *Elle*, January 8, 2019.
72. Quoted in Bottero, "Le fantasme de la femmes thaïlandaise."
73. Adila Bennedjaï-Zou, "Les ambitieuses," May 29, 2019, in *Heureuse comme une Arabe en France*, podcast, 54:00, in *LSD, la série documentaire*, France Culture, radiofrance.fr/franceculture/podcasts/lsd-la-serie-documentaire/les-ambitieuses-2426555.
74. Bennedjaï-Zou, "Les ambitieuses."
75. Simone de Beauvoir, *Le deuxième sexe* (Paris: Gallimard, 1949). In English: *The Second Sex*, trans. Constance Borde and Sheila Malovany-Chevallier (New York: Knopf, 2010), 80.

2: Real Men

1. Shere Hite, *Women and Love: A Cultural Revolution in Progress* (New York: Alfred Knopf, 1987), 26–29.
2. See Sandra Lee Bartky, *Femininity and Domination: Studies in the Phenomenology of Oppression* (New York: Routledge, 1990); Camille Froidevaux-Metterie, *Un corps à soi* (Paris: Seuil, 2021).
3. Lorraine de Foucher, "Féminicides: 'La logique patriarcale la plus pure se loge au cœur de l'intime,'" *Le Monde*, June 3, 2020.

4. See Irene Zeilinger, *Non, c'est non. Petit manuel d'autodéfense à l'usage de toutes les femmes qui en ont marre de se faire emmerder sans rien dire* (Paris: La Découverte, 2008).

5. Gloria Steinem, *Revolution from Within: A Book of Self-Esteem* (London: Bloomsbury, 1992), 26.

6. *Féminicides*, dir. Lorraine de Foucher (Paris: Radio France 2, 2020).

7. Eva Illouz, *La fin de l'amour: Enquête sur un désarroi contemporain* (Paris: Seuil, 2020), 159–60. In English: *The End of Love: A Sociology of Negative Relations* (London: Polity, 2021).

8. Judith Duportail (@judithduportail_), Instagram, December 22, 2020.

9. Liv Strömquist, *The Reddest Rose: Romantic Love from the Greeks to Reality TV*, trans. Melissa Bowers (Seattle, WA: Fantagraphics, 2023).

10. Marie-France Hirigoyen, *Femmes sous emprise: Les ressorts de la violence dans le couple* (Paris: Poche, 2006), 90

11. Hirigoyen, *Femmes sous emprise*, 87.

12. Hirigoyen, *Femmes sous emprise*, 12.

13. See Mona Chollet, "When Women Start to Talk Back," in the chapter "The Dizzy Height" in *Sorcières: La puissance invaincue des femmes* (Paris: Zones, 2018). In English: *In Defense of Witches*, trans. Sophie Lewis (New York: St. Martin's Press, 2022).

14. Hirigoyen, *Femmes sous emprise*, 83.

15. Hirigoyen, *Femmes sous emprise*, 134.

16. Annette Lucas, *À contre-coups* (Paris: Éditions Xavier Barral, 2006).

17. Lucas, *À contre-coups*,

18. Hirigoyen, *Femmes sous emprise*, 20.

19. Hirigoyen, *Femmes sous emprise*, 22.

20. Judith Duportail, "#niceguy" and "Miss Emprise," April 2020, *Qui est Miss Paddle?*, podcast, 15:00 and 14:00, Amazon Music.

21. Sophie Lambda, *Tant pis pour l'amour: Ou comment j'ai survécu à un manipulateur* (Paris: Delcourt, 2019). In English: *So Much for Love: How I Survived a Toxic Relationship* (New York: First Second, 2022).

22. Elisende Coladan, "Pervers narcissiques ou enfants sains du patriarcat?," March 1, 2019, therapie-feministe-elisende.com.

23. Hirigoyen, *Femmes sous emprise*, 25.

24. Lucas, *À contre-coups*.

25. Lucas, *À contre-coups*.

26. Mathieu Palain, "Moi, violent?," February 25, 2020, in *Des hommes violents*, podcast, 28:00, Radio France Culture..

27. *Enquête Exclusive*, "Affaire Bertrand Cantat: Le document inédit," aired on November 24, 2019, on M6.

28. Mathieu Palain, "Victime et coupable," January 15, 2020, in *Des hommes violents*, podcast, 28:00, Radio France Culture.

29. An institutional response counts for a lot. While the rate of recidivism among violent partners is 45 percent in France, it dropped to 6 percent in Douai when Luc Frémiot, who had taken an initiative for strong measures, was the prosecutor there (between 2003 and 2010). The magistrate judged that the two-day workshops served no purpose and advocated a minimum of four months (Flora Sauvage, "Violences conjugales: 'Beaucoup de femmes victimes, vivent dans des camisoles de force qui entravent leurs libertés,'" Public Sénat, May 28, 2020, publicsenat.fr.

30. John Stoltenberg, *Refusing to Be a Man: Essays on Sex and Justice* (Portland, OR: Breitenbush Books, 1989), 11–16.

31. Alexandra Lange, with Laurent Briot, *Acquittée* (Paris: Michel Lafon, 2012).

32. Lucas, *À contre-coups*.

33. Annik Houel, Patricia Mercader, and Helga Sobota, *Crime passionnel, crime ordinaire*, Sociologie d'aujourd'hui (Paris: PUF, 2003).

34. "Le crime passionnel n'existe pas en droit français," *Elle*, November 3, 2017.

35. Stoltenberg, *Refusing to Be a Man*, 22.

36. Alissa Wenz, *À trop aimer* (Paris: Denoël, 2020).

37. Lucile Cipriani, "Mort de Marie Trintignant: Nul n'a su contourner l'agresseur," *Le devoir*, September 3, 2003.

38. Quoted in Jane Ward, *The Tragedy of Heterosexuality* (New York: NYU Press, 2020), 50.

39. Palain and Laffon, "Victime et coupable."

40. Peggy Orenstein, *Girls & Sex: Navigating the Complicated New Landscape* (New York: HarperCollins, 2016), 134.

41. Claire Fleury, "La première fois qu'il m'a frappée . . . ," *Le nouvel observateur*, June 7–13, 2007.

42. Hirigoyen, *Femmes sous emprise*.

43. Lucas, *À contre-coups*.

44. Houel, Mercader, and Sobota, *Crime passionnel, crime ordinaire*.

45. Houel, Mercader, and Sobota, *Crime assionnel, crime ordinaire*.

46. Fleury, "la première fois qu'il m'a frappée . . ."

47. Anne-Sophie Jahn, "Bertrand Cantat, enquête sur une omerta," *Le point*, November 29, 2017. In January 2020, Cantat lost the case he had brought against the weekly magazine for this article.

48. "Affaire Bertrand Cantat: Le document inédit."

49. Lange, *Acquitée*.

50. Lucas *À contre-coups*.

51. Lucas, *À contre-coups*.

52. Lucas, *À contre-coups*.

53. Lange, *Acquitée*.

54. Lange, *Acquitée*.

55. Palain and Laffon, "Victime et coupable."

56. "Mrs. X at the Gaslight," season 1, episode 6, *The Marvelous Mrs. Maisel*, written by Sheila Lawrence, directed by Scott Ellis, aired November 28, 2017, on Amazon Prime.

57. Isabelle Horlans, *L'amour (fou) pour un criminel* (Paris: Le Cherche Midi, 2015).

58. Horlans, *L'amour (fou) pour un criminel*.

59. Sheila Isenberg, *Women Who Love Men Who Kill: 35 True Stories of Prison Passion*, updated edition (New York: Simon and Schuster, 1991; New York: Diversion Books, 2021), 57. Citations refer to the Diversion edition.

60. Horlans, *L'amour (fou) pour un criminel*.

61. Horlans, *L'amour (fou) pour un criminel*.

62. Isenberg, *Women Who Love Men Who Kill*, 222.

63. Horlans, *L'amour (fou) pour un criminel*.

64. Horlans, *L'amour (fou) pour un criminel*.

65. Isenberg, *Women Who Love Men Who Kill*, 152.

66. Ann Rule, *The Stranger Beside Me: The Inside Story of Serial Killer Ted Bundy* (New York: Norton, 2022), xi.

67. Horlans, *L'amour (fou) pour un criminel*.

68. Isenberg, *Women Who Love Men Who Kill*, 107.

69. Isenberg, *Women Who Love Men Who Kill*, 201.

70. Horlans, *L'amour (fou) pour un criminel*, xx.

71. Isenberg, *Women Who Love Men Who Kill*, 122–32.

72. Anne-Cécile Sarfati, "Guy Georges, l'aveu fait aux femmes," *Elle*, April 2, 2001.

73. Sarfati, "Guy Georges."

74. Patricia Tourancheau, "'Avez-vous tué . . . ?' 'Oui,'" *Libération*, March 28, 2001.

75. Quoted in Nathalie Malet, "'Il manque encore des réponses,'" *Libération*, March 28, 2001.

76. Quoted in Tourancheau, "'Avez-vous tué . . . ?'‑'Oui.'"

77. Quoted in Sarfati, "Guy Georges."

78. Horlans, *L'amour (fou) pour un criminel*.

79. RJ Parker, *Serial Killer Groupies* (CreateSpace, 2013).

80. Horlans, *L'amour (fou) pour un criminel*.

81. Horlans, *L'amour (fou) pour un criminel*.

82. Parker, *Serial Killer Groupies*. This is obviously a very partial and paradoxical view of the role of the companion of a detainee, far from the difficulties and stigmatization experienced by the women who suffer this situation.

83. Horlans, *L'amour (fou) pour un criminel*.

84. "How a Florida Woman and Convicted Serial Killer on Death Row Met and Fell in Love," ABC News, August 21, 2015.

85. "In Love with a Serial Killer: Women Who Love Men Who Kill | Loving Murderers Documentary Part 2," Java Discover, December 16, 2021, YouTube video, 55:14. Danny Rolling singing in a courtroom in 1993: "Serial Killer Danny Rolling Serenades Sondra London," Sondra London Channel, October 3, 2020, YouTube video, 1:10.

86. Isenberg, *Women Who Love Men Who Kill*, chapter 8.

87. Horlans, *L'amour (fou) pour un criminel*.

88. Lucas, *À contre-coups*.

89. Robin Norwood, *Women Who Love Too Much: When You Keep Wishing and Hoping He'll Change* (New York: Tarcher, 1985), 193–94.

90. Houel, Mercader, and Sobota, *Crime passionnel, crime ordinaire*.

91. Hélène Châtelain, Claude Faber, and Armand Gatti, "Bertrand Cantat reste des nôtres," *Le Monde*, August 16, 2003.

92. Nelly Kaprièlian, "Cantat, un héros romantique?!," *Les inrockuptibles*, September 3, 2003.

93. Valérie Toranian, "La mort de Marie," *Elle*, August 11, 2003.

94. Bernard Comment, "Je n'oublie pas qui est Bertrand Cantat," *Les inrockuptibles*, August 27, 2003.

95. Liv Strömquist, *Les sentiments du Prince Charles* and *I'm Every Woman* (Paris: Rackham, 2012 and 2018, respectively).

96. Kaprièlian, "Cantat, un héros romantique?!"

97. Elizabeth Gilbert, *Big Magic: Creative Living Beyond Fear* (New York: Penguin, 2015), 213–14. I also advise you to read her extraordinary

novel *The Signature of All Things* (Riverhead Books, 2013) and the excellent *City of Girls* (Riverhead, 2019).

98. Wenz, *À trop aimer*.

99. Gilbert, *Big Magic*, 211.

100. Mona Chollet, "Machisme sans frontière (de classe)," *Le Monde Diplomatique*, May 2005.

101. *Paris Match*, January 27, 2005.

102. *Elle* (*France*), January 31, 2005.

103. Yann Perreau, "Couple de légende: Ali MacGraw et Steve McQueen, la passion destructrice," *Elle*, April 3, 2020.

104. Manou Farine, "Couple de légende: Miles Davis & Frances Taylor, Kings of Cool," *Elle*, May 7, 2020.

105. bell hooks, *All About Love: New Visions* (New York: William Morrow, 2000), 4.

106. hooks, *All About Love*, 6.

107. Quoted in Hirigoyen, *Femmes sous emprise*.

108. Denis de Rougemont, *Love in the Western World*, trans. Montgomery Belgion (Princeton, NJ: Princeton University Press, 1940).

109. hooks, *All About Love*, 17.

110. hooks, *All About Love*, 14.

3: Guardians of the Temple

1. Annie Ernaux, *Passion simple* (Paris: Gallimard, 1991). In English: *Simple Passion*, trans. Tanya Leslie (New York: Seven Stories Press, 2011).

2. Ernaux, *Passion simple*, 53.

3. Sonia Dayan-Herzbrun, "Production du sentiment amoureux et travail des femmes," *Cahiers Internationaux de Sociologie* 72 (Jan.– June 1982).

4. See Mona Chollet, *La tyrannie de la réalité* (Paris: Gallimard, 2004).

5. Albert Cohen, *Belle du Seigneur* (Paris: Gallimard, 1968). In English: *Her Lover (Belle du Seigneur)*, trans. David Coward (New York: Penguin Classic, 2005).

6. Dayan-Herzbrun, "Production du sentiment amoureux.

7. Victoire Tuaillon, "L'amour c'est pas pour les garçons," December 1, 2017, in *Les couilles sur la table*, podcast, 34:00, Binge Audio.

8. Andre Gorz, *Lettre à D.: Histoire d'un amour* (Paris: Galilee, 2006), 2. In English: *Letter to D: A Love Story*, trans. Julie Rose (London: Polity, 2020).

9. Shere Hite, *Women and Love: A Cultural Revolution in Progress* (New York: Alfred Knopf, 1987), 7.

10. Mona Chollet, *Beauté fatale: Les nouveaux visages d'une aliénation féminine* (Paris: La Decouverte, 2012).

11. Especially Edgar Cabanas and Eva Illouz, *Manufacturing Happy Citizens: How the Science and Industry of Happiness Control Our Lives* (London: Polity Press, 2019); Julia de Funès, *Développement (im)personnel: Le succès d'une imposture* (Paris: Editions de l'Observatoire, 2019).

12. bell hooks, *All About Love: New Visions* (New York: William Morrow, 2000), 12.

13. Leïla Slimani, "Reading Is Sexy," Konbini, May 26, 2020.

14. Melody Beattie, *Codependent No More: How to Stop Controlling Others and Start Caring for Yourself*, revised and updated (2011; New York: Spiegel & Grau, 2022).

15. hooks, *All About Love*, 66.

16. Judith Duportail, "#niceguy" and "Miss Emprise," April 2020, *Qui est Miss Paddle?*, podcast, 15:00 and 14:00, Amazon Music.

17. *Les rivières*, dir. Mai Hua (2019).

18. Marie-Carmen Garcia, *Amours clandestines: Nouvelle enquête: L'extraconjugalité durable à l'épreuve du genre* (Lyon, France: Presses Universitaires de Lyon, 2021).

19. Garcia, *Amours clandestines.*

20. Garcia, Amours clandestines.

21. Jane Ward, *The Tragedy of Heterosexuality* (New York: NYU Press, 2020), 56.

22. See Céline Bessière and Sibylle Gollac, *Le genre du capital: Comment la famille reproduit les inégalités* (Paris: La Découverte, 2020) [In English: *The Gender of Capital: How Families Perpetuate Wealth Inequality*, trans. Juliette Rogers (Cambridge, MA: Harvard University Press, 2023)] as well as Titiou Lecoq's podcast about money in the couple, *Rends l'argent*, on slate.fr.

23. Eva Illouz, *Why Love Hurts: A Sociological Explanation* (London: Polity, 2012), 74.

24. Dayan-Herzbrun, "Production du sentiment amoureux."

25. Wendy Langford, *Revolutions of the Heart: Gender, Power and the Delusions of Love* (London: Routledge, 1999), 25.

26. Eva Illouz, *La fin de l'amour: Enquête sur un désarroi contemporain*

(Paris: Seuil, 2020), 71. In English: *The End of Love: A Sociology of Negative Relations* (London: Polity, 2021).

27. "Quarante ans d'évolution de la société française," INSEE, November 19, 2019.

28. Zohor Djider, "Huit femmes au foyer sur dix ont eu un emploi par le passé," *INSEE Première*, no. 1463 (August 2013).

29. Dorothy C. Holland and Margaret A. Eisenhart, *Educated in Romance: Women, Achievement, and College Culture* (Chicago: University of Chicago Press, 1992). The quotations that follow are taken from this source.

30. Colette Dowling, *The Cinderella Complex: Women's Hidden Fear of Independence* (New York: Summit Books, 1981).

31. Dowling, *Cinderella Complex*.

32. Dowling, *Cinderella Complex*, chapter 1.

33. E. L. James, *Fifty Shades of Grey* (Naperville, IL: Bloom Books, 2012).

34. Garcia, *Amours clandestines*.

35. Penelope Russianoff, *Why Do I Think I Am Nothing Without a Man?* (New York: Bantam Books, 1982). The quotations that follow are taken from this source.

36. Russianoff, *Why Do I Think I Am Nothing Without a Man?*, 44.

37. Elisa Rojas, *Mister T. et moi* (Paris: La Belle Étoile, 2020). Dialogue translated by Susan Emanuel.

38. See Claire Marin, *Rupture(s)* (Paris: Éditions de l'Observatoire, 2019).

39. Robert A. Johnson, *We: Understanding the Psychology of Romantic Love* (San Francisco: Harper, 2009), xi, 179.

40. Gloria Steinem, *Revolution from Within: A Book of Self-Esteem* (London: Bloomsbury, 1992), 58.

41. Evelyn Le Garrec, *Un lit à soi: Itinéraires de femmes* (Paris: Seuil, 1979).

42. Sophie Fontanel, *L'envie* (2011; Paris: J'ai Lu, 2013).

43. Le Garrec, *Un lit à soi*.

44. Russianoff, *Why Do I Think I Am Nothing Without a Man?*, 69.

45. Fontanel, *L'envie*.

46. Russianoff, *Why Do I Think I Am Nothing Without a Man?*, 84.

47. Samia Miskina, "La Culture du Sexe sans Engagement," March 2020, in *Sexe Club*, podcast, 30:44, Spotify.

48. Fontanel, *L'envie*.

49. Holland and Eisenhart, *Educated in Romance*.

50. Russianoff, *Why Do I Think I Am Nothing Without a Man?*, 99.

51. *Ways of Seeing*, season 1, episode 2, "Women and Art," written by John Berger, aired January 15, 1972, BBC Two. This series is available on YouTube and as a book: John Berger, *Ways of Seeing* (London: British Broadcasting Corporation and Penguin Books, 1972).

52. Jenny Tinghui Zhang, "That Feeling When Another Woman Hypes You Up," *Cut*, February 4, 2020.

53. Jane Birkin, *Munkey Diaries, 1957–1982* (London: W&N, 2020), section 1979.

54. *Crazy Ex-Girlfriend*, season 1, episode 9, "I'm Going to the Beach with Josh and His Friends!," written by Rachel Bloom, Aline Brosh McKenna, and Dan Gregor, directed by Kenny Ortega, aired January 25, 2016, on CW. The song sequence is available on YouTube: youtube.com/watch?v=P6B-r3QQw9M.

55. Gloria Steinem and Eleanor Smeal, "Why 'Mrs. America' Is Bad for American Women," *Los Angeles Times*, July 30, 2020.

56. Rupi Kaur, *home body* (Kansas City: Andrews McMeel Publishing, 2020).

57. rupi kaur (@rupikaur_), Instagram, February 26, 2021.

58. Russianoff, *Why Do You Think I Am Nothing Without a Man?*, xviii.

59. Russianoff, *Why Do You Think I Am Nothing Without a Man?*, xiv.

60. Gorz, *Lettre à D.*, 56.

61. Liv Strömquist, *Les sentiments du Prince Charles* (Paris: Rackham, 2012).

62. Emma Clit, *La charge émotionnelle et autres trucs invisibles* (Paris: J'ai Lu, 2018).

63. Erin Rodgers (@ErinMRodgers), "I want the term 'gold-digger' to include dudes who look for a woman who will do tons of emotional labour for them," Twitter, June 2, 2016.

64. Melanie Hamlett, "Men Have No Friends and Women Bear the Burden," *Harper's Bazaar*, May 2, 2019. Quoted in Ward, *The Tragedy of Heterosexuality*, 20.

65. Quoted in Langford, *Revolutions of the Heart*, 70

66. According to Stéphane Rose's observation in *En finir avec le couple* (Paris: La Musardine, 2020).

67. Miskina, "La culture du sexe sans engagement."

68. Samhita Mukhopadhyay, *Outdated: Why Dating Is Ruining Your Love Life* (Berkeley: Seal Press, 2011), chapter 1.

69. Travis L. Stork, with Leah Furman, *Don't Be That Girl: A Guide to Finding the Confident, Rational Girl Within* (New York: Gallery Books, 2008).

70. Illouz, *La fin de l'amour*, 71.

71. Mukhopadhyay, *Outdated*, chapter 4.

72. Quoted in Illouz, *La fin de l'amour*, 65.

73. Sara-Vittoria El Saadawi, "plus pute que toutes les putes: Comment je suis entrée dans la prostitution gratuite," *Diacritik*, November 28, 2017, diacritik.com.

74. Langford, *Revolutions of the Heart*, 14–15.

75. Langford, *Revolutions of the Heart*.

76. Langford, *Revolutions of the Heart*, 87.

77. Langford, *Revolutions of the Heart*, 145.

78. Carol Gilligan and Naomi Snider, *Why Does Patriarchy Persist?* (London: Polity, 2018), 9, 22, 29 (Kindle introduction). You may hear Carol Gilligan interviewed by Victoire Tuaillon: "Ce que le patriarcat fait à l'amour," November 28, 2019, in *Les couilles sur la table*, podcast, 42:00, Binge Audio.

79. Gilligan and Snider, *Why Does Patriarchy Persist?*, introduction.

80. Gilligan and Snider, *Why Does Patriarchy Persist?*.

81. Gilligan and Snider, *Why Does Patriarchy Persist?*, chapter 1.

82. Gilligan and Snider, *Why Does Patriarchy Persist?*, chapter 4.

83. Gilligan and Snider, *Why Does Patriarchy Persist?*, chapter 7.

84. Gilligan and Snider, *Why Does Patriarchy Persist?*, chapter 10.

85. *Sex Education*, season 2, episode 8, written by Laurie Nunn, directed by Ben Taylor, aired January 17, 2020, on Netflix.

86. Gilligan and Snider, *Why Does Patriarchy Persist?*, 48.

87. Hite, *Women and Love*, 5.

88. Heather Havrilesky, "'I Only Want to Date Men Who've Been Through Therapy!,'" *Cut*, February 3, 2021.

89. Havrilesky, "'I Only Want to Date Men Who've Been Through Therapy!'"

90. Havrilesky, "'I Only Want to Date Men Who've Been Through Therapy!'"

91. bell hooks, *Communion: The Female Search for Love* (New York: William Morrow, 2002), 87–88.

92. Hite, *Women and Love*, 10, 11, 43.

93. Langford, *Revolutions of the Heart*, 134.

94. Liv Strömquist, *The Reddest Rose: Romantic Love from the Greeks to Reality TV*, trans. Melissa Bowers (Seattle, WA: Fantagraphics, 2023), 152, 128, 53, 122.

95. Sophie Fontanel (@sophiefontanel), Instagram, August 12, 2018.

4: The Great Dispossession

1. Agnès Giard, "Tu m'aimes, poupée?," *Glamour*, December 2004.

2. Agnès Giard, "Une marionnette sexuelle anatomique?," *Les 400 Culs* (blog), November 23, 2020.

3. Laura Mulvey, "Visual Pleasure and Narrative Cinema," *Screen* 16, no. 3 (Autumn 1975).

4. John Berger, *Ways of Seeing* (London: British Broadcasting Corporation and Penguin Books, 1972); *Ways of Seeing*, season 1, episode 2, "Women and Art," written by John Berger, aired January 15, 1972, BBC Two.

5. I wrote a preface ("Enjoliver la domination") for the revised edition of Anne-Marie Lugan Dardigna's 1974 anthology, *femmes-femmes sur papier glacé: La presse "feminine," fonction idéologique* (Paris: La Découverte, 2019).

6. Anne-Maria Dardigna, *Les châteaux d'Éros, ou les infortunes du sexe des femmes* (Paris: Maspero, 1980), 107.

7. Dardigna, *Les châteaux d'Eros*, 108.

8. Manon Garcia, *We Are Not Born Submissive: How Patriarchy Shapes Women's Lives* (Princeton, NJ: Princeton University Press, 2023), 143, 154.

9. Barbara L. Fredrickson and Tomi-Ann Roberts, "Objectification Theory: Toward Understanding Women's Lived Experiences and Mental Health Risks," *Psychology of Women Quarterly* 21, no. 2 (June 1997), 176.

10. Fredrickson and Roberts, "Objectification Theory."

11. Fredrickson and Roberts, "Objectification Theory," 177.

12. Mona Chollet, "Les femmes sont-elles des objets?," in the chapter "The Soliloquy of the Dominant: Femininity as Subordination" in *Beauté fatale: Les nouveaux visages d'une aliénation féminine* (Paris: La Decouverte, 2012).

13. Quoted in Sophie Elmhirst, "Brazilian Butt Lift: Behind the World's Most Dangerous Cosmetic Surgery," *Guardian*, February 9, 2021.

14. Emmanuelle Ducournau, "Quand la lingerie se rhabille," *Marie Claire*, January 4, 2018.

15. Ducournau, "Quand la lingerie se rhabille."

16. Dorothée Duchemin, "Poids, cheveux blancs, visage au naturel: Le confinement a aidé des femmes à mieux s'accepter," *Slate (France)*, September 30, 2020.

17. Aniya Das, "Now That Beauty Routines Are Over, I'm Letting My 'Tache Grow Out," *gal-dem*, April 10, 2020, gal-dem.com.

18. Myriam Levain, "Journal du confinement: La revanche du jogging," *Cheek*, March 29, 2020.

19. Quoted in Audrey Renault, "Le confinement est-il l'occasion de dire fuck aux injonctions à la féminité?," *Cheek*, April 9, 2020.

20. A state theorized and described by Mihaly Csikszentmihalyi, *Flow: The Psychology of Optimal Experience* (New York: Harper and Row, 1990).

21. Fredrickson and Roberts, "Objectification Theory," 186.

22. Levain, "Journal du confinement."

23. Camille Froidevaux-Metterie, "Féminisme et confinement, du pire vers le meilleur?," *Libération*, March 24, 2020.

24. Conner Shin (@thatconnieshin), "Male authors trying to show a woman at rock bottom," Twitter, November 28, 2020.

25. And I come across these words by bell hooks: "Our feet plant us on Earth, and the well-being of our feet is the ground we must stand on if we would be self-loving. Early on in the feminist movement we called attention to the female foot and the shoes offered us by designers who for the most part would never walk an inch, let alone a mile, in female shoes. Women need to remember the importance of caring for the well-being of our feet," *Communion*, 109–10.

26. Vanessa Springora, *Le consentement* (Paris: Grasset, 2020). In English: *Consent: A Memoir*, trans. Natasha Lehrer (New York: HarperVia, 2021).

27. Springora, *Le consentement*, 90.

28. Springora, *Le consentement*, 134.

29. Springora, *Le consentement*, 168.

30. Springora, *Le consentement*, 174.

31. Springora, *Le consentement*, 177.

32. Emily Ratajkowski, "Buying Myself Back: When Does a Model Own Her Own Image?," *Cut*, September 15, 2020, thecut.com/article/emily -ratajkowski-owning-my-image-essay.html.

33. Ratajkowki, "Buying Myself Back."

34. Pauline Réage, *Histoire d'O*, followed by *Retour à Roissy* (1954 and 1970; Paris: Le Livre de Poche, 1999). In English: *The Story of O* and *Return to the Chateau*, trans. Sabine d'Estrée (New York: Ballantine, 2013), 31–32.

35. Dardigna, *Les châteaux d'Éros*.

36. Dardigna, *Les châteaux d'Éros*.

37. "Céline Sciamma et Annie Ernaux, Sœurs de Combat," *La Déferlante*, no. 1, March 2021.

38. Aurélia Aurita, *Fraise et chocolat 1* & *2* (Brussels: Les Impressions Nouvelles, 2006 and 2007).

39. This material is gathered on the site of the Collectif des Créatrices de Bande Dessinée Contre le Sexisme: bdegalite.org.

40. "*Fraise et chocolat*—L'intégrale—Aurélia Aurita—Les impressions nouvelles," ActuaBD, August 20, 2014, actuabd.com.

41. Quentin Girard, "L'amour dure '286 Jours,'" *Libération*, February 21, 2014.

42. Nancy Friday, *My Secret Garden: Women's Sexual Fantasies*, (1973; New York: Rosetta Books, 2013). The book is highly problematic in certain aspects (e.g., the chapter on "the Black man"), but it remains an essential source on a seldom-treated subject.

43. Friday, *My Secret Garden*, chapter 1.

44. Friday, *My Secret Garden*, chapter 2.

45. Kate Millett, *Sexual Politics* (New York: Doubleday, 1970).

46. I bitterly regret having formerly taken a position in favor of the penalization of clients of prostitution, because I believed in the promises being made at the time to guarantee the physical and material security of sex workers. Nor do I believe in giving up on any critical analysis of prostitution, and in particular of its signifying men's "right to sex" (who are the overwhelming majority of clients) and of a sexuality entirely devoted to satisfying their desires. It ought to be possible to combine solidarity and critique, just as we may both defend the rights of male and female employees while criticizing the wage-earning system.

47. Jonathan McIntosh, "Predatory Romance in Harrison Ford Movies," Pop Culture Detective, March 31, 2017, YouTube video, 16:59.

48. Wendy Delorme, "Merveilleuse Angélique," in Isabelle Boisclair and Catherine Dussault Frenette, eds., *Women désirantes: Art, littérature, représentations* (Montréal: Les Éditions du Remue-ménage, 2013).

49. Boisclair and Frenette, *Women désirantes*.

50. Régine Deforges, *O m'a dit: Entretiens avec Pauline Réage* (1975; Paris: Le Livre de Poche, 1985). In English: *Confessions of O: Conversations with Pauline Réage*, trans. Sabine d'Estrée (New York: Viking Press, 1979), 213.

51. Deforges, *O m'a dit*, 138.

52. Réage, *Histoire d'O*, 97.

53. Deforges, *O m'a dit*, 41.

54. Deforges, *O m'a dit*, 129.

55. Claire Richard, *Les chemins de désir* (Paris: Seuil, 2019), 78.

56. Richard, *Les chemins de désir*, 79.

57. Friday, *My Secret Garden*.

58. *Safe Word*, dir. Erika Lust (LustCinema, 2020).

59. Jean Paulhan, "Le bonheur dans l'esclavage," in Réage, *Histoire d'O*, xxiv, xxxiv.

60. Madeleine Chapsal, "Le choc d'*Histoire d'O*," *L'express*, September 1, 1975.

61. "La polémique sur *Histoire d'O* s'amplifie," *Le Monde*, September 19, 1975. MLF (feminist) activists pointed out that the film premiere coincided with a Marseille court decision to charge the perpetrators of the rape of two young Belgian lesbians simply with misdemeanors, like an attack on decency. The young women's lawyers, including the famous Gisèle Halimi, got the case transferred to the Court of Assises and made the trial a decisive moment in the recognition of rape as a crime punishable by fifteen years in prison (in 1980).

62. Dominique Aury, *Vocation: Clandestine* (Paris: Gallimard, 1999).

63. Deforges, *O m'a dit*.

64. Pauline Réage, "A Girl in Love," in *Retour à Roissy*, 207.

65. Réage, "A Girl in Love," 205.

66. Paulhan, "Le bonheur dans l'esclavage."

67. Deforges, *O m'a dit*, 73, 141.

68. St. Jorre, "The Unmasking of O," *New Yorker*, July 24, 1994.

69. Desforges, *O m'a dit*, 137–38.

70. Aury, *Vocation*.

71. Aury, *Vocation*.

72. Richard, *Les chemins de désir*, 51.

73. Delorme, "Merveilleuse Angélique."

74. Lynne Segal, "Sensual Uncertainty, or Why the Clitoris Is Not Enough," in eds. Sue Cartledge and Joanna Ryan, *Sex and Love: New Thoughts on Old Contradictions* (London: The Women's Press, 1983).

75. Cheryl Strayed, *Tiny Beautiful Things* (New York: Vintage Books, 2012).

76. Strayed, *Tiny Beautiful Things*.

77. Friday, *My Secret Garden*, xvii-xviii.

78. Friday, *My Secret Garden*, 164.

79. Richard, *Les chemins de désir*.

80. Deforges, *O m'a dit*, 81.

81. Deforges, *O m'a dit*, 146.

INDEX

Abélard, Peter, 7
Abramović, Marina, 4
actresses, 68–69, 187
ActuaBD, 236–37
L'affaire SK1, 136
age, 75
    youth, 61, 77, 78, 91
L'âge d'homme (Leiris), 28
Ageorges-Skinner, Sandrine, 131
Albert II, Prince of Monaco, 58
All About Love (hooks), 15
Allegory with Venus and Cupid, An
    (Bronzino), 223
Amnesty International, 131
L'amour sous algorithme (Duportail), 41
Angélique, Marquise des Anges, 243–44
anger, 13
Anna Karenina (Tolstoy), 45
Arbid, Danielle, 235n
Artist Is Present, The (Abramović), 4
artists, 146–52
Asakura, Keiryû, 220–21
Asian women, 78–83, 88–97
athletes, 64–65
À trop aimer (Wenz), 114–15
attachiante, 195
Aubade, 224, 227
Auffret, Séverine, 45
Aurita, Aurélia, 236–37
Aziyadé (Loti), 83

Bacchus, Ceres, and Cupid (von Aachen),
    222
Bachelor, The, 187, 196
Badiou, Alain, 2
Balzac, Honoré de, 64

Barry, John, 77
Barry, Kate, 76
Bartky, Sandra Lee, 100
Bataille, Georges, 240
Baudelaire, Charles, 63
Beattie, Melody, 161–62
Beaulieu, Baptiste, 54–55
Beauté fatale (Chollet), 225
beauty, 61, 63–64, 75, 77, 78, 160,
    187, 229, 230
Beauty and the Beast, 142
Beauvoir, Simone de, 97, 175, 224
Beineix, Jean-Jacques, 29
Belle du Seigneur (Cohen), 30–38, 144,
    154, 156, 180, 245
Bennedjaï-Zou, Adila, 95–96
Berger, Anya Bostock, 187–88
Berger, John, 187–88, 222–23
Bergman, Ingmar, 146
Bernardo, Paul, 128
Berry, Halle, 68
"Beyond Liberation: Confessions of a
    Dependent Woman" (Dowling),
    174
Bianchi, Kenneth, 130, 132
Birkin, Jane, 76–79, 189
Black, Ellie, 13
Black women, 86–93, 224
Blixen, Karen, 155
Bloom, Rachel, 35
bodily functions, 32–35
Boilet, Frédéric, 236–37
Bolin, Oscar Ray, 132, 139
Bolin, Rosalie, 132, 139
Bonder, Glenio, 37–38
Book, Shirlee, 130, 132

boots, 230–31
Bordo, Susan, 60
Bottero, Marion, 91, 94
Bougainville, Louis-Antoine de, 84
Bram Stoker's Dracula, 74
Brando, Cheyenne, 86
Brando, Marlon, 85–86, 148–49
Brazilian butt lift, 225
breast augmentation, 225
breastfeeding, 59–60
Breton, André, 63
Brice, Patrick, 131
Bronzino, 223
Bruni, Carla, 57–58, 70
Bullock, Sandra, 69
Bundy, Ted, 130–31
Byron, George Gordon, Lord, 216

Camiscioli, Elisa, 82
Campbell, Judy, 76
Camus, Albert, 252
Cannes Film Festival, 3
Cantat, Bertrand, 110–11, 114–16,
    120–21, 144–47
Carver, Raymond, 148
Cassel, Vincent, 85, 92
Cathars, 29
Catholicism, 141–42, 240, 244
Cavill, Henry, 63
Chalu, Marie-Julie, 86–87
Charlene, Princess of Monaco, 58
Charles III, 58
Charpentier, Coline, 54, 55
Châteaux d'Éros, Les (Dardigna), 223,
    240, 244
Châtelain, Hélène, 144
Chemins du désir, Les (Richard), 246
children
    abuse of, 151
    domestic violence and, 106–7,
        118–21
    having, 26, 43–44, 46, 52, 167–68

Chinese foot-binding, 61
Choisir la Cause des Femmes, 53
Christianity, 141
    Catholicism, 141–42, 240, 244
Cinderella Complex, 172
Cipriani, Lucile, 116
Cléry, Corinne, 248
Closer, 92
clothing, 227–29
    lingerie, 224, 226–27
    shoes, 230–31
Codependent No More (Beattie), 161–62
Coffin, Alice, 16, 23
cohabitation, 26, 47–56
Cohen, Albert, 36n, 37
    Belle du Seigneur, 30–38, 144, 154,
        156, 180, 245
Cohen, Bella, 36
Coladan, Elisende, 108–9
colonization, 78, 79, 82–83, 85, 86, 93,
    95, 101
Comment, Bernard, 145
"Common Program for Women," 53
Communion (hooks), 210–11
"Compulsory Heterosexuality and
    Lesbian Existence" (Rich), 16–17
Consentement, Le (Springora), 232–34,
    240
consumerist attitude toward dating, 103–4
cooking, 51–52, 55
Coppola, Francis Ford, 74
cosmetic surgery, 225
courtly love and troubadours, 29, 31, 140
Covid-19 pandemic, 43, 51–52, 179,
    227–29
Cranach, Lucas, the Elder, 187
Crawford, Joan, 68
Crazy Ex-Girlfriend, 35, 189–90
Cut, 209–10

Da Cruz, Christelle, 55
Dalida, 154–55, 157

Dardigna, Anne-Marie, 28, 33, 223, 235, 240, 244

Darrigrand, Mariette, 226

Das, Aniya, 227

dating
  sites and apps for, 34, 41, 91, 103, 195–96, 199, 225
  consumerist attitude toward, 103–4

Dauphiné libéré, 114

Davis, Bette, 68

Davis, Miles, 149–50

Dayan-Herzbrun, Sonia, 155, 157, 167–68

de Baecque, Antoine, 146

de Cleyre, Voltairine, 51, 52, 56

Delorme, Wendy, 243–44, 246, 252–53, 257, 258

Delphy, Christine, 252, 257

Deluc, Édouard, 85

Dent, Grace, 49

DePaulo, Bella, 53–54

dependence, female, 168–79, 192–93, 197
  becoming independent, 179–81

dependence, male, 192–94

Despentes, Virginie, 17, 18

detachment, 205, 207–10

Deuxième sexe, Le (Beauvoir), 97

devotion, 141, 216–18

Dhée, Amandine, 10

Diallo, Rokhaya, 87–88

Diana, Princess of Wales, 58

Dibon, Marie-Alice, 101–2

Didrikson, Babe, 66

Diter, Kevin, 158

Djian, Philippe, 29

Doillon, Lou, 76

domestic employment, 89–90

domestic tasks, 9, 53–56
  cooking, 51–52, 55

domination and submission, 58

Don Draper effect, 207–8

Don't Be That Girl (Stork), 196–97

Dostoyevsky, Fyodor, 192

Dowling, Colette, 172–74

"dumping *amoureux*," 166–67

Duncombe, Jean, 75–76

Dupond-Moretti, Éric, 129

Duportail, Judith, 41, 103, 107–8, 163, 195–96

Dupouy, Alexandre, 95–96

Dutroux, Marc, 129

economic inferiority, 67–71

Eisenhart, Margaret A., 169–71, 186

Elle, 135, 145, 149

El Saadawi, Sara-Vittoria, 199

Emmanuelle, 248

emotional needs of women, 195–97

emotions of men, 221–22
  men's detachment from, 207–10
  reverence for, 114–18, 194–95

Empire Strikes Back, The, 242, 258–59

employment, 169

L'emprise, 119–20

End of Love, The (Illouz), 50

L'envie (Fontanel), 182

Equal Rights Amendment (ERA), 190–91

Ernaux, Annie, 2, 153–56, 235–36

exercise, 62–63

L'express, 248–49

extramarital relationships, 164–65

Faber, Claude, 144

Fantôme d'Orient (Loti), 83

feminism, 15–16, 18–22, 23, 28, 53, 96, 102, 146, 156, 161, 190, 196, 197, 203–4, 216, 223, 236
  Histoire d'O and, 248–49, 252
  "pro-sex" versus "radical," 240
  red pill of, 6, 58
  sexual fantasies and, 235, 248–49, 252–56

feminist pornography, 246, 257

Femme actuelle, 228
Femme d'à côté, La, 144
Fey, Tina, 226n
fidelity, 26, 40–41
Fifty Shades of Grey (James), 175
Flaubert, Gustave
    Kuchuk Hanem and, 81–82
    Madame Bovary, 155–56, 180
Fontanel, Sophie, 182–84, 218
food, 59–61, 66
    cooking, 51–52, 55
foot-binding, 61
Ford, Harrison, 242, 258–59
Fraise et chocolat (Aurita), 236–37
Francis, Bev, 65–66
Fredrickson, Barbara L., 224, 229
Friday, Nancy, 237–39, 246, 255, 256
Froidevaux-Metterie, Camille, 100,
    227, 229
Fuller, Margaret, 7

Gainsbourg, Charlotte, 76
Gainsbourg, Serge, 77–79
Gallimard, Gaston, 251
Game of Thrones, 66–67
Gandhi, Mahatma, 101
Garcia, Manon, 58, 224
Garcia, Marie-Carmen, 54, 164, 167, 175
Gatti, Armand, 144
Gauguin, Paul, 84–85
Gauguin: Voyage de Tahiti, 85
Gay, Amandine, 86
Gay Liberation Front, 16
gay men, living arrangements of, 50–51
Gebrial, Dalia, 92
Génie lesbian, Le (Coffin), 16
Georges, Guy, 128, 132, 134–37
Giard, Agnès, 220–21
Gilbert, Elizabeth, 147, 148
Gilligan, Carol, 203–7
Godwin, William, 48
Gone with the Wind (Mitchell), 154

Gorz, André, 27–28, 46–47, 159, 193
Gorz, Dorine, 27–28, 46–47, 159, 193
Goude, Jean-Paul, 88
Grains de beauté, Les (Rezvani), 45
Grande Odalisque (Ingres), 222
Grant, Alexandra, 74
Gray, John, 21
Great Wall of China, 4
Green, Julien, 154
Groult, Benoîte, 28
Guène, Faïza, 88
Guerrilla Girls, 222
Guillemin, Marcelino, 113, 125
Guimard, Paul, 28

Haddad, Joumana, 13
Halimi, Gisèle, 53
Hamidi, Jamila, 131
Hamlett, Melanie, 195
Harcèlement moral, Le (Hirigoyen),
    101–2, 107
Harris, Joseph, 50–51
Haslam, Nick, 34
Havrilesky, Heather, 209–10
Hefner, Hugh, 166
height, 57–61, 70
Héloïse, 7
helplessness, 177
hentai, 257–58
Héritier, Françoise, 59–60
Herpin, Nicolas, 59
heterosexuality, 15–24
    deep, 20–22, 231
    misogyny and, 19–20
Heureuse comme une Arabe en France,
    94–95
Hirigoyen, Marie-France, 101–2,
    104–7, 109, 118
Histoire d'O (Réage), 235, 244–45,
    247–52, 260, 261
Hite, Shere, 99, 160, 208, 211
Hockney, David, 150

Holland, Dorothy C., 169–71, 185–86
Home Body (Kaur), 191
Homolka, Karla, 128
homophobia, 18, 20, 113
hooks, bell, 14, 15, 26, 70, 150–52, 161, 162, 210–11
Horlans, Isabelle, 128, 137
Houel, Annik, 16, 114, 119, 143, 145–46
Hua, Mai, 163
Hugo, Victor, 63
Huston, Nancy, 49

Idiot, The (Dostoyevsky), 192
Illouz, Eva, 33–34, 50, 71, 74, 102–4, 167, 169, 197–98
Inception, 243
In Defense of Witches (Chollet), 14, 176, 177, 179, 232
independence, 179–81
    detachment and, 205
Indiana Jones, 242
individualism, 161, 162
Indochina, 79
inferiority, 57–98, 106
    Asian women and, 78–83, 88–97
    Black women and, 86–93
    helplessness, 177
    physical, 57–67
    professional and economic, 67–71
Ingres, Jean-Auguste-Dominique, 222
Inrockuptibles, 116, 145
Institute for Contemporary Publishing Archives, 234
intelligence, 70
Into the Gloss, 35
introspection, 160–61
Isenberg, Sheila, 129, 133, 138, 140
Istanbul Convention, 124

Jablonski, Phillip Carl, 137
Jaeckin, Just, 248

Jaffé, Philip, 129, 141
James, E. L., 175
Johnson, Robert A., 180–81
Jones, Grace, 87–88
Judgment of Paris, 187, 190
Jung, Carl, 180
Jusqu'à la garde, 102, 111

Kahlo, Frida, 7, 40, 48–49
Kaprièlian, Nelly, 145, 147
Karpf, Anne, 62
Kaur, Rupi, 191–92
Kiffe ta race, 88
Kleiner, Véronique, 59
Klossowski, Pierre, 240
Kuchuk Hanem, 81–82
Kunakey, Tina, 92

Lady Comes to Her Lover's House in a Rainstorm, A, 1–2
Lamb, Caroline, 215–16
Lambda, Sophie, 108
Landru, Henri Désiré, 128
Lange, Alexandra, 113, 119–20, 122–25
Langford, Wendy, 8, 200–204, 211–12
Lavoine, Marc, 79
Lawrence, D. H., 239
Lecoq, Titiou, 75
Le Garrec, Évelyne, 52–53, 182
Legrand, Xavier, 102
Leiris, Michel, 28
lesbians, 15–19, 21, 51, 257
Lesseps, Emmanuèle de, 16, 22, 24
Lettre à D (Gorz), 27–28, 47, 159, 193
Levain, Myriam, 227, 229
Libération, 144, 237
Lindon, Vincent, 75
lingerie advertisements, 224, 226–27
"little wives," 82, 85, 89
living arrangements, 26, 47–56
London, Sondra, 130, 139
Loti, Pierre, 79–83, 94

love, 2–9, 12–15, 138–39, 211
  falling in, 200–204, 212
  longer-term, 26–27, 38–47, 50, 51
  male attitudes toward, 158–60, 164
  passion versus, 151
  revolution and counter-revolution in, 200–205, 213
  separating sex from, 197–98
love, women's attitudes toward, 153–219
  caregiver role and, 165–66
  dependence and, 168–79, 192–93
  "dumping *amoureux*" and, 166–67
  maternity and, 167–68
  and relationships with other women, 185–92
  sentimentality and, 198
Love Actually, 55–56
Love in the Western World (Rougemont), 29
love stories, 7, 25–30
Lust, Erika, 246, 247
Ly, Grace, 88–89, 93

MacGraw, Ali, 149, 150
MacKinnon, Catharine, 58
Macpherson, Elle, 62
Madama Butterfly (Puccini), 79
Madame Bovary (Flaubert), 155–56, 180
Madame Chrysanthème (Loti), 79–83, 94
Madame Figaro, 228
Mad Men, 207–8
Madmoizelle, 228
Madonna, 62
Magnotta, Luka Rocco, 137
Mailer, Norman, 239, 240
male gaze, 222, 223, 227, 228
Mandiargues, André-Pieyre de, 223–24
Manne, Kate, 117
Manson, Charles, 128
Mara, Rooney, 150
Marcos, Ferdinand, 89

Mariage de Loti, Le (Loti), 83, 84
Marie Claire, 75, 226
Marsden, Dennis, 75–76
Marshall, Garry, 175
Marvelous Mrs. Maisel, The, 72–73, 127
Matrix, The, 6, 74
Matzneff, Gabriel, 232–34, 240
Mazursky, Paul, 177
McIntosh, Jonathan, 242–43
McQueen, Steve, 149, 150
Men Are from Mars, Women Are from Venus (Gray), 21
Mercader, Patricia, 16, 114, 119, 143, 145–46
Mere Preferences Argument (MPA), 92–93
#MeToo movement, 9, 226, 232
Metropolitan Museum of Art, 222
Miller, Alice, 162
Miller, Henry, 239, 240
Millet, Kate, 240
Miskina, Samia, 184
misogyny, 29, 36, 97
  heterosexuality and, 19–20
  internalized, 131
Mister T. et moi (Rojas), 178
Moix, Yann, 75
Monde, 53
monogamy, 40
Motocyclette, La (Mandiargues), 22–23
Mouglalis, Anna, 62
Mrs. America, 190–91
Mukhopadhyay, Samhita, 196–98
Mulvey, Laura, 222
Munch, Edvard, 146
murderers, attraction to, 120–21, 127–43, 167, 180
murders of abusive partners, 119, 123
murders of women, 6, 105, 114
  as crimes of passion, 143–46, 151
  "feminicide" term for, 143
  see also violence, domestic

muscles, 62–63, 65
Museum of Modern Art, 4
music, 45
Musset, Alfred de, 7
My Secret Garden (Friday), 237–39, 255

narcissism, 102–3, 108
narcissistic restoration, 203
National Institute of Statistics and
  Economic Studies (INSEE), 104
Nehring, Cristina, 6–9, 14, 40, 48
New York, 174
New Yorker, 13, 251
New York Times, 58
Nolan, Christopher, 243
Normal People, 25–26
Norwood, Robin, 142
Notre-Dame de Paris (Hugo), 63
Nouvelle revue française, 244n
novels, 168
nuclear family, 52, 53
nudes, 222

objectification, 224, 229, 231–32
open relationships, 39–40
orgasm, 10, 199, 238, 239, 253
Orientalism (Said), 81
Oscars, 68–69
Outdated (Mukhopadhyay), 196
Out of Africa (film), 155
Ouvrir la voix, 86
Ovidie, 246

Pajon, Léo, 85
Pakora, Sabine, 87
Papin, Line, 79
Paris, 231
Parisien, 135
Paris match, 57–58, 144, 149
Parvati, 216

passion, 236
  crimes of, 143–46, 149, 151
  love versus, 151
  Rougemont on, 29–31, 143, 151,
    180, 181
  Passion simple (Ernaux), 2, 153–56,
    235–36
patriarchy, 23, 24, 203–6
  deep heterosexuality and, 22
  "healthy children of," 108–9
Paulhan, Jean, 235, 244n, 247–51, 260,
  261
Paulus, Caroline von, 79
Pays lointains, Les (Green), 154
Peck, M. Scott, 150
Phèdre (Racine), 154
Philippines, 89–90
Phillips, Adam, 148
philosophy, 161
Phoenix, Joaquin, 150
physical inferiority, 57–67
Piaf, Édith, 154
Picasso, Pablo, 146
Pikul, Mary Bain, 7–8, 132
Pivot, Bernard, 232
Playboy, 166
Polanski, Roman, 146–47
Pollack, Sydney, 155
Pollock, Jackson, 146
Pons, Frédérique, 135–37
pornography, 246, 247, 257
  hentai, 257–58
*Pourquoi les femmes sont-elles plus petites
  que les hommes?*, 59
power, balance of, 67–71
Preciado, Paul B., 63
preferences, romantic and sexual,
  92–93
Pretty Woman, 175
Prince, Richard, 234
professional inferiority, 67–71
Progrès, 114

prostitutes, 83, 89
psychological attacks, 105–6
Psychology in the Bathroom (Haslam), 34
puberty, 224
Public, 62
Puccini, Giacomo, 79
Pygmalion, 220

Queen's Gambit, The, 230
Questions féministes, 16
Qui est Miss Paddle?, 107

Racine, Jean, 154
Radwańska, Agnieszka, 64
Rády, Krisztina, 120–21, 145
Ramsey, Franchesca, 89
rape, 100, 117, 243, 244, 258–59
    conjugal, 107
    in fantasies, 254, 255, 258–61
Ratajkowski, Emily, 234
Raymond, Michel, 60
Réage, Pauline, *Histoire d'O*, 235, 244–45, 247–52, 260, 261
Reddest Rose, The (Strömquist), 215–17
Reeves, Keanu, 74–75
Renard, Noémie, 61
Revolution from Within (Steinem), 101, 181–82
Rezvani, Danièle "Lula," 43–44, 46–47, 159
Rezvani, Serge, 43–45, 47, 159
Rich, Adrienne, 16–17
Richard, Claire, 246, 252, 257
Rilke, Rainer Maria, 49–50
rivalry
    female, 187–92
    male, 190, 192
Rivera, Diego, 7, 40, 48–49
Rivières, Les, 163
Robbe-Grillet, Alain, 240

Roberts, Tomi-Ann, 224, 229
Rodgers, Erin, 195
Róisín, Fariha, 35
Rojas, Elisa, 178
Rolling, Danny, 130, 139
romance literature, 168
Roman d'une maison, Le (Rezvani), 44–45
Rooney, Sally, 25
Rougemont, Denis de, 29–31, 37, 40–42, 140, 143, 151, 180, 181
Rubens, Peter Paul, 187
Rule, Ann, 131
Russianoff, Penelope, 177, 179, 183, 184, 186, 192–93
Ryder, Winona, 74–75

Safe Word, 247
Said, Edward, 81
Saint Phalle, Niki de, 150
St. Vincent Millay, Edna, 7
Sand, George, 7
Sarkozy, Nicolas, 57–58
Sastre, Peggy, 60
scarcity mentality, 191–92
Schapiro, Miriam, 172
Schlafly, Phyllis, 191
Schlesinger, Peter, 150
Schultz, Jason, 20
Schwarzenegger, Arnold, 65
Sciamma, Laurent, 20, 231
Scott, Travers, 40
security paradox, 212
Segal, Lynne, 253, 257
self-esteem and self-confidence, 11, 78, 100–101, 107–8, 212, 213
self-help books, 161–63, 195
self-love, 162–63
self-respect, 217
sentimentality, 14, 28, 198
sex dolls, 220–21
Sexe Club, 184

Sex Education, 206–7
sexual activity, 182–85, 197–200
  hookup culture and, 199
  separating love from, 197–98
sexual dimorphism, 60–61
sexual fantasies of men, 222, 252
sexual fantasies of women, 235, 237–47,
  250, 252–61
  cultural influences on, 243–45,
    252–53, 258
  feminism and, 235, 248–49, 252–56
  of lesbians, 257
  masochistic, 252, 253, 256–58
  rape in, 254, 255, 258–61
  transgression in, 246–47, 257
sexual harassment, 226
sexual identity, re-creation of, 112
sexual orientation, 18–19
shame, 34, 35, 100
Sharapova, Maria, 64
Shiva, 216
shoes, 230–31
Skinner, Hank, 131
Sklar, Julia, 51
slavery, 83, 86, 93
Smeal, Eleanor, 190–91
smiling, 62
Snider, Naomi, 203–6
Sobota, Helga, 16, 114, 119, 143,
  145–46
social status, 67–71, 77
Soumahoro, Maboula, 86
Spadoni, Carol, 137
Spectre, 243
Springora, Vanessa, 232–34, 240
Sprinkle, Annie, 246
Star Wars, 242
Staszak, Jean-François, 85
Stefani, Gwen, 62
Steinem, Gloria, 64–66, 73–74, 101,
  181–82, 190–91
Stoltenberg, John, 111–12, 114

Strayed, Cheryl, 254–55
Strömquist, Liv, 10, 103, 146, 193–94,
  215–17
"Strongest Woman in America, The"
  (Steinem), 64–65
students, study of, 169–72, 185–86
submission and domination, 58
Swank, Hilary, 62, 69

Tahiti, 84–85
Tant pis pour l'amour (Lambda),
  108
Taraud, Christelle, 82
Taylor, Frances, 149–50
Tcherkézoff, Serge, 84
Tellier, Frédéric, 136
Teriipaia, Tarita, 85–86, 148–49
Testino, Mario, 226
thinness, 60–62, 64
Thurier, Pauline, 57
Tinder, 34, 41, 195–96, 199
Tinguely, Jean, 150
Tolstoy, Leo, 45
Toranian, Valérie, 145
Touraille, Priscille, 59, 60
Tragedy of Heterosexuality, The (Ward),
  17–22
Traître, Le (Gorz), 159
37°2 le matin, 29
Trintignant, Marie, 110–11, 114–16,
  120–21, 144–46, 149
Trintignant, Vincent, 115
Tristan and Isolde, 29–31, 140
Trivers, Robert, 60–61
Trois dames de la Kasbah, Les (Loti), 83
Truffaut, François, 144
Trump, Donald, 19, 189
Tuaillon, Victoire, 161

Ulay, 4
Unmarried Woman, An, 177
Ursulet, Alex, 135–36

vahine, 83–84
validation, 184
Vaujour, Michel, 131
Vaujour, Nadine, 131
Véron, Laélia, 62
Vindication of Love, A (Nehring), 6–9
Vindication of the Rights of Woman, A
    (Wollstonecraft), 14
violence, domestic, 11, 60, 99–152,
    162, 212
  abuser's friends and family and,
    121–26
  children and, 107–8, 118–21
  condescendence toward victims of,
    140
  contrition phase in, 112
  effacement of victims in, 114–18
  group therapy for men imprisoned
    for, 67–68, 110, 111
  journalists' distortion of, 143–46
  justice system and, 123, 124, 126
  masculine identity and, 112–13
  men's emotions and, 114–18
  and men's status as husband and
    father, 106–7
  outside intervention and, 122–23
  passion as excuse for, 143–46, 149,
    151
  psychological, 105–6
  tormented artist excuse for, 146–52
  victims' empathy and self-abnegation
    and, 132–37
  warnings from former partners and,
    123
  women murdered in, 6, 105, 114,
    1143–46

women's inability to defend their
    interests in, 118–21
women's murder of abusive partner
    in, 119, 123
voice, 62
von Aachen, Hans, 222
Voyage autour du monde (Bougainville),
    84

Wallis, Samuel, 84
Wang, Ping, 61
Ward, Jane, 17–22, 166, 231
Ways of Seeing, 187–88, 222
We (Johnson), 180
Wenz, Alissa, 114–15, 147
Why Does Patriarchy Persist? (Gilligan
    and Snider), 203–6
Wild (Strayed), 254
Williams, Serena, 64
Winslet, Kate, 68
Witherspoon, Reese, 68–69
Wittig, Monique, 17, 252
Wollstonecraft, Mary, 14, 48
women's relationships with other
    women, 185–92
work force, women in, 169
writers and artists, tormented,
    146–52

Yourcenar, Marguerite, 36n
youth, 61, 77, 78, 91

Zaharias, George, 66
Zeniter, Alice, 63–64
Zhang, Jenny Tinghui, 188–89
Zheng, Robin, 90, 92–93

ABOUT THE AUTHOR

© Mathieu Zazzo

Mona Chollet is a Franco-Swiss writer and journalist. She is the author of *In Defense of Witches* and lives in Paris, France.